AMERICAN INDIANS

Answers to
Today's Questions

Also by Jack Utter —

Wounded Knee & The Ghost Dance Tragedy

AMERICAN INDIANS

Answers to Today's Questions

Jack Utter

NATIONAL WOODLANDS PUBLISHING COMPANY
Lake Ann, Michigan

Additional copies of this book may be ordered through bookstores, from the publisher, or

Publishers Distribution Service
6893 Sullivan Road
Grawn, MI 49637
(800) 345-0096

Cover design and sketches by Angela Saxon
Computer-drawn maps by Michael Blume

AMERICAN INDIANS: Answers to Today's Questions

First Edition: April 1993

Publisher's – Cataloging in Publication Data

Utter, Jack.
    American Indians: answers to today's questions / Jack Utter
    p. cm.
    Includes bibliographical references and index.
    Preassigned LCCN: 92-62877.
    ISBN 0-9628075-2-4 (soft)
    ISBN 0-9628075-3-2 (casebound)
    1. Indians of North America – Government relations. 2. Indians of North America – Politics and government. 3. Indians, Treatment of – North America. I. Title.

E93.U88 1993   970.004'97
                                    QBI93-20112

93 94 95 96 97   10 9 8 7 6 5 4 3 2

*To all Americans and our greater
understanding of each other*

CONTENTS

Contents of Part II

THE QUESTIONS

SECTION C: TREATIES AND AGREEMENTS

SECTION D: MYTH, MISINFORMATION, AND STEREOTYPE

SECTION G: LAND, RESOURCES, AND ECONOMICS

SECTION H: LEGAL STATUS AND TRIBAL SELF-GOVERNMENT

Section I: The Bureau of Indian Affairs

Section J: Health

Section K: Education

LIST OF FIGURES (MAPS)

LIST OF APPENDIXES

PREFACE

*Are American-born Indians who live on reservations citizens of the
U.S. or are they not? I recall that, when Ronald Reagan was President, he once told some Russian university students that Indians
are not citizens.*

F. R., Oklahoma City, Oklahoma
In *Parade Magazine,* July 21, 1991
(Scott 1991)

*Ignorance is one of the greatest barriers to understanding between
two peoples. If we don't understand each other, if we do not know
the culture, the language, or the history of each other, we are unable
to see each other as human beings with value and dignity. This is
especially true in relations between Indians and non-Indians.*

William C. Wantland (1975)
former Attorney General
Seminole Nation of Oklahoma

Apparent in the first quotation–and discussed in the second–is
something I call *innocent ignorance.* All of us have it to some degree,
whether non-Indian or Indian. Most non-Indians tend to know much
less about Native Americans and their culture than the latter know
about non-Indians. This is understandable because Euro-American
society has so overwhelmingly dominated and intruded upon Native
society. A key objective of this book, therefore, is to help fill part of
the gap that often exists between public perception and Indian reality.

I began the project by searching out and chronicling common misperceptions about many legal, social, historical, political, and cultural aspects of life for indigenous Americans. Later, help came from numerous people, both Indian and non-Indian, through comments, suggestions, and criticisms, as well as the kind provision of the right reference material at the right time. Ultimately, I endeavored to "stand on the shoulders of giants" to get a better view of the many questions, answers, and other information needed to complete this wide-ranging publication.

A partial list of my "giants" includes such writers and scholars as Felix Cohen, Vine Deloria, Jr., Ruth Underhill, Walter Echo Hawk, D'Arcy McNickle, William Sturtevant, James Mooney, Wilcomb Washburn, Francis Prucha, Tim Giago, Robert Utley, Robert Williams, Jr., Edward Spicer, John Collier, David Getches, Carl Waldman, Alvin Josephy, Jr., Kirke Kickingbird, Sharon O'Brien, Theodore Taylor, David Case, and Charles Wilkinson. Knowledge gained from their works and those of many others, along with government documents and information from non-government organizations, provided the foundation for most of the book. I hope what follows will broaden readers' views and stimulate further inquiry.

A note about laws and court cases cited in this book:

Readers who are unfamiliar with the manner in which laws are cited may find the following statement helpful if they wish to learn more about laws referred to in this book. Legislation can be cited in three different ways. For example, the National Environmental Policy Act of 1969 is cited as (1) Public Law (P.L.) 91-190, (2) 83 Stat. 852, or (3) 43 USC 4321. The first citation indicates that the act was the 190th law passed by the 91st Congress. The second tells us that the act is found in Volume 83 of the U.S. Statutes at Large, beginning on page 852. The third citation indicates that the law has been codified in Volume 43 of the U.S. Code (USC), beginning at Section 4321. All three methods are correct; they simply allow someone to find them in different sources. In this book, you will find laws cited in all of these ways.

The names of court cases are italicized. In the Bibliography, information provided after the italicized name of the case will allow interested readers to learn more if they consult with a documents librarian at a library which carries legal reference materials.

ACKNOWLEDGMENTS

No book, especially one of this nature, is ever an individual effort. Information, encouragement, and assistance in helping me understand Native issues, and in assembling this publication, came from many sources. In the alphabetic list below, I have attempted to recognize those from whom I've learned, or who provided essential assistance in one form or another. Without doubt, some sources have been overlooked, and I sincerely regret any omissions.

I am especially grateful to Joanne Schultz for her untiring effort in reviewing and editing the manuscript, and in compiling the index.

Acknowledgment of individuals, agencies, or organizations does not necessarily equate with endorsements from them.

Administration for Native
    Americans
Alaska Federation of Natives
Alvin (Tonto Apache)
American Indian Anti-Defamation
    Council
American Indian Movement
Brian Aranjo
Association on American Indian
    Affairs
Tina Begay (Apache/Navajo)
Michael Blume
Margery Brown
Senator Ben Nighthorse Campbell
    (Northern Cheyenne)
Rita and Paco Cantu
Anthony Castillo (Tohono O'odham)
Joseph and Nathan Chasing Horse
    (Sicangu Lakota)
Congressional Research Service
Argyll Conner (Oklahoma Cherokee)
    & Dixie Conner
Dennis (Tonto Apache)

Mary Derrick (Navajo)
Merle and Betty Finch
Paula Fleming
Phil Garcia (Laguna)
Gayle Hartmann
Wilson Hunter (Navajo)
Indian Arts and Crafts Board
Indian Country Today (including
    the Lakota Times)
Indian Health Service
International Indian Treaty
    Council
Leonard Peltier Defense Committee
Library of Congress
National Anthropological Archives
National Congress of American
    Indians
National Indian Education
    Association
National Indian Gaming
    Commission
National Indian Media Association
National Indian Policy Center

National Indian Youth Council
Native American Rights Fund
Navajo Nation
Agnes Nichols (Chugachmuit
    Aleut)
Evelyn Pickett (Oklahoma
    Cherokee)
Bob Robideau (Chippewa) &
    Paulette D'Auteuil-Robideau
Jackie Rich
Michael Rios (Tohono O'odham)
Dr. John D. Schultz
Jeff Silverman
Smithsonian Institution
Dyanne Stanley (Eastern Cherokee)

Tatanka Oyaté (multi-tribal)
Mililani Trask (Native Hawaiian)
Dr. Brock Tunnicliff
U.S. Bureau of Indian Affairs
U.S. Fish and Wildlife Service
U.S. House Subcommittee on
    Native American Affairs
U.S. National Park Service
U.S. Senate Select Committee on
    Indian Affairs
University of Arizona Library and
    College of Law
Colonel Leon and Jacqueline Utter
Phyllis Utter
Yavapai-Prescott Indian Tribe

INTRODUCTION

The amount of material that has been published on the general topic of American Indians is staggering. Any good-sized library is likely to have thousands of books and documents on the subject. Despite this abundance of information, American Indians have been described by some observers as "the unknown minority." Considering the average person's contact with and knowledge about today's Indians, this description would appear to be accurate.

Unfortunately, the majority of Americans have gained their knowledge about Indians from fictional movie and television "westerns" and from history books which frequently limit discussion about Indians to the Indian wars of the 18th and 19th centuries. Relatively few people, for example, have been exposed to enough factual information to know the answers to such basic contemporary questions as.

> Who is an Indian? Are all Native Americans Indians? Are Indians indeed citizens? What percentage of the population is Indian? How many tribes are there? How many reservations are there? Do most Indians live on reservations? Does the United States still make treaties with Indian tribes? Why are Indian tribes treated differently from other groups? Who are the Inuit and Aleut people? What is Indian country? What is the primary mission of the Bureau of Indian Affairs?

This book does not attempt to "reinvent the wheel" in answering these questions and the many others appearing between its covers. It takes information from various sources and makes that information more readily available to readers. Also, unlike some works that say a lot about a limited number of topics, this project does the opposite by saying a little about a lot of topics. Readers who desire further study are encouraged to obtain more in-depth publications, like many listed in the Bibliography.

The book is divided into three main parts. Part I is the shortest and was composed, in part, as a brief response to the 1992 observance of the Columbus Quincentennial. It also touches on the question of Indian origins. The main purpose of Part I, however, is to help the reader understand why the issue of "discovery" has had so great an impact on American Indians.

Part II contains 115 questions and answers covering a wide array of issues. Descriptive materials consist of maps, photographs, and text relating to contemporary and historical issues. These are distributed throughout the book.

To better comprehend the current relationship between American Indians and the federal government–and where that relationship is apparently headed–it is necessary to have some understanding of its past. To this end, Part III contains a summary history of government policies regarding American Indians, extending from the end of the British colonial period to the present. Collectively, this history and the other segments of the book are designed to provide a broad introduction to many interesting–and sometimes surprising–topics germane to American Indians. A principal goal of this book is to foster new perceptions which will help bring America's image of Native people out of the 19th century.

PART I

THE DISCOVERY ISSUE

A few solitary white sails, far out on the blue water, are seen with mysterious awe by the Indian from the Atlantic shore, appearing like huge monsters from the spirit world.

They move toward the land!

From out their sides pour forth a new, unheard-of race....

Henry Howe, 1851
In *Historical Collections of the Great West*

> *Navajo Community College, founded in 1968, was the first institution of higher learning established on an American Indian reservation. Not long after the college was started, its president, Ned Hatathli, was asked what made NCC different. He paused, then said: "We don't teach that Columbus discovered America."*

"Who *really* discovered America?" The answer to that question may seem obvious since this is a book about American Indians. However, in light of the importance which Euro-Americans placed, centuries ago, on the word "discovery," the reader will find that the question is *not* trivial. In fact, it lies at the heart of many of the problems which Indians have faced since long before the United States became a nation—and which continue to confront them today.

THE AGE OF DISCOVERY

The 1992 observance of the Columbus Quincentennial might well have helped many Americans understand why Ned Hatathli referred to the discovery issue as he did. Though the voyage of Christopher Columbus was an outstanding navigational achievement, he never set foot on or even saw the North American continent. Nonetheless, he did trace the Central American coast from Honduras to Panama on his last voyage; and he even landed on the northern coast of South America during his third voyage in 1498, thinking it was an island.

Columbus first made landfall on October 12, 1492, on a small island in the Bahamas, southeast of Florida. It was already inhabited by the Arawak people. Because he felt he had found an archipelago off the coast of Asia—most likely India—Columbus gave these people the name "Indios," the Spanish word for Indians.

On several occasions during his travels, in what we now call the West Indies, Columbus took his men and Indian scouts on expeditions in search of Japan, which he felt was in the region. Up to the time of his death in Spain, on May 21, 1506, Christopher Columbus was convinced he had reached the fringe of Asia. Though he wasn't first, and he was mistaken about his whereabouts, Columbus stands out as the one man who inaugurated Europe's "Age of Discovery," which forever changed Native lifeways in the Western Hemisphere.

The distinction of being the first recorded European of the discovery era to walk the shores of North America usually falls to John Cabot. Sailing in the name of Henry VII of England, Cabot reached the far northeast coast of North America on June 24, 1497. When he arrived at Cape Bauld, Newfoundland, he claimed the land for King Henry. After a hasty exploration of the region, Cabot returned to England in August with three kidnapped Micmac Indians. Unlike Spain's quick response to Columbus' explorations, however, England did not effectively follow through on Cabot's claim for more than a century. It is ironic that John Cabot, whose real name was Giovanni Caboto, was an Italian whose birthplace was Genoa, the reported home city of Columbus.

Though these 15th century explorations took place in what is now called the discovery era, credit for even earlier European landings rightfully goes to the Scandinavian explorers of the 10th and 11th centuries.

VIKINGS AND SKRAELINGS

Adam of Bremen, the German historian, wrote briefly in 1070 A.D. of the Norse voyages to North America that occurred 60 to 80 years earlier. Detailed written descriptions of the Nordic explorations were not available until the Norse "sagas" were first set down in the 1200s. Two of these, the "Saga of Erik the Red" and the "Saga of the Greenlanders," describe the Vikings' arrival in North America and their early contacts with Native inhabitants.

According to the "Saga of the Greenlanders," Bjarni Herjolfsson first sighted North America (northeast Canada), which the Vikings called "Vinland," in 986 A.D. He had been blown off course while sailing from Iceland to Greenland. Fourteen years later, Leif Ericsson sailed on a westward expedition from Greenland. He eventually landed in Newfoundland where he and his 35 men wintered before their return voyage.

One of the first Viking encounters with Native Americans–to whom the Norsemen referred with the vague term "Skraelings"–was that of Thorvald Ericsson, Leif's brother. About the year 1003, Thorvald led a voyage to Leif's former camp in Newfoundland. Several expeditions were made from the camp over a two-year period. On the final trip, the Vikings found three skin boats upside down on a beach with nine Native men hiding under them. Eight of these men were summarily slaughtered, but one escaped to get help. A small navy of skin boats, bearing numerous warriors, brought a counter-attack. A shower of arrows rained on the Norsemen who were in their own vessels. Thorvald was mortally wounded. Before dying, however, he urged his men to return to Greenland–which they did. Thus ended what is perhaps the earliest-described encounter between Europeans and Native Americans. Other contacts, both violent and peaceful, occurred before the Vikings ultimately quit their Vinland adventures about 1020.

Who were those Native Americans and where did they come from? And, who were the Natives encountered by the Spanish and British hundreds of years later?

THE FIRST AMERICANS

Many archaeologists believe that nomadic hunters of Asian Mongoloid stock first arrived in North America between 20,000 and 35,000 years ago. Still others believe the earliest arrivals had to have been 40,000 or even 100,000 years ago. Most scientists theorize that prehistoric peoples used the so-called Bering "land bridge" (and perhaps an "ice bridge" and the Aleutian Islands) on migrations to North America. Apparently, no massive migration occurred similar to that which took place when the American West was "won." Over thousands of years, small bands and extended family and tribal groups probably crossed the land bridge searching for and following the game animals on which they depended for survival.

The Bering Strait, separating Siberia from Alaska, is named after Vitus Bering, a Danish sea captain. He made the first recorded passage through the strait in August 1728, on a voyage of exploration for the Russian Czar, Peter. The strait, roughly 150 feet deep, is only about 50 miles wide at its narrowest point and is bisected by two tiny islands, the Diomedes. This geography allowed Eskimos, in historic times, to cross the strait in their stout skin umiaks. In much earlier times, however, a boat would not have been needed for the crossing.

During the ice ages, ocean levels were lowered because much of the earth's water was tied up in glacial ice. This resulted in exposure of large land areas and creation of a "land bridge" between Asia and North America. The idea of such a bridge of land between Siberia and

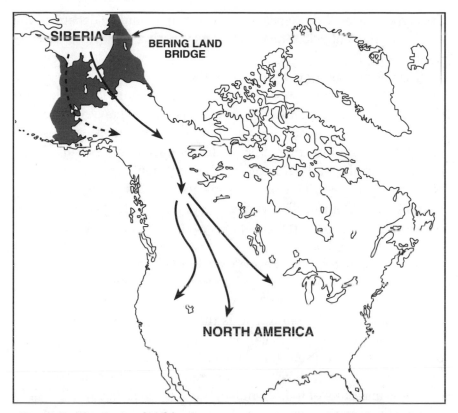

Figure 1. The Bering land bridge migration theory is depicted on the map shown above. Shading represents the area where it is believed the ocean floor was exposed during certain glacial periods, thus allowing routes of access between Asia and North America. Scientists believe migration may have occurred in either or both directions.

Alaska conjures up thoughts of a narrow strip of land tenuously connecting the two continents. However, glaciologists and other scientists have proposed that the Bering land bridge was perhaps 1,000 or more miles wide during the last glacial period. (See Figure 1.) This would have allowed ample opportunity for land crossings between the continents for those who may have been inclined to make the trek.

In a logical twist to the Bering land bridge theory, Vine Deloria, Jr., the Indian author, political scientist, theologian, and lawyer, has presented an interesting conjecture. He wrote that scientists "cannot tell which way the foot prints were pointing and it may well be that Asia was populated from the Western Hemisphere" (Deloria 1989).

This type of provocative speculation can help stimulate debate on the issue and prevent scientific complacency with a one-way theory of migration.

Despite the amount of theorizing, there is no consensus about the origins of humankind in the Americas. For example, the Mormon Church and some Jewish scholars (see Glaser 1973) have claimed that American Indians–referred to as "Lamanites" by the Mormons–are descendants of a lost tribe of Israel. In contrast, many North American tribes profess a beginning on the continent. For instance, the Navajo people describe coming from beneath the earth in the area roughly equivalent to their current reservation. The precise time of this origin is unclear, and it is not of great importance in the traditional Navajo view of life.

Most scientists today, however, agree that the earliest migrants to cross the Bering land bridge came from Siberia and were probably the first humans to set foot on North America. If anyone "discovered" this part of the world, it was these ancestors of Native Americans. When Europeans began arriving, thousands of years later, descendants of the prehistoric pioneers were living throughout the hemisphere and had developed hundreds of distinct cultures. Little did these ancestors of today's Indians realize that "discovery" would become *the* central issue in whether or not they could survive as sovereign peoples, maintaining control of their lives and their land.

THE DOCTRINE OF DISCOVERY

National celebrations of European arrival in the Western Hemisphere cause resentment among many Native Americans who are aware of the so-called "doctrine of discovery." This doctrine is the European-invented legal theory upon which all claim to, and acquisition of, Indian lands in North America is ultimately founded.

During the discovery era's fierce international competition for new lands, a need arose for some commonly acknowledged principle by which rights–as between European nations–could be established. The main purpose for developing such a principle was to avoid war over conflicting claims and settlements.

In the earliest years, the competing powers relied on grants from the Pope. The prevailing belief, stated by King Duarte of Portugal, was "whatever is possessed by the authority and permission of [the

Pope] is understood to be held in a special way and with the permission of almighty God" (Williams 1990, p. 70). But the Pope's international authority was lessening with the growing protestant movement and other world developments. Some new system had to be adopted.

Over time, and through many agreements, grants, and charters, the European nations established the principle that initial *discovery* of lands gave title therein to the government whose subjects, or by whose authority, the discovery was made. This title, ignoring the Native peoples, was good against all other European or civilized (i.e., Christian) governments. It could be secured by possession of the land through the continued presence of the government's citizens or representatives somewhere within the bounds of the claimed area.

The United States officially embraced the discovery doctrine in 1823 through the Supreme Court case of *Johnson v. McIntosh*. The following paragraphs, which conclude this opening section of the book, are excerpts from that precedent-setting case in federal Indian law. They begin by addressing the proclaimed superior right of Euro-American governments to sell Indian lands—despite the fact that Indians might claim and be living on them. The last paragraph leaves no doubt as to the U. S. view of the legal effect of European discovery.

> While the different nations of Europe respected the right of the Natives, as occupants, they asserted the ultimate dominion to be in themselves; and claimed and exercised, as a consequence of this ultimate dominion, a power to grant the soil, while yet in possession of the Natives. These grants have been understood by all, to convey a title to the grantees, subject only to the Indian right of occupancy. [For which some form of compensation was usually paid.]
>
> No one of the powers of Europe gave its full assent to this principle, more unequivocally than England. The documents upon this subject are ample and complete.
>
> Thus, all the nations of Europe, who have acquired territory on this continent, have asserted in themselves, and have recognized in others, the exclusive right of the discoverer to appropriate the lands occupied by the Indians. Have the American States rejected or adopted this principle?
>
> By the treaty which concluded the war of our revolution, Great Britain relinquished all claim, not only to the government, but to the "property and territorial rights of the United States,".... By

this treaty, the powers of government, and the right to the soil, which had previously been in Great Britain, passed definitely to these States.

The United States, then, have unequivocally acceded to that great and broad rule by which its civilized inhabitants now hold this country. They hold, and assert in themselves, the title by which it was acquired. They maintain, as all others have maintained, that discovery gave an exclusive right to extinguish the Indian title of occupancy, either by purchase or by conquest; and gave also a right to such a degree of sovereignty [over Indians and their land], as the circumstances of the people [of the U. S.] would allow them to exercise.

As the reader will come to see, many issues which concern American Indians today derive ultimately from the international "legal fiction" known as the doctrine of discovery.

> *They made us many promises, more than I can remember....*
> *They never kept but one: They promised to take our land,*
> *and they took it!*
>
> Red Cloud
> Lakota Sioux Chief

[Primary sources for Part I are: Axtell 1988; Bradford 1973; Ceram 1971; Encyclopaedia Britannica 1990; Farb 1968; Getches, Rosenfelt, and Wilkinson 1979; League of Women Voters 1976; MacNeish 1971; Mooney 1928; Service 1963; Thomas 1899; United States Commission on Civil Rights 1981; Waldman 1985; Williams 1990; Wrone and Nelson 1973.]

PART II

QUESTIONS & ANSWERS

The issues and the problems that confront Indian people on a day-to-day basis are extremely complex. It takes a lifetime of education to even begin to understand them.

Tim Giago 1991b
Member of the Oglala Lakota Nation and
Publisher of the weekly *Indian Country Today*
(including *the Lakota Times*)

INTRODUCTION

For readers who are accustomed to historical or ethnological books about American Indians, some of the material in Part II may seem comparatively technical or legalistic. The reason has to do with the contemporary nature of most of the subject matter.

Those who do not experience the phenomenon of everyday life in Indian country cannot have a clear understanding of just how extensively government and laws affect American Indians. Their lives are deeply intertwined in the workings of–and unceasing conflicts among–federal, tribal, state, and local laws and governments. In the federal area alone, more than 300 treaties have been ratified, more than 5,000 Indian laws passed, more than 2,000 relevant court cases decided, and at least 500 attorneys general opinions rendered. Thus, any serious effort to discuss widely ranging topics relating to Indian America cannot avoid topics and explanations that are both technical and legalistic.

It is appropriate to ask, "How were the following questions selected?" Some were taken from among the questions most frequently asked of the U. S. Bureau of Indian Affairs (BIA) by the public. Others were developed through the author's own experience, and still more were recommended by reviewers of the first draft of the book. The common thread, of course, is that all the questions are relevant to the nation's uncertain concept of Native American people.

Part II begins with what would seem to be a simple question: Who is an Indian? Its answer, however, clearly shows just how complex is the modern world of Native Americans.

SECTION A: THE INDIAN PEOPLE

> *It should be remembered that aboriginal tribes never considered themselves "Indians" in a racial sense, but as separate nations.*
>
> Underhill 1974

A-1. *Who is an Indian?*

Before first European contact, the answer to "Who is an Indian?" was easy. Nobody was. "Indian" is a European-derived word and concept. Prior to contact, Native American people were not Indians but were members of their own socio-political and cultural groups—Delaware, Comanche, Yurok, Tlingit, or Chugach, for example, or sub-groups thereof—just as there were Frenchmen, Germans, Englishmen, and Italians in Europe. With the landing of the Europeans, an immediate dichotomy arose that was previously unknown in the hemisphere. Instantly the Native people lost some of their identity when they were all lumped together under a single defining word. The distinction between Native and non-Native peoples resulted in a highly significant legal, political, and social differentiation that remains with us today and is embodied in this first question.

Today in the U.S. there may be 10 to 20 million people with some Indian blood, but only a small percentage identify themselves as being primarily Indian (Taylor 1984). Also, no single definition of "an Indian" exists—socially, administratively, legislatively, or judicially.

The end purpose of the question "Who is an Indian?" is usually the determining factor in deciding which of the multiple definitions is used (Cohen 1982). For U.S. census purposes, as one example, an Indian is anyone who declares himself or herself to be one. Thus, the concept of *Indian* as used by the Bureau of the Census does not denote a scientific or biological definition but, rather, is an indication of the race with which a person identifies.

Tribal groups, themselves, have differing criteria for who is an Indian of their tribe. The Cherokee of Oklahoma require proof only of descent from a person on the 1906 tribal roll—no matter how small the percentage of Indian blood may be. Other tribes specify one-half, one-fourth, or another degree of blood for membership (Taylor 1984).

From a strictly ethnologic standpoint, if a person is, say, 3/4 Caucasian and 1/4 Indian, that person would normally not be considered an Indian. Yet, for many legal and social purposes, such a person will be an Indian, as might someone with a lesser quantum of Indian blood (Cohen 1982).

Many federal laws and regulations define "Indian," and these various definitions take on great significance when they control the distribution of funds and services or regulate the application of civil and criminal law. As the first of several examples, the BIA *generally* defines an Indian as an individual who is a member of an Indian tribe, band, or community that is "recognized" by the federal government; who lives on or near a reservation; and who is of 1/4 or more Indian ancestry (Bureau of Indian Affairs 1987a).

Another example relates to the situation where federal assistance is provided for Indian health care education. The definition provided in the Indian Health Care Improvement Act of 1976 is considerably broader than the definition used by the BIA. The act defines "an Indian" as anyone who is a member of a "recognized" tribe, with no mention of blood quantum. An individual may also be considered Indian if he or she belongs to a tribe, band, or group that has been terminated since 1940, regardless of whether or not the individual lives on or near a reservation. Another category includes those members of tribes which are recognized now–or may be recognized in the future–by the state in which they reside. In addition, anyone who is a descendant, in the first or second degree, of any of these individuals also qualifies. Eskimos, Aleuts, or other Alaska Natives are considered Indians. Anyone considered by the Secretary of the Interior to be Indian for any purpose qualifies. And, finally, anyone who is determined to be Indian under regulations promulgated by the Secretary of Health and Human Services also is considered to be an Indian.

The Indian Education Act of 1972 employs a relatively broad definition of "Indian." It includes all of the following: people of one-eighth blood ancestry and higher who are members of Indian tribes and groups, residents of state reservations, urban Indians, Indians from "terminated" tribes, and self-identified Indians.

In the Indian Arts and Crafts Act of 1990, "Indian" is defined by Congress, for the purposes of the act, as "any individual who is a member of an Indian tribe, or…is certified as an Indian artisan by an Indian tribe." There is no blood quantum requirement. A "tribe" is also defined to include those tribes and Alaska Native villages recognized by the federal government, those formerly recognized, and tribes or groups recognized by a state government when there is no federal recognition.

As indicated above, federal definitions have included Alaska Natives under the broad heading of "Indians" when discussing BIA and other agency programs affecting Indians. Therefore, "Indians" is sometimes employed as a generic term for all Native peoples of the continental United States. At other times, the term refers only to Native Americans in the 48 states, while "Alaska Natives" is used to distinguish the Indian, Eskimo, and Aleut people of Alaska.

To avoid the great confusion associated with the question of who is an Indian, Felix S. Cohen (1982)–the renowned chronicler of American Indian Law–suggested that a practical and basic *legal* definition of an Indian would be one which sets two essential qualifications: (a) some of the individual's ancestors lived in what is now the United States before the first Europeans arrived and (b) the individual is recognized as an Indian by his or her tribe or community.

COMPARATIVE EXAMPLE OF "WHO IS AN INDIAN" FOR SIX FEDERAL PURPOSES, REGARDING MEMBERS OF THE FEDERALLY RECOGNIZED NAVAJO TRIBE OF THE SOUTHWEST AND THE NON-FEDERALLY RECOGNIZED CATAWBA TRIBE OF SOUTH CAROLINA

	"Indian" for these purposes					
Blood degree	Census Bureau Indian Count	BIA Services	Indian Arts & Crafts Authentication	Regulations Re: Obtaining Eagle Feathers for Religion	Administr. for Native Americans Programs	BIA Hiring Preference
4/4 Navajo	YES	YES	YES	YES	YES	YES
1/4 Navajo	YES	YES	YES	YES	YES	YES
1/8 Navajo	YES	NO	MAYBE	NO	YES	MAYBE
4/4 Catawba	YES	NO	YES	NO	YES	YES
2/4 Catawba	YES	NO	YES	NO	YES	YES
1/4 Catawba	YES	NO	YES	NO	YES	NO

NOTE: The Catawba Tribe is scheduled to become federally recognized during 1993.

A-2. *How do American Indians view themselves in the context of the larger society?*

Over the past two decades, a number of Indian acquaintances have made it clear to the author that they see themselves as tribal members first, Indians second, and Americans third. Even so, they are aware of being all three at once. They have also stated that this view is widely held in Indian country. Social scientists and the courts have referred to this understandable phenomenon as "community consciousness" (Weatherhead 1980; *Mashpee Tribe v. New Seabury Corp.* 1979).

A few non-Indians have suggested that this attitude, at first glance, may seem "unpatriotic." Actually, it tends to show an extraordinary patriotism that does not break faith with ancestral nations, centuries, or millennia older than the U.S., and that expands to embrace additional allegiances. In addition, one of the conceptual requirements of tribalism long recognized by the U. S. government is that tribes are "distinct political communities" and the "members owe immediate allegiance to their…tribes" (U.S. Department of the Interior 1894, p. 664).

A-3. *Are all Native Americans Indians?*

No. The term "Native American" is widely recognized as meaning a person who is of a tribe or people indigenous to the United States. It is most frequently applied to American Indians in the 48 coterminous states, but it also includes Alaska's three ethnological groups—Indians, Eskimos, and Aleuts. (Eskimos are also called Inuit.) Native Hawaiians are also considered to be Native Americans.

The federal government, through the Department of Health and Human Services, includes a broader definition for "Native Americans" within its regulations for the Native American Programs Act (1975). That definition lists the four groups referenced above and also names "Native American Pacific Islanders." The latter are defined as "American Samoan Natives and the indigenous peoples of Guam [Chamorros], the Commonwealth of the Northern Marianas, and the Republic of Palau" (Administration for Native Americans 1991a & b).

Guam is a U.S. territory. The other areas named are present and former Pacific Island Trust Territories of the U.S.

In the remainder of this book, unless specifically noted otherwise, "Native Americans" is used to refer *only* to the indigenous people of Alaska and the lower 48 states.

A-4. *How do the major Native American groups generally differ?*

According to the Asian migration theory, the parent stock of today's Indians is considered to have migrated to North America thousands of years before those of the Aleuts and Eskimos (Sutton 1985). The Aleuts are thought to have come second, and the Eskimos most recently, but still in prehistoric times. Distinct cultural, linguistic, and genetic differences exist between American Indians, as one group, and Eskimos and Aleuts as another.

More often than not, the word "Indian" conjures up images similar to this photograph of a Kiowa chief from the central plains, circa 1870s. Lone Wolf was nationally known for fighting the White Man—but more in the courts than on the battlefield. In the famous U.S. Supreme Court case of *Lone Wolf v. Hitchcock* (1903), he was unsuccessful in his efforts to get the U.S. government to uphold treaties it had made with the Kiowa and Comanche tribes.

PHOTO COURTESY OF THE SMITHSONIAN INSTITUTION

In the lower 48 states, all of the indigenous people are of *Indian* heritage. In Alaska, the Indian people are grouped into two main classifications: (1) the Athapaskan tribes, e.g., Ahtna, Koyukon, Kutchin, Tanana, etc., of interior Alaska, and (2) the southeast coastal tribes–Eyak, Tlingit, Haida, and Tsimshian (Waldman 1985).

Eskimos and *Aleuts* differ from each other, both genetically and by their unrelated languages, but they developed comparable sea-hunting cultures. The similarities are considered by some to be greater than the differences (Bureau of Indian Affairs 1966; Damas 1984).

Eskimos (or Inuit) are generally people of far northern, western, and southern Alaska. They have traditionally lived along the coasts of the Bering Sea, Arctic Ocean, and Gulf of Alaska, as well as up some of the rivers that flow into these waters, and on the islands of St. Lawrence, Nunivak, and Kodiak. (See Damas 1984.)

Aleuts are the traditional people of the western Alaska Peninsula and the Aleutian chain of islands. They were the first Alaska Natives to come under non-Native domination when Russian fur traders began to enslave them in the mid-1700s. They suffered greatly under early Russian domination and are estimated to have lost as much as 80 percent of their population to disease and violence by the end of the 18th century (Bureau of Indian Affairs 1966; Arnold 1976). Most Pacific Eskimos (i.e., those of southern Alaska) are now called Aleuts.

Native Hawaiians, also considered to be Native Americans, are descendants of the Polynesians who migrated to the Hawaiian Island chain many centuries ago. In at least two pieces of federal legislation regarding education and health care (respectively, Title IV of the Elementary and Secondary Education Act amendments of 1988 and the Native Hawaiian Health Care Act of 1988), Congress has defined a Native Hawaiian as being "a descendant of the aboriginal people, who, prior to 1778 [the year of first European contact], occupied and exercised sovereignty in the area that now comprises the State of Hawaii, as evidenced by: (i) genealogical records, (ii) Kapuna (elders) or Kam'aina (long-term community residents) verification, or (iii) birth records of the state of Hawaii."

Houghton (1989) published a law journal article supporting the recognition of legal "Indian status" for Native Hawaiians. He suggested this be done under the general laws which recognize the political existence of the three other major Native American groups. A

An Eskimo, or "Inuit" woman from Alaska territory, 1908. Considered "Indian" under broadly applicable federal law, the Inuit are ethnologically distinct from Indians, as are the Aleut people of Alaska. Also, the socio-political organization of the Inuit and Aleut people was based not on tribes but on small groups of extended families. Today it is largely based on a corporate model, following passage of the Alaska Native Claims Settlement Act (1971). Photo by F. H. Nowell

PHOTO COURTESY OF THE SMITHSONIAN INSTITUTION

majority of Native Hawaiians disagrees with Houghton's "Indian" approach to resolving the lingering questions of their legal status (Trask 1992).

For further discussion on Native Hawaiians, refer to Appendix 1 for a brief summary of basic Hawaiian issues.

A-5. *What is the Indian population of the United States?*
In 1990, through the Census Bureau's system of self-identifying, there · were 1,959,234 individuals identified as Indians, including Alaska Natives. This is 0.8% of the total U. S. population of 248,709,873. The "Indian" population breaks down ethnologically to 23,797 Aleuts, 57,152 Eskimos, and 1,878,285 Indians.

A-6. What is the Indian population in each of the 50 states and Washington, D.C.?

STATE	TOTAL POPULATION OF STATE	INDIAN & ALASKA NATIVE POPULATION	PERCENT OF STATE'S TOTAL
Alabama	4,040,587	16,506	0.4
Alaska	550,043	85,698	15.6
Arizona	3,665,228	203,527	5.6
Arkansas	2,350,725	12,773	0.5
California	29,760,021	242,164	0.8
Colorado	3,294,394	27,776	0.8
Connecticut	3,287,116	6,654	0.2
Delaware	666,168	2,019	0.3
Florida	12,937,926	36,335	0.3
Georgia	6,478,216	13,348	0.2
Hawaii	1,108,229	5,099	0.5
Idaho	1,006,749	13,780	1.4
Illinois	11,430,602	21,836	0.2
Indiana	5,544,159	12,720	0.2
Iowa	2,776,755	7,349	0.3
Kansas	2,477,574	21,965	0.9
Kentucky	3,685,296	5,769	0.2
Louisiana	4,219,973	18,541	0.4
Maine	1,227,928	5,998	0.5
Maryland	4,781,468	12,972	0.3
Massachusetts	6,016,425	12,241	0.2
Michigan	9,295,297	55,638	0.6
Minnesota	4,375,099	49,909	1.1
Mississippi	2,573,216	8,525	0.3
Missouri	5,117,073	19,835	0.4
Montana	799,065	47,679	6.0
. Nebraska	1,578,385	12,410	0.8
Nevada	1,201,833	19,637	1.6
New Hampshire	1,109,252	2,134	0.2
New Jersey	7,730,188	14,970	0.2
New Mexico	1,515,069	134,355	8.9

New York	17,990,455	62,651	0.3
North Carolina	6,628,637	80,155	1.2
North Dakota	638,800	25,917	4.1
Ohio	10,847,115	20,358	0.2
Oklahoma	3,145,585	252,420	8.0
Oregon	2,842,321	38,496	1.4
Pennsylvania	11,881,643	14,733	0.1
Rhode Island	1,003,464	4,071	0.4
South Carolina	3,486,703	8,246	0.2
South Dakota	696,004	50,575	7.3
Tennessee	4,877,185	10,039	0.2
Texas	16,986,510	65,877	0.4
Utah	1,722,850	24,283	1.4
Vermont	562,758	1,696	0.3
Virginia	6,187,358	15,282	0.2
Washington	4,866,692	81,483	1.7
Washington, D.C.	606,900	1,466	0.2
West Virginia	1,793,477	2,458	0.1
Wisconsin	4,891,769	39,387	0.8
Wyoming	453,588	9,479	2.1
Totals	248,709,873	1,959,234	

A-7. *Is the Indian population increasing or is it decreasing?*

It is definitely on the increase. Ninety years ago the U. S. Indian population hit an all-time low of about 250,000. The 1990 census count was 1,959,234. Besides being much greater than the 1900 low, it represented an increase of 37.9% over the 1,420,400 Indians counted in 1980. Part of the increase in recent decades has been attributed to a greater willingness of people to identify themselves as Indians.

The numbers of full-bloods among American Indians are increasing in some tribes and decreasing in others. For example, among the Kaw Tribe of Oklahoma (formerly known as the Kansa), only six full-bloods remained in 1991; yet there are many thousands more Navajo full-bloods than there were in the last century. This is primarily because the Navajos have been relatively isolated from large non-Indian populations in the past and because their population has increased greatly since the late-1800s.

A-8. *How many Indians live on reservations?*

The most recent census reported that 437,431 Indians–or 22.3% of the total–live on legally designated reservations or associated trust lands. Another 10.2% (200,789) live within "Tribal Jurisdiction Statistical Areas," which are former reservation areas in the state of Oklahoma where tribes retain certain types of tribal jurisdiction.

In Alaska, except for one small reservation in the far southeastern part of the state (Annette Island Reserve), there are no designated Indian reservations. Therefore, for census purposes, "Alaska Native Village Statistical Areas" have been identified by the Bureau of the Census. They coincide with living areas of tribes, bands, clans, groups, villages, communities, or associations that have been recognized in some way by the federal government. The Native people in these Statistical Areas make up 2.4% of the total U.S. Indian population, or 47,244 individuals. They account for 55% of the population of Alaska Natives.

One last population statistic is that for "Tribal Designated Statistical Areas." These are home areas delineated by tribes outside of Oklahoma who do not have reservations. They account for 2.7% of the Indian population, or 53,644 people. Therefore, a total of 1,220,126 Indian people–or 62.3% of all Indians–reside *outside* all official categories of Indian areas identified by the Census Bureau.

A-9. *How many non-Indians live on reservations?*

The total population (all races) for reservations and trust lands is 808,163. Subtracting Indian residents leaves a population of 370,732 non-Indians, or 45.9% of the total, on average. But the range of percentages of non-Indians on Indian lands varies widely from a low of less than 1% to as high as 100% in isolated situations.

Various reasons account for the large percentage of non-Indian residents. Inter-marriage is responsible for some of the non-Indian count, as is non-Indian employment or certain land-leasing programs. The most notorious reason, however, is the "allotment system" established by the government in 1887 and rigorously pursued into the 1930s. Under this system, many tribes' lands within legally established reservation boundaries were divided up by government agents and assigned to individual Indians. Left-over "excess" lands, amounting to millions of acres, were sold to non-Indians. The exterior boundaries of many of these "allotted" reservations have remained the same. Ownership of these lands has gone partially or primarily to non-Indian settlers, their descendants, and successors, who make up much of the non-Indian population on allotted reservations. The Flathead Reservation of western Montana is typical. There, the Indian population is 5,130; but non-Indians (living on what is now private, non-Indian land within the original and still valid boundaries of the reservation) account for another 16,129 people, or 76% of the residents. An example from the other end of the scale comes from Jemez Pueblo in New Mexico 99.3% of the Pueblo's 1,750 residents are Indian.

A-10. *Do many Indians live in urban areas?*

Yes. Most Indians, like most other Americans, live in what the Census Bureau defines as urban or suburban settings. At least 50 metropolitan areas in the United States have Indian populations ranging in size from 4,000 to nearly 90,000 individuals. These 50 areas, alone, are home to 740,000 Indian people. Listed below, in alphabetical order, are the 25 U.S. "metropolitan statistical areas" with the highest Indian populations. Their relative rankings, as to Indian numbers, are also given. (Data are from the 1990 census.)

Metropolitan Statistical Area	Indian Population (Includes Alaska Natives)	Ranking
Albuquerque, NM	16,296	14
Anchorage, AK	14,569	16
Chicago, IL–into IN & WI	15,758	15
Dallas–Ft. Worth, TX	18,972	11
Denver, CO	13,884	17
Detroit, MI	17,961	12
Fort Smith, AR–into OK	9,054	22
Houston–Galveston, TX	11,029	21
Los Angeles–Anaheim–Riverside, CA	87,487	1
Milwaukee–Racine, WI	8,522	23
Minneapolis–St. Paul, MN–into WI	23,956	8
New York, NY–into Long Island, NJ & CT	46,191	3
Oklahoma City, OK	45,720	4
Philadelphia, PA–into NJ, DE, & MD	11,307	19
Phoenix, AZ	38,017	6
Portland, OR–into Vancouver, WA	13,603	18
Sacramento, CA	17,021	13
Salt Lake City–Ogden, UT	8,337	25
San Diego, CA	20,066	10
San Francisco–Oakland–San Jose, CA	40,847	5
Seattle–Tacoma, WA	32,071	7
Tucson, AZ	20,330	9
Tulsa, OK	48,196	2
Washington, DC–into VA & MD	11,036	20
Yakima, WA	8,405	24

A-11. *What was the Native population of the Americas in 1492?*

Several 20th century researchers have attempted to estimate what the aboriginal population of the Western Hemisphere was on the eve of Columbus' arrival. Much of their work has been summarized and critiqued by Denevan (1976), who opens page one of his informative book as follows.

> How many Indians were there? No one will ever know, but can't we at least agree on whether there were few or many? Apparently not yet, for on few questions of history do so many authorities continue to differ so greatly. The reasons for attempting to know are numerous and important. It would not be an overstatement to hold that almost every major investigation of pre-Columbian cultural evolution and ecology, of the European conquest, and of colonial social and economic history must ultimately raise the question of Indian numbers. Thus the effort to determine those numbers continues, and as the quality of the research improves, the trend is toward acceptance of the higher numbers.

Denevan compiled a table of population estimates from five noted researchers who published their data between 1924 and 1966. The table is reproduced here in slightly modified form.

Some Estimates of Aboriginal American Population, ca. 1492					
	Kroeber (1939)	Rosenblat (1954)	Steward (1949)	Sapper (1924)	Dobyns (1966)
			(in millions)		
North America	0.9	1.0	1.0	2.0-3.5	9.8-12.3
Mexico	3.2	4.5	4.5	12.0-15.0	30.0-37.5
Central America	0.1	0.8	0.7	5.0-6.0	10.8-13.5
Caribbean	0.2	0.3	0.2	3.0-4.0	0.4-0.6
Andes	3.0	4.8	6.1	12.0-15.0	30.0-37.5
Lowland South America	1.0	2.0	2.9	3.0-5.0	9.0-11.2
Hemisphere Total	8.4	13.4	15.5	37.0-48.5	90.0-112.6

Denevan believes it is reasonable to estimate that somewhere between 50 and 100 million Natives inhabited the Western Hemisphere at the time Columbus arrived. He points out, however, that Magnus Morner, a respected expert, calculates the number to have been 33 million. The controversy continues.

A-12. Was military conflict the greatest single reason Native population declined during the conquest era?

Apparently not. It seems most historians believe that introduced disease was the major killer of Native Americans. Single epidemics often reduced Indian communities by half or more, and many tribes were completely wiped out in a matter of decades (Denevan 1976).

In 1837, for example, smallpox swept through a 1600-member Mandan tribe in the upper plains. Only 31 people survived (Capps 1973). Smallpox was the most notorious killer, but other, newly introduced diseases also became common causes of mortality. Among them were measles, whooping cough, chicken pox, bubonic plague, typhus, diphtheria, amoebic dysentery, influenza, and parasitic worms (Denevan 1976). Surviving tribes which had been exposed longest began to develop some resistance to new diseases by the 17th century. Nondisease factors contributing to population decline included military conflict, mistreatment, starvation or malnutrition, depression and loss of vigor or will to live, and exportation into slavery.

A-13. What is "The Indian Problem" mentioned so often in U.S. history books and government documents through the 1960s?

> *There is, I insist, no problem as created by the Indian himself. Every problem that exists today in regard to the Native population is due to the white man's cast of mind, which is unable, at least reluctant, to seek understanding and achieve adjustment in a new and significant environment in which it has so recently come.*
>
> Luther Standing Bear, 1933
> quoted in Worton 1974, p. 121

"The Indian Problem" is a term of antiquity that, with its various phrasings, predates the establishment of the United States by centuries. In fact, it goes right back to the time of first European contacts with Native Americans during the 1490s and early-1500s.

The term's meaning has changed over time; but, as long as there was a frontier, one description covered all frontier settings: "How were the newly arrived immigrants to deal with the Native inhabitants of the land?" (Deloria and Lytle 1984).

At the earliest stages of addressing "the Indian problem," the primary issue, as the Spanish identified it, was whether or not the Indians were fully human. If so, what rights did Indians have that should be respected by the "civilized" nations of the world? Decisions made one way or another would obviously have profound effects on Indian policy.

There were those, like Gonzalo Fernández de Oviedo y Valdez, who could be counted among supporters of the less-than-human argument. Oviedo was a royal officer, notary, and historian in the West Indies whose many official duties included the branding of Native slaves—for which he was paid a small amount of gold for each Indian branded. Oviedo's opinion is made evident in the following quotation from one of his histories, written in the early 1500s, and decrying the Indians and their culture.

> Their marriages are not a sacrament but a sacrilege. They are idolatrous, libidinous, and commit sodomy. Their chief desire is to eat, drink, worship heathen idols, and commit bestial obscenities. What could one expect from a people whose skulls are so thick and hard that the Spaniards had to take care in fighting not to strike [an Indian] on the head lest their swords be blunted? [Williams 1990, p. 94.]

On the other side of the argument were men like the Dominican scholar Franciscus de Victoria (or Vitoria), whose advice on royal policy as it related to Indian affairs was sought by the Spanish king. In 1532, Victoria delivered a lecture titled "On the Indians Lately Discovered" in which he established three main points that were later partially adopted by Spain and other nations which colonized North America. Cohen (1942b) and Williams (1990) described Victoria's three points in the following manner:

1. The Native inhabitants of the Americas possess natural legal rights as free and rational people. ("Rational" was frequently equated with "human.")
2. The Pope's grant to Spain of title to the Americas was baseless and could not affect the inherent rights of Indian inhabitants.
3. Only transgressions by the Indians against the Spaniards' natural rights to travel, trade, and "sojourn" in the Indians' lands

could justify a war against the Indians and the taking of their property through the right of conquest. (This was often interpreted by Spaniards in the New World–that is, by those who even bothered to consider it–to mean that *any* objections to their activities by Native peoples justified Spanish retaliation.)

Victoria's discourse did not halt the injustices and atrocities committed against the indigenous peoples. Nonetheless, it served to temper official hemispheric policies toward Natives (as bad as some of these policies were) in the early stages of policy development.

By the time the United States became a nation, the Indian tribes were generally considered to be impediments to civilization and "the Indian problem," as the U.S. government generally interpreted it, had two facets: (1) how to best develop trade with the Indians, and (2) how to most effectively obtain their land for national expansion. This early characterization of the problem evolved over the next two centuries to include: how best to (a) remove the tribes from the settled parts of the country, (b) conquer them, (c) establish and keep them on reservations and away from American society, (d) take their reservation lands away, (e) extinguish their culture and absorb them within American society, (f) reorganize them for renewed self-government, (g) terminate their self-government, and (h) establish opportunities for Indian tribes to determine for themselves what their futures should be.

Alvin M. Josephy, Jr. (1968), in *The Indian Heritage of America*, wrote about "the Indian problem." What he penned was appropriate for the times and warrants repeating–especially considering recent setbacks in the U.S. Supreme Court relative to freedom of religion for Indians and, potentially, other Americans. (See *Lyng v. Northwest Indian Cemetery Protective Association* 1988, and *Oregon v. Smith* 1990.)

> [The] Indian has survived, still posing to the white conqueror a challenge that not all non-Indians, particularly in the United States, wish happily to tolerate, even, indeed, if they understand it: acceptance of the right to be Indian. That right suggests, at heart, the right to be different, which in the United States runs counter to a traditional drive of the dominant society. Ideally, the American Dream in the United States offers equal opportunities to all persons; but in practice the opportunities imply a goal of sameness, and the Indians, clinging to what seems right and best

for them, have instinctively resisted imposed measures by non-Indians designed to make them give up what they want to keep and adopt what they have no desire to acquire. That has been–and continues to be–the core of the so-called "Indian problem" in the United States, which many Indians characteristically refer to as "the white man's problem." [Emphasis added.]

From the present author's point of view, two important points should be made. First, employing the generic term "the White Man" to distinguish Indians from the rest of American society is no longer sufficiently inclusive–for the U.S. is fast becoming a nation where racial minorities will make up the majority. Secondly, to characterize what might be called "the Indian problem" of today, one could reasonably say the non-Indian views it from a somewhat benign position and describes the problem as being one of *clarifying* existing Indian rights. The Indian, on the other hand, would justifiably view the problem as being one of having to rigorously *defend* existing Indian rights and actively *reclaim* past rights.

A-14. What are "the year" and "the century" of reconciliation?

They began in South Dakota when publisher Tim Giago and other Indian leaders urged Governor George Mickelson to pronounce 1990, the centennial of the Wounded Knee massacre, as a year of reconciliation between Indians and non-Indians within the state. The governor embraced the idea and enthusiastically made the designation. The "year" concept has since been expanded to a declared "century" of reconciliation in South Dakota, where frequent animosity between non-Indians and Indians, as well as among different factions of Indians, has been an unfortunate reality since the mid-1800s.

A step similar to the highly commendable one taken in South Dakota was taken in the U.S. Congress in the form of a resolution for a national year of reconciliation. The resolution, which passed both houses, speaks for itself and is reproduced on the following page. It was introduced by members of the South Dakota delegation and their House and Senate supporters. President Bush signed the resolution into effect on May 11, 1992.

102d CONGRESS
1st SESSION   **S. J. RES. 222**

JOINT RESOLUTION

To designate 1992 as the "Year of Reconciliation Between American Indians and non-Indians."

Whereas 1992 will be recognized as the quincentennial anniversary of the arrival of Christopher Columbus to this continent;

Whereas this 500th anniversary offers an opportunity for the United States to honor the indigenous peoples of this continent;

Whereas strife between American Indian and non-Indian cultures is of grave concern to the people of the United States;

Whereas in the past, improvement in cultural understanding has been achieved by individuals who have striven to understand the differences between cultures and to educate others;

Whereas a national effort to develop trust and respect between American Indians and non-Indians must include participation from the private and public sectors, churches and church associations, the Federal Government, Tribal governments and State governments, individuals, communities, and community organizations;

Whereas mutual trust and respect provides a sound basis for constructive change, given a shared commitment to achieving the goals of equal opportunity, social justice and economic prosperity; and

Whereas the celebration of our cultural differences can lead to a new respect for American Indians and their culture among non-Indians: Now, therefore, be it

Resolved by the Senate and House of Representatives of the United States of America in Congress assembled,

That 1992 is designated as the "Year of Reconciliation Between American Indians and non-Indians." The President is authorized and requested to issue a proclamation calling upon the people of the United States, both Indian and non-Indian, to lay aside fears and mistrust of one another, to build friendships, to join together and take part in shared cultural activities, and to strive towards mutual respect and understanding.

Section B: Indian Tribes

> *By a "tribe" we understand a body of Indians of the same or similar race, united in community under one leadership or government, and inhabiting a particular though sometimes ill-defined territory....*
>
> U.S. Supreme Court
> In *Montoya v. United States* 1901, p. 266

B-1. *What defines an Indian tribe?*

The term "tribe" is commonly used in two senses—an ethnological sense and an official political sense. Distinguishing between them is important because the latter has far-reaching legal consequences.

Before the federal government developed official definitions for an Indian tribe, the term was purely ethnologic. A tribe was a group of indigenous people, bound together by blood ties, who were socially, politically, and religiously organized according to the tenets of their own culture, who lived together, occupying a definite territory, and who spoke a common language or dialect.

Originally, the question of official political delineations arose in connection with treaty relations. It was necessary to determine which groups were tribal political entities in order to negotiate treaties of peace or land acquisition on a government-to-government basis. Later, federal legislation to regulate Indian affairs, to allow claims for Indian depredations, to permit claims by Indians against the government, and to protect Indian property and other rights required determinations of which groups were affected by particular statutes (Cohen 1982).

Establishment of the Indian reservation system and the placement of tribes on reservations sometimes created new tribal identities. On some reservations, two or three ethnologically autonomous tribes were placed together and had to form a new political identity to deal with the U.S. government. Occasionally this led to great tribal stress or even warfare with the U.S., e.g., the Modoc War of 1873. In still other cases, a tribe might be broken up and spread over two or more reservations (e.g., the Chiricahua Apaches) to be politically absorbed into the "tribe" established for the particular reservation.

Today, after centuries of cultural and political interference by Euro-Americans, the term "tribe" might apply to a distinct group within an Indian village or community, the entire community, or a large number of communities. It might also refer to several different groups or villages speaking different languages but sharing a common government, or a widely scattered number of villages with a common language but no common government (Taylor 1984).

Legally, no universal definition for the generic term "tribe" exists in the U.S. Constitution, federal statutes, or regulations. Nonetheless, the term is specifically found in the Constitution, in hundreds of statutes, and in numerous regulations. In most instances, a question of a tribe's political existence can now be resolved by reference to a treaty, legislative agreement, statute, or executive order of the President "recognizing" the tribe at some time in the past. In other cases, the definition of "tribe" will depend in part on the context and the purpose for which the term is used (Cohen 1982). Occasionally, a court may find that there have been sufficient dealings by agents of the federal government (such as the BIA) with an Indian group that, over time, the group should be "recognized" as a tribe. This type of ruling has to be consistent with the overall intent of Congress in its broad constitutional authority over Indian affairs.

Canby (1981) provided a reasonable, contemporary, and concise definition to keep in mind as a basic initial response to the question of "What is an Indian tribe?" He wrote: "At the most general level, a tribe is simply a group of Indians that has been recognized as constituting a distinct and historically continuous political entity for at least some governmental purposes." By far, the most significant and valuable recognition is that of the U.S. government.

B-2. *What is the significance of federal "recognition" of an Indian tribe?*

Recall that, with the break-up of the Soviet Union in 1991, a number of the former republics declared their independence and immediately sought to obtain diplomatic "recognition" by other nations of the world, including the United States. Once granted by a nation, initially through a formal declaration, this recognition becomes the official acceptance of one nation by another as a fellow sovereign government. It is the starting point for an ongoing government-to-government relationship.

This international form of recognition is the historic foundation of our federal government's recognition of Indian tribes. It is a legacy from early colonial days when tribes were considered entirely independent nations with whom inter-governmental relations were to be observed and maintained. In its earliest years, the U.S. adopted this same policy from the precedent set by the British. But, by the early 1800s, all of the remaining independent Indian nations east of the Mississippi were subdued—through disease, conquest, pacification, and assimilation—and became "domestic dependent nations," as declared by the U.S. Supreme Court in 1831 (*Cherokee Nation v. Georgia*). Without realizing it, the other tribes which eventually came under U.S. jurisdiction as the country expanded also inherited dependent nation status. This occurred once they were recognized as tribes by the U.S. government through treaty negotiations or other official interactions. Recognized tribes, therefore, became semi-sovereign political entities whose level of self-government has varied over the years according to the policies of Congress, in addition to the effects of Supreme Court decisions.

Under regulations published in 1978, the Bureau of Indian Affairs can administratively "acknowledge" the existence of an Indian tribe. Acknowledgment is essentially the same as recognition. Perhaps because of its international flavor, however, "recognition" seems to be left mostly to use by Congress and the President.

Recognition or acknowledgment really have the same effect. They establish that a tribe exists as a unique political entity which has a formal relationship with the United States government—a relationship that is ultimately traceable to the Indian Commerce Clause and the Treaty Clause of the U.S. Constitution (Art. I, Sec. 8, Cl. 3 and Art. II, Sec. 2, Cl. 2, respectively). Recognition also establishes that a recognized tribe has certain inherent rights and powers of self-government and is entitled to specific benefits and services enumerated in various federal laws. Further, rights reserved or granted to tribes by treaties, executive orders of the President, or special acts of Congress, or rights verified through the judicial process, may be available to the tribe and its members. Finally, recognition also means that a tribe becomes subject to the extremely broad powers that Congress has in dealing with Indian tribes.

B-3. *How many tribes have federal recognition?*

As of January 1993, the official BIA count of politically recognized Indian tribes was 515. This number includes 318 "tribal entities" in the lower 48 states, which are described as Indian tribes, bands, villages, communities, and pueblos. (See Appendix 2.) The remaining 197 recognized entities are in Alaska.

The number for Alaska is slightly misleading, however. Though this number includes all of the politically recognized tribes, communities, bands, clans and villages, perhaps 300 more "Native Entities" in Alaska are "eligible to receive services from the United States Bureau of Indian Affairs" (Office of the Federal Register 1988). The difference is that, at present, these additional bands, villages, and communities, though eligible to receive services, are not politically recognized. (A list of those eligible appears in Appendix 3.) The main reason for this exception is that Congress has passed certain laws which apply only to Alaska Natives and their special circumstances. These laws make Native groups eligible for certain BIA programs even though they may not be officially recognized as tribes or may not be able to prove their historical existence as tribes. Absence of historical documentation on a number of Alaska groups would make it very difficult, if not impossible, for them to comply with such a requirement.

B-4. *Are any tribes not officially recognized by the federal government?*

Yes. Even though the great majority of ethnologically identifiable tribes in the U.S. are officially recognized by the federal government, some are not. Perhaps as many as 200 or more tribal entities are not recognized (O'Brien 1989). Reasons have varied. A few Indian groups which never made war on the U.S. may never have had the opportunity to get recognition through the treaty process. Others were so physically or socially isolated that nobody outside the local area ever officially noticed them. And, there were those who chose to keep to themselves and avoid contact with the United States, sometimes for fear of hostilities. Then there are tribes which once had been federally recognized but whose recognized status was terminated by Congress. In at least 26 instances, tribes are recognized by the states in which they reside, in the absence of federal recognition, and some may be satisfied to retain this status.

Nonetheless, a significant number of the Indian groups currently not recognized by the federal government desire recognition. Roughly 100 self-identified Indian tribes, at this writing, have active petitions for acknowledgment as "tribes" before the Secretary of the Interior. Some will be successful in the long and tedious process and some will not, the latter because they do not meet the regulatory requirements. At this time, the two most recent tribes to be successful with their requests for Congressional recognition or their petitions for acknowledgment by the Interior Department are the Mechoopda Indian Tribe of Chico Rancheria, California (April 1992) and the Aroostook Band of Micmac Indians of Maine (November 1991). Three Indian tribes from California were recognized in September 1991.

Generally, unless an Indian group currently desiring federal recognition can gain independent acknowledgment of its tribal status from Congress, it must comply with the Interior Department's petition process. The steps to be taken are set forth in Title 25 of the Code of Federal Regulations (CFR), Part 83, "Procedures for Establishing That An American Indian Group Exists As An Indian Tribe." These procedures are summarized in Appendix 4.

Members of some of the unrecognized tribes have asked Congress to reform the process of conferring recognition. They claim the administrative procedures: (1) are too burdensome with respect to documentation requirements, (2) are too costly to comply with (up to $500,000 for genealogical and historical research), (3) take far too long (up to a decade or more), and (4) are controlled by recognized tribes who want to keep other legitimate Indian groups from sharing in governmental privileges. In 1991, Senator John McCain of Arizona introduced a bill to transfer administrative authority for tribal recognition from the BIA to an independent commission. The BIA has stated that it is working to reform the procedures and, therefore, does not support the Senator's idea. Representatives of a number of recognized tribes say the present rules should be maintained to keep the process "respectable" (Lick 1991).

B-5. *What benefits and services are available to federally recognized tribes?*

The two main federal agencies which provide benefits and services to recognized Indian tribes are the Bureau of Indian Affairs (BIA) and the Indian Health Service (IHS). The BIA is a unit of the U.S. Department of the Interior and the IHS is a branch of the U.S. Department of Health and Human Services (USDHHS). Major benefits and services provided by these agencies include, but are not limited to, the following: medical and dental care, grants and programs for education, housing programs, aid in developing tribal governments and courts, resource management, and other services based upon tribal needs and interests. Some of the latter range from police protection and other law enforcement activities to economic development. With the federal government's policy of self-determination for tribes, a policy which has been evolving since the 1960s, numerous federal agencies have joined with tribal governments in providing services and benefits, just as they do with government entities like cities, counties, and states. To describe all the specific agencies and programs involved would require a separate book. The major players, including those within the USDI and USDHHS, are within the Departments of Agriculture, Education, Housing and Urban Development, Justice, Labor, and Transportation. The Environmental Protection Agency has also expanded its consultation and assistance roles in Indian country.

B-6. *What responsibility or accountability comes with federal recognition of an Indian tribe?*

A recognized tribe has a responsibility to provide some level of formalized government for its people—one that identifies and responds to the people's needs and goals as prescribed by the tribe's culture, laws, and capabilities, and by applicable federal law. This tribal government role can be much like that of other governments in the American system, be they local, state, or even the federal government. Frequently, larger tribes' activities involve programs relating to law enforcement, education, health care, employment, emergency services, transportation, housing, environmental protection, tribal courts, land and resource management, taxation, and social services. At the same time, these and less comprehensive tribal governments are often delimited by, and must remain consistent with, the many federal laws and regulations pertaining to Indian tribes. Among such laws are those affecting Indian government organization, disbursement of grants and other funds, the major crimes acts, civil rights legislation, and laws relating to Indian lands and other properties held in trust by the federal government.

B-7. *How is tribal membership determined?*

In the past, the government was directly involved in membership requirements of federal tribes. Federal officials decided, on a person-by-person basis, who was to be considered a member. The determinations, theoretically, were made through "good faith" evaluations.

Today it is generally the tribes which define who is and who is not a member–though Congress ultimately has authority to intervene. Tribal decisions on membership, however, are still influenced by past and present federal policies.

A formalized enrollment process exists for each tribe and is administered by the BIA or the tribe. The process varies among tribes but it is typically established by a tribal constitution, tribal law, or a separate tribal roll document approved by the federal government. Sophisticated methods of electronic record-keeping are often used.

As a caveat, the legal aspects of present-day tribal enrollment are entirely inconsistent with traditional concepts of tribal membership (Deloria 1974a). This concerns some Indian people so much that they refuse to participate in the official "federally sponsored" tribal enroll-ment process. A representative sentiment is: "This is not our way. We never determined who our people were through numbers and lists. These are rules of our colonizers...I will not comply with them" (Churchill 1991, p. 12, quoting Leonard Peltier, Ojibwa–Sioux).

Cohen (1982) reports that the courts have consistently declared one of an Indian tribe's most fundamental powers is that of determin-ing its own membership. A tribe may grant, deny, revoke, and qualify membership. Specific requirements may be established by custom, written law, treaty with the U.S., or intertribal agreement.

No single set of criteria exists which establishes tribal member-ship. Some tribes accept relationship through the mother, and others through the father, while many accept a tribal tie through either par-ent. The requirements concerning blood quantum also vary. In some instances, only a trace of Indian blood is required. Determining factors are those of (1) being a direct descendant of a previously or currently enrolled tribal member of Indian heritage and (2) being able to docu-ment this relationship adequately. Other tribes require one-half or more Indian blood, and some may have a rule that a tribal member must have been born on the tribe's reservation. For some tribes, adop-tion is another method of obtaining membership. This latter method may or may not lead to eligibility for tribal or federal government ser-vices, depending on the laws of the tribes and the Indian heritage of the adopted individual.

An excellent example of tribal membership rules appears in the Navajo Tribal Code and is reproduced in Appendix 5.

B-8. *What are the basic consequences of tribal membership?*

Official tribal membership is highly significant in a cultural sense. In addition, it is almost always a prerequisite for an Indian who needs to make use of education, training, health, and other assistance programs offered by tribal, state, or federal governments. Membership may bring the individual under tribal jurisdiction for certain criminal and civil matters. It can also make him or her subject to certain federal jurisdiction not otherwise applicable, though enrollment is less critical in this area. In other words, federal jurisdiction may apply if the individual concerned is not an enrolled tribal member but is found by the court to be "an Indian."

Tribal membership permits qualified individuals to take advantage of the preferences which the Bureau of Indian Affairs and the Indian Health Service have toward the hiring of Indians. Verifiable state or federal tribal membership also allows a person to legally produce and sell "Indian made" arts, crafts, and related products in accordance with the Indian Arts and Crafts Act of 1990 (discussed in a later section). Under this act, non-enrolled or non-authenticated artists and craftspersons—as well as museums and retailers—which knowingly misrepresent "Indian made items" are subject to substantial criminal penalties.

Finally, payments to tribal members under statute and treaty depend on enrollment, as do tribal voting rights and the capacity to be an elected tribal official. In addition, allotments of tribal land to individuals for living areas and for economic purposes can be made only to enrolled members (Park 1975).

B-9. *What are the largest and smallest Indian tribes in the U.S.?*

Officially, the largest Indian tribe in the U.S. is the Navajo Nation. The Indian population of the Navajo *Reservation* (including members of other tribes) is reported to be 143,405 (U.S. Bureau of the Census 1991). A tribal official recently quoted this author the number 146,001. The same official stated that a recent low estimate of the total Navajo population, on and off the reservation, was 167,000 but the number of people who qualify for enrollment may be as high as 215,000. The disparity is because not all Navajos are registered with the tribe, and many have moved to different regions of the country.

The Oklahoma Cherokee Nation, with about 120,000 enrolled members, is closest in population to the Navajo. It is noteworthy that the Oklahoma Cherokees no longer have a reservation. They were forced to relinquish it when Oklahoma became a state in 1907.

Determining the Indian population by tribe–as opposed to reservation–is difficult. During the 1990 census, for example, the Census Bureau counted tribal memberships for the first time. In the table which follows, population data for the largest tribes are at variance with those presented above because of the way the census counts were made. The Census Bureau counted as "Indian" everyone who said he or she was Indian, and then the individual was asked for tribal affiliation. There were 542 tribes counted, but two of them–Cherokee and Navajo–made up 25 percent of the total number of Indians counted. Although the Cherokee tribe is listed as the largest, its official enrollment is less than the Navajo, and Cherokee tribal officials acknowledge the Navajo as the largest tribe. Tribes listed in the table are those which the Census Bureau identifies as the largest American Indian tribes. Tribal enrollment numbers are often notably smaller.

LARGEST AMERICAN INDIAN TRIBES (as identified in the 1990 Census, through self-reporting)					
Cherokee	308,132	Tlingit	13,925	Ottawa	7,522
Navajo	219,198	Seminole	13,797	Ute	7,273
Chippewa	103,826	Athapaskans	13,738	Colville	7,140
Sioux	103,255	Cheyenne	11,456	Yuman	7,128
Choctaw	82,299	Comanche	11,322	Winnebago	6,920
Pueblo	52,939	Paiute	11,142	Arapaho	6,350
Apache	50,051	Salish	10,246	Shawnee	6,179
Iroquois	49,038	Yaqui	9,931	Assiniboine	5,274
Lumbee	48,444	Osage	9,527	Pomo	4,766
Creek	43,550	Kiowa	9,421	Sac and Fox	4,517
Blackfoot	32,234	Delaware	9,321	Miami	4,477
Canadian/		Shoshone	9,215	Yurok	4,296
Latin American	22,379	Crow	8,588	Omaha	4,143
Chickasaw	20,631	Cree	8,290	Nez Perce	4,113
Potawatomi	16,763	Yakima	7,850	Eastern tribes	3,928
Tohono O'odham	16,041	Houma	7,810		
Pima	14,431	Menominee	7,543		

The second most populated *reservation* in the U.S., with respect to Indians, is Pine Ridge, of the Oglala Lakota (Sioux) Nation. In 1990, some 11,182 Indian residents comprised 91.7% of the reservation's total population.

Determining the smallest tribe is difficult. It is likely to be one of several California *rancheria* groups which have half-a-dozen or fewer members. For example, Buena Vista Rancheria, near Sacramento, had only one tribal resident listed with the BIA in 1989. Other tiny tribal acreages in California and elsewhere have no residents.

B-10. *What is a "terminated" tribe?*

"Termination" is used to describe a specific policy toward Indian affairs, the popularity for which peaked in Congress in 1953 and resulted in the infamous House Concurrent Resolution 108. Simply stated, the policy goal of HCR 108 was to end the federally recognized status of Indian tribes and their trust relationship with the United States "as rapidly as possible." Many of the policy's naive but sometimes well-intentioned supporters were convinced they were finally going to solve "the Indian problem" through yet another form of forced assimilation—making the Indian people become just like "other citizens."

Approximately 100 Indian tribes, bands, and rancherias were thus "terminated," i.e., their official recognition as tribes ended; their special relationship with the federal government ended; they were fully subjected to state laws; and their lands were converted to private ownership, being sold in most instances.

With no formalized tribal organization, tribal lands, federal health care services, BIA education programs, or other benefits (except for frequently inadequate investments or short-lived monetary settlements), these people were set adrift. Generally, the results were disastrous.

Government enthusiasm for termination began to wane in the late-1960s. Many of the terminated tribes then began scratching and clawing their way back up through the bureaucracy to "recognized" status. The Ponca Tribe of Nebraska is among the most recent to regain federal recognition, on October 31, 1990–only 37 years after the termination resolution was passed by Congress!

B-11. *What is the President's official policy toward American Indian tribes?*

First, some background. Presidents historically played a much more direct and active role in Indian affairs than is the case today. Nonetheless, in modern times, the president does set the tone of the administration. If the president is perceived as being favorable toward Indian causes, as was President Lyndon B. Johnson, then the executive branch tends to adopt this positive attitude. However, if the president is uninterested (as were Eisenhower and Carter), or even hostile (as was Reagan), the executive branch will also tend to reflect an indifferent attitude (Deloria and Lytle 1984).

On June 14, 1991, President Bush issued his administration's official policy on American Indians. It was drafted by Interior Department officials, who will eventually do the same for President Clinton. The basic thrust of the Clinton policy may not vary greatly from the previous administration's, though it will likely present some changes in detail.

President Bush's concise statement, reproduced in full on the next page, is the most recent in a series of relatively positive White House policies that began with Lyndon Johnson (1968) in his historic special address to Congress on "The Forgotten American." Hopefully, Indian policy under President Clinton may be even more enlightened.

B-12. *Who are the Five Civilized Tribes and how did they get their name?*

The Oklahoma Indian nations referred to as the Five Civilized Tribes are the Creek, Choctaw, Chickasaw, Cherokee, and Seminole. Their

Reaffirming the Government-to-Government Relationship Between the Federal Government and Tribal Governments

On January 24, 1983, the Reagan-Bush Administration issued a statement on Indian policy recognizing and reaffirming a government-to-government relationship between Indian tribes and the Federal Government. This relationship is the cornerstone of the Bush–Quayle Administration's policy of fostering tribal self-government and self-determination.

Quasi-Sovereign Domestic Dependent Nations

This government-to-government relationship is the result of sovereign and independent tribal governments being incorporated into the fabric of our Nation, of Indian tribes becoming what our courts have come to refer to as quasi-sovereign domestic dependent nations. Over the years the relationship has flourished, grown, and evolved into a vibrant partnership in which over 500 tribal governments stand shoulder to shoulder with other governmental units that form our Republic.

This is now a relationship in which tribal governments may choose to assume the administration of numerous Federal programs pursuant to the 1975 Indian Self-Determination and Education Assistance Act.

Office of Self-Governance

This is a partnership in which an Office of Self-Governance has been established in the Department of the Interior and given the responsibility of working with tribes to craft creative ways of transferring decision-making powers over tribal government functions from the Department to tribal governments.

Office of American Indian Trust

An Office of American Indian Trust will be established in the Department of the Interior and given the responsibility of overseeing the trust responsibility of the Department and of insuring that no Departmental action will be taken that will adversely affect or destroy those physical assets that the Federal Government holds in trust for the tribes.

I take pride in acknowledging and reaffirming the existence and durability of our unique government-to-government relationship.

Personal Liaison

Within the White House I have designated a senior staff member, my Director of Intergovernmental Affairs, as my personal liaison with all Indian tribes. While it is not possible for a President or his small staff to deal directly with the multiplicity of issues and problems presented by each of the 510 tribal entities in the Nation now recognized by and dealing with the Department of the Interior, the White House will continue to interact with Indian tribes on an intergovernmental basis.

Permanent Relationship

The concepts of forced termination and excessive dependency on the Federal Government must now be relegated, once and for all, to the history books. Today we move forward toward a permanent relationship of understanding and trust, a relationship in which the tribes of the nation sit in positions of dependent sovereignty along with other governments that compose the family that is America.

ancestral lands covered a broad area of the southeastern U.S., east of the Mississippi River. Of the five, the Seminole tribe did not come into existence until the latter part of the 1700s. At that time, White pressure forced a fusion of smaller groups of resisting Creeks, Apalachicolas, Alabamas, and others into a tribal alliance which was identified separately by the federal government (Spicer 1969; Worton 1974).

During the late-1700s and early-1800s, in a political and social attempt to cope with overwhelming White encroachment, all five tribes adopted many of the customs and institutions of the settlers in their original homelands. These new lifeways included Christianity, individual land holdings, routine farming and stock raising, formal schooling, town living, Euro-American housing, road building, written constitutions, formal legal codes, and even Black slavery. Therefore, they were called "civilized" by their White neighbors and the national government.

This effort to stave off what proved to be the inevitable worked only so long. All the tribes were eventually forced to give up their lands during the 1820s to 1840s and move to reservations in the Indian territory west of the Mississippi. However, some of their tribesmen managed to stay behind in small and often isolated communities.

B-13. *Who are the Six Nations?*

The Six Nations constitute the Iroquois League, or Confederacy, of the Senecas, Mohawks, Onondagas, Cayugas, Oneidas, and Tuscaroras. They refer to themselves as the Haudenosaunee, or "People of the Longhouse." Their primary homelands are in central and western New York state. Before 1722, the Iroquois League consisted of the Five Nations, a name which some people have confused with the Five Civilized Tribes. In that year, the Tuscaroras joined the League after migrating north from the Carolinas where colonists and colonial militia had brought military actions against them (Spicer 1969).

Farb (1968) provided an overview of Iroquois constitutional government which suggested a significant resemblance to the United Nations. In the mid-1700s, the sophisticated political organization and powerful confederacy of the Iroquois strongly impressed several future revolutionaries like Benjamin Franklin and others. They went on to formulate the United States' first national government under the Articles of Confederation and borrowed at least some of their ideas from experiences with the Iroquois (Grinde 1977; Larabee 1961). One of the great traits of the Iroquois has been their tenacity in clinging to important aspects of their culture and self-government in the face of fierce and continual opposition and repression over the centuries. The same can be said for most of the other surviving tribes.

SECTION C: TREATIES AND AGREEMENTS

WHAT IS A TREATY?

The word "treaty" has more than one meaning. Under the principles of international law, the term broadly refers to any agreement, compact, alliance, convention, act, or contract between two or more independent nations with a view to the public welfare. This would include agreed-to terms of peace, alliance, boundary establishment, trade, or other issues of mutual interest. Such a treaty would normally be "formally signed by commissioners properly authorized and solemnly ratified by the...sovereigns or the supreme power of each state" (Black's Law Dictionary 1990). Specific means of ratification vary widely among nations and between agreements. Also, there is no set form for treaties. Most, however, including Indian-U.S. treaties, usually contain five elements: (1) a preamble, (2) terms and conditions, (3) provisos (special conditions, usually referring to some time in the future), (4) consideration (the exchange of something of value), and (5) signatures, seals, and marks (Kickingbird, et al. 1980).

Under the United States Constitution, technical application of the term "treaty" is more restrictive than in international law. It refers to those international agreements concluded by the President with the advice and consent of the Senate, provided it is ratified by "two thirds of the Senators present...." (Article II, Sec. 2, Cl. 2, U.S. Constitution). These are commonly referred to as "Article II treaties," which are binding on the states and others as "the supreme law of the land" (Article VI, Cl. 2).

C-1. *How did the U.S. begin its treaty-making policy with Indian tribes?*

> *A treaty is…to be read…in the light of that larger reason which constitutes the spirit of the law of nations.*
>
> U.S. Department of the Interior 1894, p. 665

The U.S. adopted the practice of negotiating formal treaties with Indian tribes directly from customs that were established by Great Britain and its colonial governments. At least 175 treaties had been concluded by these governments between 1607 and 1776. When the first colonists arrived in Virginia and Massachusetts, they were "shaking on the beach," as one Indian aptly described the situation to this author. They were in desperate need of four things in order to survive even their initial few months on the continent–land, food, shelter, and protection from attack. To secure these necessities the colonists began to negotiate formal agreements, both oral and written, with the powerful Indian tribes in their vicinities. This early treaty-making–which was acknowledged, encouraged, and later expanded by the British government–technically served to recognize tribal entities as members of the international community with sovereign powers to "treat" with, or contract with, European governments and their agents.

For the next 200 years, through the period of the American revolution and on into the War of 1812, major Indian tribes, or alliances of tribes, were considered to hold the balance of power in their part of the world. These tribes, such as the great Iroquois confederacy in the north and the Creek federation in the south, had survived disease, conquest, and assimilation. The British, French, and, later, the U.S. then competed to secure treaties with the strategic tribes.

The first treaty between the United States and an Indian tribe was the treaty with the Delaware Nation, dated September 17, 1778. A comparatively short document, it is reproduced in Appendix 6. This interesting agreement, which pre-dates the Constitution, even contains a provision that would allow other tribes to join the Delawares "and to form a state whereof the Delaware nation shall be the head, and have a representation in Congress"–but only with the approval of Congress.

Before 1815, the Delawares and other tribes negotiated their U.S. treaties from a position of some power. This was because they still exercised a good deal of control over the frontier and had the choice of allying with the British. When the War of 1812 ended and the British withdrew from U.S. territory, the tribes' bargaining power was reduced and U.S. policy began to reflect it.

The format for Indian-U.S. treaties and the procedures for putting them into effect were the same as for U.S. treaties with foreign nations. After the U.S. Constitution was ratified in 1789, all treaties ratified with Indian tribes were "Article II treaties." (See "What Is A Treaty?" at the beginning of this Section.) They were legally considered to have the same status, force, and dignity as the highest level of agreements with sovereign nations. As a result, the originals of Indian treaties were maintained by the Department of State after the Senate approved them. Each treaty file contained an original signed copy of the treaty (including the sometimes intriguing totem marks of the Indian signers), the presidential proclamation of it, the Senate resolution ratifying the treaty, and a printed copy of the treaty (Hill 1981). The original Indian treaties are now housed in the National Archives in Washington, D.C.

C-2. Does the U.S. still make treaties with Indian tribes?

No. The last official treaty with an Indian tribe, which the U.S. Senate ratified, was the Nez Perce treaty of August 13, 1868. In an obscure rider to an Indian appropriations bill, Congress abolished constitutional treaty-making with Indian tribes in 1871 (16 Stat. 566). The abrupt language of the statute reads:

> Hereafter, no Indian nation or tribe within the territory of the United States shall be acknowledged or recognized as an independent nation, tribe, or power with whom the United States may contract by treaty: **Provided, further,** That nothing herein contained shall be construed to invalidate or impair the obligation of any treaty heretofore lawfully made and ratified with any such Indian nation or tribe....

Several political forces were behind this action. In the early 1860s, for example, there were Union reactions to alliances made with the Confederacy by some of the southern Indian tribes. Colonel Ely S. Parker, Commissioner of Indian Affairs in 1869, believed that treaty-making by the Indians was a "farce" because he perceived a lack of sovereignty on their part. (Parker was the Seneca Indian who had served as General Grant's aide during the Civil War.) A third force included influential representatives of Protestant churches who felt treaty-making only served to perpetuate the "savage life" of the tribes. These people believed they were "called" to eliminate the Indians' culture. A fourth, and perhaps most important, force behind terminating the formal treaty process with Indian tribes was the U.S. House of Representatives. That body was tired of having no role in treaty-making; yet it had to appropriate funds to meet treaty obligations. The House wanted—and got—an equal voice in Indian affairs. As stated in the quotation above, the 1871 law did not in any way repeal or modify treaties that had been ratified prior to that date. If the 1871 legislation were to be fully repealed by Congress, formal treaties between the U.S. and Indian tribes would not seem to be barred by law. Some government officials, however, have said that Indians' U.S. citizenship now would legally preclude entering into new treaties (Deloria 1974a).

PHOTO COURTESY OF THE SMITHSONIAN INSTITUTION

The Treaty of Fort Laramie, negotiated in 1868 with the Sioux and Arapaho, was one of the last five Indian-U.S. treaties. The Indians (left to right) are Packs-His-Drum, Old-Man-Afraid-Of-His-Horses, and Red Bear.

C-3. *How have Indian tribes viewed the treaties they entered into with the U.S.?*

Historically, tribes viewed treaties as ways of preserving themselves as a people (Deloria and Lytle 1984). They sought two specific things from the federal government. One was a recognition of their rights to their specific homelands. The other was a commitment from the government to protect and defend their rights within those homelands from encroachment by non-Indians.

With the end of official treaty-making, most tribes came to view their treaties as sacred pledges on the part of the U.S. Later generations regarded the treaties as having the symbolic and moral significance associated with the Declaration of Independence and the Constitution. The federal government's unremitting antiseptic attitude toward the treaties, i.e., considering them to be routine legal documents that are subject to easy change and abrogation, is a continuing point of great concern among the tribes which have treaties with the U.S. (Kvasnicka 1988).

C-4. *Are Indian-U.S. treaties real treaties?*

Yes, although history shows that the terms of many treaties were not taken seriously. Many were violated by non-Indian civilians and government representatives even before the ink of the signatures was dry. It is also apparent that some treaties were unilaterally changed by members of the executive branch and the Senate, after the Indians had agreed to them, but before ratification. Nonetheless, it is abundantly clear– from numerous Supreme Court cases, historical actions of the President, and numerous acts of Congress–that Indian-U.S. treaties are solemn treaties according to international law. They are also unquestionably treaties according to the more restrictive standards of the United States Constitution.

A well-known international law publication, containing more than 230 volumes (Parry 1969), indexes all the treaties available from throughout the world that have been negotiated in the past several centuries. Listed, in chronological order with the rest of the world's treaties, are the treaties the United States has made with Indian tribes. British and French publications which reprint international state papers also contain copies of Indian-U.S. treaties (Meyer 1984). (See Kappler 1904 for the texts of Indian-U.S. treaties.)

Millions of non-Indian Americans who own lands once ceded to the U.S. by Indian tribes, through treaties and "agreements" (as discussed in subsequent questions), ultimately hold valid title to their lands based on the validity of the treaties and agreements.

C-5. *What rights to land and related resources did treaties give to Indian tribes that the tribes did not already have?*

None. It was the Indian tribes which granted the U.S. rights to lands–generally in exchange for peace, protection, less desirable lands, annuities, rations, manufactured goods, and services. This is sometimes a confusing concept for non-Indians to understand at first, but it is straightforward.

Indian tribes with which the U.S. made treaties were considered to have specific prior rights of ownership in their lands, which they had held long before the U.S. became a nation. Non-Indians often call these Native land rights "Indian title," "rights of occupancy," or "aboriginal rights." The U.S. government wanted to acquire most, if not all, of the tribes' lands for various reasons, e.g., to re-sell or grant to settlers, commercial interests, or others some time in the future. Through 1871, the treaty process was the main legal way to do this.

When a treaty involved some sort of land transfer (many, but not all, did), it typically stated in one section that the tribe or tribes concerned would "cede, relinquish, and convey to the United States all their right, title, and interest..." in a large tract of specified land, often exceeding millions of acres. (Quote is from Yakima Nation Treaty 1855.) Often, a subsequent section of the treaty would "reserve" a smaller area of the Indians' lands which they would keep for the use and occupancy of the tribe(s). Thus a "reservation" was created out of what was left. The Indian tribes, as recognized governments, retained or reserved the sovereign rights they had not granted to the U.S.

A brief quote from the milestone Supreme Court case of *United States v. Winans* (1905) summarizes the overall point: "[T]he treaty was not a grant of rights to the Indians, but a grant of rights from them...." The frequently heard term "treaty rights" thus refers to rights explicitly and implicitly retained by the tribe and not to rights granted by the U.S. government. It also refers to those obligations which the government owed the tribe in exchange for its lands as well as other consideration received from the federal government.

> *Treaty rights...have so many twists and turns as to make any statement on treaties appear to be an over-simplification.*
>
> Deloria 1974b, p. 59.

C-6. *How many official treaties did the U.S. make with Indian tribes?*

From the first Indian-U.S. treaty in 1778 to the end of official treaty-making in 1871, the U.S. Senate ratified 370 Indian treaties (some sources report 371). At least another 45 were negotiated with tribes during the same period but were never ratified by the Senate (Bureau of Indian Affairs 1903; Institute for the Development of Indian Law 1973). Even so, some of the unratified treaties took legal effect, as determined by the U.S. Court of Claims (Kvasnicka 1988).

C-7. *What is the present status of the Indian-U.S. treaties?*

Some were superceded by more recent treaties, some have been entirely abrogated (nullified) by acts of Congress, some have been partially abrogated, and all have been affected in one way or another by federal legislation and court decisions.

Whether abrogated or not, all of the treaties provide the foundation for the expanding body of United States law known as Federal

Indian Law. As Kickingbird et al. (1980, p. 45) have stated: "Treaties form the backdrop of the past, confirm rights of the present, and provide the basic definitions for the evolving future."

A recent confirmation of this statement was the multi-faceted role played by the 1854 "Treaty of Medicine Creek" in the "Puyallup Tribe of Indians Settlement Act" passed by the U.S. Congress in 1989. This legislation affirmed a negotiated settlement of conflicting Indian and non-Indian land claims. It also recognized several other important claims of the Puyallup Tribe of Washington state.

Treaties like that of Medicine Creek will obviously continue to influence Indian law. Those who question their validity solely because of the treaties' age are also, indirectly, questioning the validity of our 200-year-old Constitution, which not only pre-dates them but authorizes their negotiation and ratification.

C-8. *After 1778, were there other notable American Indian treaties besides those made with the U.S. government?*

Yes. In the 1830s and early-1840s, for example, several treaties of "Peace and Amity" were entered into by Comanches and the independent Republic of Texas (Demallie 1977). But, the most famous non-U.S. treaties were those from the Civil War era.

In 1861, attorney Albert Pike was named Commissioner of the Confederate States to the Indian Nations west of Arkansas. Pike competently negotiated more than a half-dozen treaties of "Friendship and Alliance" with the Five Civilized Tribes and with other so-called eastern and western tribes in the old Indian Territory, e.g., Osage, Shawnee, Seneca, Quapaw, Comanche, Wichita, Caddo, and Delaware (Gibson 1977).

The Confederate treaties with tribes in the Indian Territory were all similar. Their effect was to establish, through the Confederacy, the same rights and obligations that had been secured under U.S. treaties. Tribes were required to furnish troops to help defend Indian Territory against invasion by Union forces or by Indian tribes which were Union sympathizers. In turn, the Confederacy promised to protect the tribes from invasion or internal disorder. Another provision of the treaties allowed for tribal delegates to be accepted into the Confederate Congress. Of course, with the dissolution of the Confederacy at the end of the Civil War, all of the treaties became moot (Harlow 1935).

> *There shall be perpetual peace and friendship, and an alliance offensive and defensive, between the Confederate States of America and all their States and people, and the Cherokee Nation and all the people thereof.*
>
> Article I of the Confederate
> "Treaty with the Cherokees"
> October 7, 1861

C-9. *Can and do Indian tribes make treaties with each other?*

Yes. The practice of making inter-tribal alliances and other agreements has been going on as long as there have been tribes. This governmental function is an inherent right, included in that part of the tribes' sovereignty which they have not surrendered to the United States, and of which they have not otherwise been deprived. Among the most famous inter-tribal treaties of historic times was the Iroquois alliance, negotiated and ratified some 400 years ago. For the tribes involved, the Iroquois alliance served much the same function as the U.S. Constitution (Deloria and Lytle 1984).

Treaty-making between tribes has been all but dormant in this century. Since the termination days of several decades ago, however, new needs and renewed tribal confidence and vigor may bring about a resurrection of this time-honored and functional tool of government-to-government relations.

In fact, on October 1, 1991, four Oklahoma Indian tribes announced an historic inter-tribal treaty to improve law enforcement services within each of their adjoining jurisdictional areas (Anquoe 1991b). The Sac and Fox, Iowa, Kickapoo, and Citizen Band Potawatomi agreed to cross-deputize their police officers and provide cooperative and coordinated police training and services. This treaty affects 1600 square miles of eastern Oklahoma, representing the four combined tribal territorial areas. It is also possible that the treaty has set a modern precedent and inaugurated a new era in inter-tribal relations.

C-10. *What is an Indian-U.S. "agreement" as opposed to a treaty?*

After official treaty-making ended in 1871, the federal government continued negotiating with various tribes in just the same manner as it had for treaties. The end products of these negotiations, which most often had the primary purpose of achieving further reductions in Indian lands, were officially referred to as "agreements." It was sometimes difficult, however, to tell how the agreements differed from many of the earlier treaties. These agreements were submitted to both the Senate *and* the House of Representatives for ratification, whereas "treaties" had been ratified only by the Senate, under Article II of the Constitution. Agreements were occasionally approved by Congress in separate laws for the single purpose of ratification. The majority, however, were attached as riders to appropriations bills.

C-11. *Are formal Indian-U.S. "agreements" still made?*

Yes and no. The agreement era, which began in 1871, ended just over 40 years later, in 1913. That year, Congress amended and "ratified" an agreement, the last of that particular kind, between the United States and the Wiminuche Band of Southern Ute Indians. There was no specific policy to put an end to these types of agreements. The U.S. halted the practice, apparently, because it had obtained all the land and other concessions it wanted for that period. Later agreements have been referred to and treated as regular legislation.

A new, and somewhat different, agreement era seems to have begun as a result of (1) self-determination policies initiated in the late-

1960s and (2) associated efforts by tribes to reclaim lost rights. The Alaska Native Claims Settlement Act of 1971 was, in effect, the largest "Indian" agreement ever ratified by Congress. Also, as recently as 1989, Congress enacted legislation to ratify a major agreement "between the Puyallup Tribe of Indians, Local Governments in Pierce County [Washington], the State of Washington, the United States of America, and certain private property owners." Though it was designated a "Settlement Act," one major stated purpose of the legislation was to "ratify" an agreement to which the Puyallup Tribe and the federal government, among others, were parties. The traditional agreements of the late 19th and early 20th centuries primarily addressed such things as Indian land cessions to the U.S. and government annuities to the tribes. The newer "settlement agreements," which are likely to be negotiated and ratified into the foreseeable future, are apparently concerned with tribal land claims, water rights, resolution of conflicts involving Indians and non-Indians, and certain other issues related to tribal self-determination. (The more recent "Seneca Nation Land Claims Settlement," which was passed by Congress in 1990, involved another agreement in New York state. In this one, however, the U.S. served primarily as mediator for the Seneca Nation, the City of Salamanca, and the State of New York.)

C-12. *How many of the traditional Indian-U.S. agreements were made and what is their legal status?*

Between 1871 and 1913, at least 98 traditional agreements were negotiated and 96 of them were ratified by Congress. Unless abrogated later, each agreement remains law in its original form or as otherwise modified or amended by subsequent legislation.

In the 1975 U.S. Supreme Court case of *Antoine v. Washington*, the subject of the legal status of traditional Indian-U.S. agreements was addressed. The court found as follows: "Once ratified by Act of Congress the provisions of the agreements become law, and like treaties, the supreme law of the land." Further, some of the 1871-1913 agreements are indexed in the international treaty publications referred to in the answer to question C-4 (Hill 1981; Meyer 1984).

The Supreme Court added another twist to the question of the legal status of older Indian-U.S. agreements in the case of *Waldron v. United States* (1905). Interpreting the status of the Great Sioux Agreement of 1889 (25 Stat. 888), the Court stated flatly that, while the agreement "appears in form as an independent legislative act of the government, it was and is a treaty or contract made by the United States and the Sioux Nation of Indians."

SECTION D: MYTH, MISINFORMATION, AND STEREOTYPE

> *To kill an error is as good a service as, and sometimes even better than, the establishing [of] a new truth or fact.*
>
> Charles Darwin

D-1. *How did the United States government acquire America?*

This question is answered best with a quote by Felix S. Cohen (1947, p. 34-35), the most renowned expert in federal Indian law.

> Every American schoolboy is taught to believe that the lands of the United States were acquired by purchase or treaty from Britain, Spain, France, Mexico, and Russia, and that for all the continental lands so purchased we paid about 50 million dollars out of the federal treasury. Most of us believe this story as unquestioningly as we believe in electricity or corporations. We have seen little maps in our geography books showing the vast area that Napolean sold us in 1803 for 15 million dollars and the various cessions that make up the story of our national expansion. As for the original Indian owners of the continent, the common impression is that we took the land from them by force and proceeded to lock them up in concentration camps called "reservations."
>
> Notwithstanding this prevailing mythology, the historic fact is that practically all of the real estate acquired by the United States since 1776 was purchased not from Napolean or any other emperor or czar but from its original Indian owners. What we acquired from Napolean in the Louisiana Purchase was not real estate, for practically all of the ceded territory that was not privately owned by the Spanish and French settlers was still owned by the Indians, and the property rights of all the inhabitants were safeguarded by the terms of the treaty of cession. What we did acquire from Napolean was not the land, which was not his to sell, but simply the power to govern and tax....

Cohen concluded his discussion on this point by emphasizing the distinction between a *transfer of governmental power* and a *sale of land*. As for the lands comprising the Louisiana Territory, he contrasted the

15 million dollars paid to Napolean with the 20-times-this-amount eventually paid to Indian tribes. The former payment was for a cession (transfer) of political authority over the territory; the latter was to extinguish Indian title to the lands they ceded from within the area. Figure 2 illustrates how people generally believe the U.S. obtained the nation's land from Europeans. Figure 3, however, shows how the U.S. actually acquired title to most of the country through Indian land cessions. But even this does not present the broader story. About 180 separate tribal land areas were judicially recognized through Indian land claims, thus further subdividing most of the 67 areas shown in Figure 3. This was done because more than just 67 tribal entities had claims against the government for taking their lands without compensation. (See Prucha 1990a.) For example, nine

Figure 2. The United States obtained its lands in a number of ways. This map shows how the major blocks of land came under U.S. government control. It does not, however, show how most of the land was *actually* acquired through cessions from Native Americans. (From Coggins and Wilkinson 1981.)

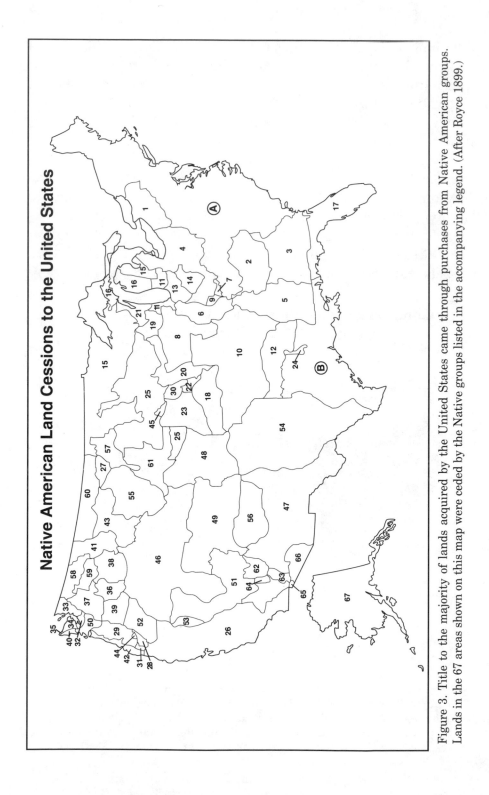

Figure 3. Title to the majority of lands acquired by the United States came through purchases from Native American groups. Lands in the 67 areas shown on this map were ceded by the Native groups listed in the accompanying legend. (After Royce 1899.)

Legend for Native American Land Cessions to the United States

Code numbers on map correspond with the tribes listed below, for land cessions in the United States after 1776.

1. Iroquois
2. Cherokee
3. Creek
4. Wyandot, Delaware, Chippewa, and allied tribes
5. Choctaw, Chickasaw
6. Kaskaskia
7. Delaware
8. Sauk, Fox
9. Piankashaw
10. Osage
11. Ottawa, Chippewa, Potawatomi
12. Quapaw
13. Potawatomi
14. Miami
15. Chippewa
16. Ottawa, Chippewa
17. Seminole
18. Kansas
19. Winnebago
20. Sauk, Fox, Sioux, Omaha, Iowa, Oto, Missouri
21. Menominee
22. Oto, Missouri
23. Pawnee
24. Caddo
25. Sioux
26. California Indians
27. Sioux Cheyenne, Arapaho, Crow, Assiniboine, Gros Ventre, Mandan, Arikara
28. Rogue River
29. Umpqua, Kalapuya
30. Omaha
31. Chastacosta et al.
32. Nisqually, Puyallup et al.
33. Duwamish, Suquamish et al.
34. Challam
35. Makah
36. Walla Walla, Cayuse, Umatilla
37. Yakima
38. Nez Perce
39. Confederated Tribes of Middle Oregon
40. Quinault, Quileute
41. Flathead et al.
42. Coast Tribes of Oregon
43. Blackfoot, Flathead, Nez Perce
44. Molala
45. Ponca
46. Shoshoni
47. Apache
48. Arapaho and Cheyenne
49. Ute
50. Chehalis, Chinook et al.
51. Paiute
52. Klamath et al.
53. Washo
54. Comanche, Kiowa
55. Crow
56. Navajo
57. Arikara, Gros Ventre, Mandan
58. Methow, Okanagan et al.
59. Coeur d'Alene et al.
60. Gros Ventre, Blackfoot, River Crow
61. Sioux, Northern Cheyenne, Arapaho
32. Hualapai
63. Yuma
64. Mojave
65. Cocopa
66. Papago, Pima, Maricopa
67. Alaska Natives

NOTE: The area designated "A" on the map corresponds to lands already acquired by the British, through treaty, purchase, warfare, etc., prior to the American Revolution. The area designated "B" represents land which Spain and France had acquired earlier from Indians.

million acres in the western portion of unit 47 (on the map) were declared by the federal government to have been original homelands of the Yavapai tribe, not the Apaches.

D-2. *How did the term "Red Man" come into use?*

It did not originate from self-descriptions by Native Americans. And, contrary to many beliefs, it did not begin with Columbus. He described the complexion of the Native people he encountered as "the color of the inhabitants of the Canaries [Canary Islands], neither black nor white..." (Wrone and Nelson 1973, p. 35).

The truth is that "red man" did not come into frequent use until the late-1700s. Further, it was not until the early-1800s that "red" became a universally accepted color label for American Indians. Before this time, descriptions given of the color of Indians varied, and rightly so. In fact, Indians vary in color from a deep, rich brown to what would technically be considered a "white" complexion.

From the 1400s through the 1600s, colonists employed cultural (not color) descriptions to identify the indigenous people of America. The use of "Indians," "Natives," and "savages" was common. When color was referred to, it was most often "tawny," "olive," "copper," and "brown." Russet, yellow, and white were sometimes used, and occasionally black. The term "red" is conspicuously absent in the literature describing Indian complexions for the first 200 years or so of European presence on the continent.

Many prominent figures from Europe and colonial America of the 17th and 18th centuries commented on Indian color at one time or another. In 1643, for example, Roger Williams of Rhode Island, in common with a number of contemporaries, said the Indians in his area were white. William Penn, in the 1680s, inconsistently described Indians as black and as the color of "Italians." In the 1720s, the English naturalist, Richard Bradley, wrote of American Indians as "a sort of White Men...." In the mid-1700s, Benjamin Franklin summed everything up in his own way by saying "all" of the Indians were "tawny," which the dictionary describes as yellowish brown or tan, e.g., the color of a lion.

A clear turn toward "red" in descriptive terminology can be traced to Europe in the mid-1700s. European naturalists were rigorously working at classifying the world's known species of plants and animals. Charles Linnaeus, of Sweden, was perhaps the most notable of these naturalists. He used primary colors to label the four basic human groups he identified. Though he actually wrote little about his human classifications, what he did write on the subject gained wide acceptance. Linnaeus' four human groups were: *Europaeus albus* (white), *Americanus rubescens* (red), *Asiaticus fuscus* (yellow), and *Africanus niger* (black).

Beginning about 1750, the well-read people in Europe and America began to use the term "red man," or variations thereof, with more frequency. Usage of "red" began to proliferate by 1775, when average colonials, as well as some of the Indian people in contact with them, also picked up the term. This was perhaps due to overhearing it or from seeing Indians in what was referred to as red "war paint" during the many conflicts of the time. (Application of pigments to the skin for various reasons was common among American Indians. Historically, however, the term "war paint" has been too broadly applied to that use of pigments.)

At the time, three clearly identifiable "races" were found on the continent. One consisted of "white" colonists, and a second was "black" slaves. Describing Indians as "red" was a convenient outflow of pre-existing and very strong social, cultural, and racial distinctions. Thomas Jefferson, who wrote of the "white, red, and black" races may have been the first public spokesman to use the tri-color metaphor for the races of early America.

Vaughn (1982, p. 948), the main source for this information, summarizes his research on the "red" question as follows:

> The precise reason for the gradual adoption of red, instead of tawny or some other hue, can only be surmised.... Not until the second half of the eighteenth century did "red" emerge as a fairly common label. By 1765 some Indians may have adopted the primary color label for themselves.... By the 1760s the continuing association of red bodypaint and an almost perpetual enmity –later heightened by the War for Independence–made "redskin" the most plausible epithet. Linnaeus' use of red gave additional impetus. Although the reasons for his choice remain obscure,

most likely he sought a primary color to parallel the other races' black, white, and yellow. Red was the obvious candidate because Indians used red stains so widely and because it avoided the confusion that might have come from such colors as brown, olive, and tawny, which were sometimes applied to racial subgroups.... In any event, [Thomas] Jefferson and some of his contemporaries used "red" as a racial category in the 1770s and 1780s, a trend that spread rapidly.... In the middle of the nineteenth century, James Fenimore Cooper's *The Redskins* (1846) and anthropologist Henry Rowe Schoolcraft's *The Red Race in America* (1847) symbolically marked Caucasian America's full recognition, in both fiction and science, of Indians as innately red and racially distinct.

D-3. *Was scalping introduced by Europeans?*

This controversial issue was actively debated in the 1960s and 1970s, and it has resurfaced in the 1990s (Associated Press 1991g). In a research paper published in 1986, James Axtell and William C. Sturtevant, two highly respected authors, say the answer is no. Many of the tribes in North and South America engaged in the practice of taking scalps or heads, as trophies, before the arrival of Europeans in the Western Hemisphere. This is not to say the practice of scalping victims or adversaries wasn't encouraged and promoted by Europeans. It was. Bounties were offered for Indian heads or scalps by Euro-Americans in various parts of North America from the 1600s to the 1800s. Frontiersmen and soldiers were also known to take heads or scalps without financial inducement. Even a few Indians were known to scalp other Indians for the bounty money offered by non-Indians (Wrone and Nelson 1973). It should be pointed out, however, that scalping was not practiced by all tribes.

In one widely cited book, Indian author Vine Deloria, Jr. (1969, p. 6) stated that scalping was "introduced prior to the French and Indian War by the English...." In support, he cited a scalp bounty offered in 1755 by Massachusetts. However, 220 years before this particular bounty was offered and 85 years before the English pilgrims landed, Jacques Cartier was shown "the skins of five men's heads, stretched on hoops, like parchment." In 1535, Cartier was making his second voyage up the St. Lawrence River when his Iroquois hosts in Quebec presented the five scalps taken from their enemies, the Micmacs. This and other convincing data regarding the widespread existence of scalping prior to European influence are cited by Axtell and Sturtevant (1986). (For a description of the traditional practices of trophy-taking and counting coup among the plains tribes, see Grinnell 1910.)

D-4. *Is it true that Indians are more susceptible to the intoxicating effects of alcohol than are non-Indians?*

No. As far back as the 1950s this myth was being refuted by research (Worton 1974). More recently, what people have stereotypically attributed to racial susceptibility has been tied directly to a particular consumption pattern that some Indians, like some non-Indians, tend to follow. Indian as well as non-Indian experts in the field of substance abuse refer to the pattern as binge drinking.

The binge pattern among Indians began to develop long ago in various groups whose members were encouraged by circumstances to drink hard and fast any liquor they acquired (Reynolds 1991). One function of this drinking style was to reduce the chances that authorities would discover and confiscate the alcoholic beverages. Depending on the circumstances, Indians could not legally acquire and consume alcohol in the same ways that non-Indians all around them could. This remains true for many reservation Indians.

Binge drinking seems to continue among some Native American communities for two basic reasons. First, legal restrictions of the past encouraged it for so long that it may have become a consumption norm in some circles. Second, the pattern is still encouraged indirectly by the prohibitions against alcohol which tribes have in place on various reservations. On reservations where alcohol is not sold, Indians must go to border towns off the reservations to obtain it. Of those who do, some drink quickly in order to finish before returning to the reservations, where their purchases might be confiscated. This scenario often leads to high profile problems in the border towns and on the roads back to the reservations. Media coverage reinforces the stereotype of the Indian.

The binge pattern does lead to one set of statistics that is much higher, per capita, for Native Americans than it is for other population groups, i.e., the rates of alcohol-related problems such as arrest, accidents, death, and illness (Reynolds 1991; Rhoades, Hammond, Welty, Handler, and Ambler 1987). Some tribes are addressing alcohol-related problems by legalizing the sale of alcohol on their reservations. Advocates suggest that tribal control of alcohol sales will reduce the border-town syndrome, bootlegging, and perhaps other elements of the alcohol abuse equation (Associated Press 1991h).

D-5. *Are reservation Indians required to stay on their reservations?*
As surprising as it may seem, some people still believe that many, if not most, Indians are somehow confined by the government to reservations (O'Brien 1989; Bureau of Indian Affairs 1991a). This, of course, is not true. More than two-thirds of all Indians do not live on reservations. But, whether they live on a reservation or not, all Native Americans can move about as freely as other Americans. This was not always the case, however.

In the 19th century, especially during the 1860s through the 1890s, the government routinely issued orders that prevented individuals and entire tribes from leaving the boundaries of their reservations without special permission. In fact, such a decree was the specific administrative action that led to the Battle of the Little Bighorn in 1876 and the killing of Sitting Bull in 1890. Similar orders played a part in other bloody conflicts, like the Wounded Knee Massacre in 1890. In each instance, the government was worried about Indian activities. It issued reservation confinement orders and then followed up with force.

By the beginning of the 20th century, confinement of entire tribes was no longer practiced. However, many individual Indians essentially became long-term prisoners of war. Two of the most notable were Joseph (Nez Perce) and Geronimo (Chiricahua Apache). They died in 1904 and 1909, respectively, after spending decades in forced exile on reservations far from their homelands.

Joseph, who repeatedly tried to gain permission to return to his native Idaho, once said, "I have asked some of the great white chiefs where they get their authority to say to the Indian that he shall stay in one place. They cannot tell me" (Capps 1975, p. 185). Perhaps the misconception that may still exist about reservation confinement is nothing more than a holdover from the reality of the late 19th and early 20th centuries.

D-6. *What is the "politically correct" term to use in referring to American Indians?*

The important social question as to how to refer courteously to the first Americans warrants some exploration. To reduce potential confusion, the eye-opening answer will be divided into three sections: Lower 48 States, Alaska, and Hawaii.

Lower 48 States

A lot of Anglo-American terminology has been used over the past 500 years to distinguish the Indian people of North America from non-Natives. It is instructive to review some of these appellations (those that are printable), especially the older ones appearing in numerous historic documents. They include:

Indians	West Indians	Savages
Heathens	Americans	Natives
Barbarians	Old People	Virginians
Wild People	Brutish People	Country People
Naturals	Inhabitants	Old Inhabitants
Red Devils	Indigenous People	Tawny Serpents
Redskins	Red Men	Aborigines

Obviously, nearly all of these terms fell into disuse long ago. Historically, however, "Indians" appears to have been most often employed. It is significant that, into the early and perhaps mid-18th century, the terms "Indians" and "Americans" were equivalent. Until then, "Americans" was not applied to those people of European heritage in North America (Vaughn 1982).

The more common of the acceptable modern terms that have been used to designate indigenous Americans (of the contiguous 48 states) include "Indians," "American Indians," "Native Americans," "Amerinds," and "Amerindians." Axtell (1988) says that Canadian social scientists are fond of the last two terms, but he and many others consider them to be awkward jargon. He also reports that reservation and rural Indians generally prefer "Indian" over "Native American." Axtell further suggests that urban Indians and non-Indian urban dwellers, along with federal grant and college application writers, frequently prefer "Native American."

Deloria (1974b, p. 6) states that "Indian Americans," as opposed to "American Indians," is not a welcome term in Indian circles because it was derived from the "melting pot" social theory–a concept injurious to tribalism. Deloria's further comments, largely in agreement with Axtell's, are as follows:

> Just what "Indians" are to be called today remains a subject of great debate. Anthropologists have attempted to call us "Amerindians" or "Amerinds," but the phrase has not caught on. A great many younger Indian people have tried to popularize the phrase "Native Americans," but the older generation feels ill at ease with this name. In all probability no name other than "Indians" will ever satisfy most of the people known popularly as "Indians."

Since Deloria wrote those remarks, use of the name "Native Americans" has grown widely among Indians and non-Indians, but especially among the latter. Many non-Indians (e.g., Wills 1991) now mistakenly believe that it is the only correct term to use when referring to American Indians.

Tim Giago (1991c), publisher of the largest Indian advocacy newspaper in the country, states that the editorial policy of *Indian Country Today* includes use of the terms "American Indian," "Indian," and "Native American." The preference is to use individual tribal affiliations whenever possible, e.g., Lakota, Onondaga, Pomo, etc. This is a good rule to follow in all situations where applicable. Several of Mr. Giago's comments on the nomenclature issue are worth quoting:

> We are, more and more, pulling away from using Native American, because, as so many phone calls and letters have

pointed out to us, and correctly so, anyone born in America can refer to themselves [sic] as Native American.

We realize the word "Indian" is a misnomer, but for generic purposes, we are forced to use it when speaking of many different tribes. American Indian is also acceptable in Indian country.

Any politically correct thinker who believes Native American is the preferred identification tag for the Lakota or any other tribe is wrong. Most of us do not object to the use of Indian or American Indian. And as I said, Native American can be used by any American native to this land.

Alaska

In Alaska, "Natives" and "Alaska Natives" are the widely accepted terms for the three ethnologic groups of indigenous people Eskimos, Aleuts, and Indians (Price 1978; Alaska Native Claims Settlement Act of 1971; Case 1984).

The Alaskan people who are still commonly referred to by Natives and non-Natives as "Eskimos" are now also called "Inuit." In 1977, at the Inuit Circumpolar Conference held in Barrow, Alaska, the term Inuit ("the people") was officially adopted as a preferred designation when collectively referring to Eskimos (Damas 1984). "Eskimo" has long been considered to have come from an eastern Canadian Algonquian term which means "raw meat eaters." Some, but not all, Inuit would rather it not be used. Major subgroups of Alaska's Eskimos are the North Slope Inuit (Inupiat), the Central Alaskan Inuit (Yup'ik), and the southern or Pacific Inuit (Sugpiaq). A number of Sugpiaq (e.g., on the Kenai Peninsula and Kodiak Island) have come to accept and prefer the "Aleut" designation mistakenly applied to them by the Russians in the late-18th and early-19th centuries (Lantis 1984).

"Aleut" is the acceptable designation for the people of the western Alaska Peninsula, the Pribilof Islands, and the Aleutian Island chain. The name is of Russian origin and was probably borrowed from the Native village of Alut, located on the Kamchatka Peninsula of the Russian far east. Russian fur traders used "Aleut" to identify the people of the Aleutian Islands. The two major linguistic divisions of Aleuts are the Atkan (western) and Unalaska (eastern) branches (Lantis 1984).

"Indians" native to the Cook Inlet and interior regions of Alaska commonly refer to themselves as "Athapaskans," a broad ethnologic term. There are, however, a number of major Athapaskan groups, e.g., Kutchin, Koyukon, Nabesna, Han, Tanana, Holikachuk, Kolchan, Ingalik, Tanaina, and Ahtna (Prucha 1990a; Waldman 1985). Indian people of southeast coastal Alaska are often referred to as "Southeast Villagers" or "Southeast Natives, " but their preferred tribal names, in north-to-south order, are Eyak, Tlingit, Haida, and Tsimshian.

Hawaii

The indigenous people of Hawaii prefer the terms "Hawaiians," "Hawaiian Natives," or "Native Hawaiians" over "Native Americans." In fact, some Hawaiians take such offense at being called "Native Americans" that the term is almost considered to be "fighting words" (Trask 1991). The reason is simple. Many Native Hawaiians harbor great resentment over the 1893 coup, orchestrated by American businessmen, which overthrew the government of the independent nation of Hawaii and led to annexation of Hawaii to the United States five years later. Annexation also led to great misery, hardship, and economic loss for the dispossessed Native Hawaiians and many of their descendants.

D-7. Do Indians serve in the military?

Yes. Indian men and women have the same obligations and opportunities for military service as other U.S. citizens. Indeed, they have a long history of serving with the nation's armed forces, dating back to the Revolution.

After the recent War with Iraq, the Bureau of Indian Affairs (1991a) updated its still incomplete information on Indian veteran history. It reported that about 3,000 Indian military personnel served in the Persian Gulf theatre of operations. Three Indian men were among those killed in action. A total of 24,000 Indian men and women were in the military in 1990 just prior to Operation Desert Storm.

During the Viet Nam War, 41,500 Indians served in the armed forces. Many of these people have helped organize important Indian veterans' groups, like the Navajo Nation Viet Nam Veterans. Also, thousands of Indians served in Korea, where one Indian soldier was awarded the Congressional Medal of Honor.

During World War II, about 25,000 Indian men and women were in the military, mostly the Army. They served on all fronts in Europe and Asia and were awarded at least 215 medals for valor, including two Congressional Medals of Honor. The most famous Indian exploit of World War II involved the Navy Department's use of Navajo Marines as "code talkers." Trained as battlefield radiomen, these Navajos converted military radio traffic to a special classified version of their own language and conversed without fear that the Japanese could break their "code." Stallings (1963) reported instances of Indian language, such as Choctaw, being employed as "code" for battlefield telephone use in World War I, but this was done on the initiative of soldiers in the field and apparently had no official military sanction.

Approximately 8,000 Indians were in the military during World War I. Their valor and demonstrated patriotism moved Congress to pass the Indian Citizenship Act of 1924.

Indian soldiers were also active in the Civil War, on both sides. For example, Colonel Eli Parker, a Seneca, was an aide to General Grant. Parker attended General Lee's surrender at Appamattox on April 9, 1865, and served as secretary, recording the conditions of surrender. Stand Watie, a Cherokee, was the last Confederate general to surrender, on June 23, 1865. One more Confederate Indian unit, in what was probably the final act of the war, surrendered in mid-July (Harlow 1935).

Today, approximately one in four adult Indian men is a veteran, and just over 45 percent of current tribal leaders are veterans.

D-8. *What offends many Indians about sports mascots such as the Washington "Redskins?"*

Not all Indians are offended. Some Eastern Cherokees, for example, have come out publicly in support of the Redskins, Kansas City Chiefs, Cleveland Indians, and Atlanta Braves. The tribe's principal chief, Jonathon Taylor, unabashedly states that the sports teams are good for the tribe's crafts business which recently sold 300,000 mass-produced headdresses.

The Kansas City Chiefs professional football team is called "The Tribe." This is an example of what many—but not all—Indians consider to be inappropriate use of the Indian image. Photo © Costacos Bros. Sports.

Nonetheless, tens of thousands of Native Americans are clearly offended by the use of Indian mascots, though not in every instance —such as at some Indian schools. A major concern is racism, blatant or not. And, there is offense taken at what are seen as stereotypical and disrespectful antics by fans and players. Charlene Teters (1991), a Spokane with the National Congress of American Indians, makes a point when she argues, "These symbols must be seen for what they are: relics from a time period when racism and manifest destiny were the common basis for decisions affecting Indian people. [They] honor neither Indian or non-Indian [and] should have gone by the wayside with Little Black Sambo and the Frito Bandito."

A third point of contention is the inappropriate use of items like pipes, body paint designs, and feathers, all of which are considered sacred in traditional Native American cultures.

Non-Indians are responding with, "Why haven't you complained before?" Some Native Americans have, but nobody would listen. People need to understand the heavy cloud of repression that has hung over Indian country for so long, just as slavery and racism bottled up the voice of Black America. It was only 20 years ago that the cloud over Indian country began to lift in any significant way. Growth of the mascot controversy indicates that more Native Americans are feeling free to express their concerns publicly about things that have bothered them for a long time. Media interest, stirred by the Columbus Quincentennial, has also stimulated the exercising of Native Americans' long-dormant right to freedom of expression.

One of those speaking out on Indian issues is Tim Giago, Oglala Lakota (Sioux) and publisher of *Indian Country Today*, a weekly newspaper which includes *The Lakota Times*. Printed below, with permission, is a pertinent editorial from Mr. Giago's "Notes from Indian Country" (1991a). It exemplifies the Indian point of view about some of the things Native Americans find offensive in the highly charged and symbolic issue of Indian sports mascots. Mr. Giago affirms a concern for racism but moves on to address religious aspects of the mascot issue that are sometimes overlooked.

MASCOTS, SPIRITUALITY, AND INSENSITIVITY

Indians as mascots has been a point of contention for many years among Native Americans.

Most of our ranting and raving has fallen on nearly deaf ears lo these many years.

Suddenly, as the Atlanta Braves fought their way to the World Series, other voices picked up our indignant shouts and the issue has taken on national stature.

As a columnist and newspaper editor, these are the things we have struggled to get on the front pages of the national media for years and we are pleased to see it become a national issue.

As an American Indian writer who has spent much of his life "covering the coverage," it does my heart good to get this kind of support, support vitally needed by the Indian people if we are to see change.

The media has centered its attention on whether the sham rituals and painted faces in the stands at Braves' baseball games border on racism. In our minds (Indians) it does, but there is another side of this coin I have written about that needs to be expanded at this time.

The sham rituals, such as the wearing of feathers, smoking of so-called peace pipes, beating of tom-toms, fake dances, horrendous attempts at singing Indian songs, the so-called war whoops, and the painted faces, address more than the issues of racism. They are direct attacks upon the spirituality (religion) of the Indian people.

Suppose a team like the New Orleans Saints decided to include religious rituals in their halftime shows in keeping with their name. Would different religious groups feel insulted to see these rituals on national television?

For instance: suppose Saints' fans decided to emulate Catholicism as part of their routine. What if they carried crosses, had a mascot dressed up like the Pope, spread ashes on their foreheads, and displayed enlarged replicas of the sacramental bread of Holy Communion while drinking from chalices filled with wine?

Would Catholics consider these routines anti-Catholic?

Eagle feathers play an important role in the spirituality of Native Americans. Faces are painted in a sacred way.

The Pipes that became known to the white man as "peace pipes" are known to most Indians who use them as part of their spirituality as Sacred Pipes. ...To most tribes of the Great Plains the Pipe was, and is, their Bible.

Because the treaties signed between the sovereign Indian nations and the U.S. government were so sacred and so important to the Indian nations, the signing was usually attended by the smoking of a Sacred Pipe.

This spiritual gesture was intended to show the white man that the document just signed was a sacred one and would be treated as such by the Indian people.

Since most of the treaties were intended to bring about peace between white man and Indian, the *wasicu* (white man) called the Sacred Pipe a peace pipe.

The point I hope to make here is that there is a national insensitivity when it comes to the religious beliefs, traditional values and the culture of the American Indian.

It is bad enough that America sees nothing wrong in naming football teams after the color of a people's skin. Jack Kent Cooke [owner of the Redskins] considers the name Washington Redskins complimentary to the Indian people.

Would he consider a team called the Minnesota White-skins complimentary to the white race?

The Christian Bible says, "Do unto others as you would have them do unto you." Would God-fearing Christians use sports mascots that would insult the Jewish people, Muslims, Buddhists, Shintoists, Hindus or any other minority religious group?

If not, then why in the world would they do this to the indigenous people of the Western Hemisphere, the American Indian?

As we approach the Quincentennial of Columbus, it is important that America take a long, hard look at itself and its dealings with Native Americans over the past 500 years.

Most foreigners, particularly those from countries that have been colonized by others (African nations), look upon America as a nation with two faces.

One face it shows to the world as a land of democracy and freedom, the other it shows to its indigenous peoples as uncaring, greedy, dictatorial and often-times racist.

By the time December 31, 1992, rolls around, most of us will be sick of Christopher Columbus, revisionists, and politically correct thinkers, but that doesn't mean there is not a whole lot of truth in the things Native Americans are complaining about.

Stop insulting the spirituality and the traditional beliefs of the Indian people by making us mascots for athletic teams. Is that asking so much of America?

Tim Giago
© *1991 Lakota Times*

D-9. What stereotypical images are associated with Indians, and are some Native Americans also guilty of stereotyping?

Ugh. Me Gettum, Kemo Sabe?
Tonto, *The Lone Ranger*, 1933

Sometimes it was hard to believe that this strange bloody-minded red race was human at all. It was as if giant lizards had come on horses, mouthing and grunting their unearthly language that so few white men had ever understood
From the 1957 "western" novel *The Unforgiven*
Stedman 1982, p. 118

The Savages are utter Strangers to distinctions of Property, for what belongs to one is equally others! ...Money is in use with none of them....They'll tell you that amongst us [Whites] the People Murder, Plunder, Defame, and betray one another....They think it unaccountable that one Man should have more than another....'Tis vain to remonstrate to them how useful the Distinction of Property is for the support of a Society....In fine, they neither quarrel, Nor Fight, Nor Slander one another.

Quoting Baron de Lahontan, who helped invent the European version of "The Noble Savage" for the 18th century era of European Enlightenment
Leland 1990, p. 145-145

A stereotype may be defined loosely as a somewhat fixed or unvarying image which people have about something—be it an object, a set of beliefs or actions, or a group of people. The image can be uncomplimentary because it is frequently applied to all members of the same category, regardless of how true it is. Thus, stereotyping is often associated with prejudice. Most stereotyping overemphasizes one or more characteristics which may be partly true, and this often results in distortions about those characteristics.

In the Indian world, for example, everyone would agree that there were Plains tribes with horse-riding, feather-bonnetted warriors and that some of these tribes were viewed as a threat to White expansion. That, in itself, is not a distortion. It became a stereotype in motion pictures and television by endless repetition. It also occurred through the ignoring of hundreds of other Native societies, the other kinds of Indian–White relationships, Indian societies in their own terms, and the crucial roles of women among Native American peoples (Price 1978).

Indian stereotypes are so numerous that hundreds of works address the issue, and entire volumes have been written on the subject. Books with titles like *Shadows of the Indian* (Stedman 1982), *The White Man's Indian* (Berkhofer 1979), and *The Invented Indian* (Clifton 1990) make informative and provocative reading.

Stereotypes applied to Native Americans over the past 500 years show that Native people have been variously defined as innocent children of nature, subhuman demons, untrustworthy thieves, noble savages, bloodthirsty murderers, royal princesses, human curiosities, unfeeling stoics, natural-born warriors, innately inferior humans, shiftless wanderers, vanishing vestiges of the stone age, wild animals, oppressed and promiscuous "squaws," lazy parasites, incompetents, devil worshippers, completely democratic egalitarians, loyal "Men Friday," born bearers of wisdom, magical healers, depraved drunkards, born mystics, automatic knowers of nature, threats to female virtue, supernaturals, favored "pets" of the government, the enemy, racist "white-bashers," the antithesis to "civilization," and the bearers of a holy message to mankind. Throughout history, it seems, Native Americans have been routinely regarded as almost anything but true-to-life men, women, and children, who are as individualistic and human as any other people on earth (Josephy 1982).

Stereotypical images are used to attract the attention of tourists where so-called "trading posts" and other curio shops are found. Some of these establishments do not even carry genuine Indian items. While not ill-intentioned, these totems are not always well received by Native Americans.

Another stereotypical theme about Indians in the late 20th century is that of the "true Indian" archetype. This idea was nurtured by the attractively done motion picture *"Dances With Wolves."*

> "Spontaneous, Natural, Timeless, Original" have been the most common ways of characterizing the True Indian[s] as human beings, identifying what is specific to them with the additional provisos that True Indians live close to and in harmony with nature, and are just as agreeably fused with one another socially in conflict-free consensual communities.
>
> Simard 1990, p. 354-355

Viewing today's Native Americans through impossible, non-Indian expectations is grossly unfair. Indians today simply do not fit the images portrayed in the "true Indian" stereotype. As Schickel (1975) wrote, "Total goodness is also less than human."

With the exception of certain Alaska Natives, few Native Americans today live mostly "off the land." In fact, some non-Indians live "closer to nature" than do most Indians. Because of 500 years of uninvited change, most Native Americans reside in or near urban settings. All use one form or another of modern transportation and buy

modern groceries. And, all have varying degrees of personal, inter-
personal, and social conflict affecting their lives. Indians, Inuit, and
Aleuts are human beings who possess the same general strengths and
frailties as everyone else. They also have the same aspirations to take
their self-defined and deserved place in the world without undesired
interference or involvement by the larger society.

As to the matter of stereotyping *by* Indians, it obviously occurs
among many. In the "them-and-us" scenario necessary for stereotyping to take place, the "them" is the "White Man." Naturally, this omits
the millions of Hispanics, African Americans, and Oriental Americans who will collectively constitute the majority of American society
in the 21st century. The stereotypical view which many Indians have
of White society is that *it* always has the flaws. It is guilty of racism,
historical injustices, continuing legal injustices, environmental pollution, introduction of alcohol and the death penalty, culture-crushing,
genocide, the killing off of Native religions, etc. Typical of stereotyping, there is frequently little room for someone defined as a "White
Man" to have an individuality separate from the massed wrongs of
the past and present. Whatever is wrong with "White" society is perceived as not being part of Native culture. This allows Indians to
maintain claims of moral superiority over the majority race.

One has to admit to an overwhelming amount of historical and
often continuing motivation for Indian stereotyping of the "White
Man." The Lakota scholar, Vine Deloria (1970, p. 44), however, has
thoughtfully criticized stereotyping by Indians and other minorities.
"They must not fall into the same trap by simply reversing the
process that has stereotyped them. Minority groups must thrust
through the rhetorical blockade by creating within themselves a sense
of 'peoplehood'." These are words of wisdom for everyone.

Section E: Culture and Religion

> *So what is it you guys want...? Secrets? Mystery?...I can tell you right now there are no secrets. There's no mystery. There's only common sense.*
>
> Oren Lyons, Onondaga elder
> Comments to two non-Indian "seekers"
> In Wall and Arden 1990, p. 64

E-1. *Do American Indians have a common cultural heritage?*

From a nationwide perspective, the general answer would have to be "no." The stereotypical image of horse-mounted warriors, wearing "war bonnets" and hunting bison, is far from being representative of the diverse cultural heritage of all Native Americans.

At the time of first European contact, in the 15th century, hundreds of Native cultures existed in what is now the U.S. The fact is, there were as many individual cultures as there were tribes and smaller, self-sufficient living groups.

Anthropologists, archaeologists, and ethnologists have developed a broad system of 10 culture areas to classify the many Native cultures of America's past. (See Figure 4.) These areas were identified on the basis of such things as geographical influence, family and kinship systems, seasonal life, economic structure, and other factors (O'Brien 1989). Information relevant to these culture areas and the people who lived within them may be found in many thousands of books and articles published during the past century. Perhaps the best all-around source is the Smithsonian Institution's multi-volume work that is being published under the title "Handbook of North American Indians." Nearing completion, this 20-volume encyclopedic series summarizes what is known about the prehistory, history, and cultures of the indigenous peoples of North America. Most of the 11 volumes on the culture areas are now available through many libraries and book stores. (An easily accessible overview of early Native culture is provided in the October 1991 issue of *National Geographic*. Other good starting places are: Encyclopaedia Britannica 1990; Owen, Deetz, and Fisher 1967; Spicer 1982; Waldman 1985.)

   Though the identified culture areas help in modern understanding of the old cultures, it should be noted that they would have had
no useful meaning for Native peoples of the past. Tribal territories
were sometimes vague or changing. There was often much regional
movement of tribes and transfer of cultural traits from one area to
another. Interestingly, people of the same language family commonly
lived in different cultures or even inhabited separate ends of the continent. The Athapaskan-speaking groups of the Subarctic and the
Southwest are good examples.

   Despite the diversity of traditional cultures, there are two broad
phenomena which show a similarity in today's Native Americans
across the continent. These are: (1) nature-based, traditional lifeways
and (2) a shared response to Euro-American society (Owen, Deetz,
and Fisher 1967; Deloria 1973). With increased travel, communication,
and inter-tribal marriage in the latter part of the 20th century, the
amount of cross-cultural sharing and blending is also on the increase.

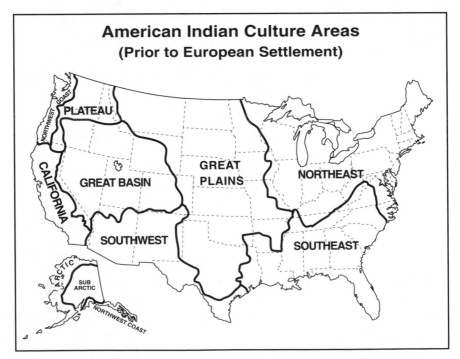

Figure 4. The ten broad culture areas recognized for pre-Columbian American
Indians on the basis of geography, kinship systems, seasonal life, economy, etc.
(After Prucha 1990a.)

E-2. *What is the basic philosophical difference between American culture at large and traditional Native American culture?*

Recognizing that the two "cultures" are actually collections of numerous sub-cultures, a broad and contrasting comparison can nonetheless be made. Simply stated, traditional Native cultures (beyond the basic issues of survival) generally have had the acquisition of wisdom and the development of spiritual awareness as their philosophical goals. On the other hand, the larger American society is philosophically inclined toward acquisition of information and the development of profit—the latter being in financial or material form.

One caveat to remember is that there are no completely traditional Native cultures left in the United States. Many tribal groups, however, are philosophically close to their traditional past. The Hopi of Arizona and the traditional Kickapoo of south Texas are two examples. In addition, most Native groups which have not clung to their pasts still consider wisdom and spiritualism their guiding ideals.

One further point is that western culture generally tends to measure its advancement by the distance it places between itself and nature. In contrast, traditional Native cultures tend to view greater closeness to the natural world and its cycles as a measure of significant achievement.

E-3. *Why are so many non-Indians especially interested in traditional Indian cultures, arts, and crafts?*

One can only surmise an answer, but this question addresses a truly ironic phenomenon. This country oppressed the Native people for so long through military, social, legal, and economic measures. Yet, there is a surprisingly large segment of the population which, indeed, greatly admires the cultures of the first Americans.

In part, this admiration may stem from the romanticism which Americans associate with the larger nation's origins. The great human drama which unfolded as colonial America clashed with hundreds of smaller Native nations has always been a captivating theme. Many also recognize an inherent quality in the traditional social and material culture of Native Americans that is generally lacking in our modern society. But, there is probably something much deeper.

Dr. Carl Sagan has said that humankind has always had a desire to feel connected with the cosmos. It is only in the last millennium that western society began to abandon the truly elemental life–a life that continued to be lived by a few Inuit in Alaska and Canada as recently as the early 1950s. Also, it is only in the 20th century–a mere snippet of the total period of human existence–that television, radio, telephone, airplane, automobile, and other machines have come to dominate the world. Could it be that, just below the surface of the popularity of Native culture, lies a faint human memory of an earlier era–when the "connectedness" Carl Sagan talks about was strongly felt by *all* people?

To explain this by example, T.C. McLuhan published what became an immensely popular book–*Touch the Earth* (1971). It consists, primarily, of beautiful photographs of American Indians taken at the turn of the century by renowned photographer Edward S. Curtis. The photographs are accompanied by selected quotations which describe a kinship with nature and unity with the elements. One could reasonably submit that many who acquire and read *Touch the Earth*, like the non-Indians who are actively interested in Native cultures, are vicariously trying to do as the title states.

Anthropology professor Alice Kehoe (1990) takes the explanation of the Indian popularity phenomenon one step farther. She ascribes much of it–as many others have–to "cultural primitivism," or the discontent of the civilized with civilization. "[H]undreds of thousands of Europeans and Americans, alienated by our culture...look to representations of non-Western cultures for 'authentic' experiences. To gain 'genuine' culture, they seek...Asian or American Indian" (Kehoe 1990, p. 194-195). This has also led to the relatively recent "Wanabe" syndrome. It is exemplified by thousands of "new age" non-Indians who want to be Indians in a spiritual sense. Unfortunately, in at least some instances, they interfere with the very cultures they so admire. (See, for example, Camp 1992 and Little Eagle 1992.)

Since passage of the sometimes controversial Indian Arts and Crafts Act of 1990, the work of Native American artisans has enjoyed a great degree of protection from counterfeit competition. Here, Evalena Henry, Master Basket Weaver, is shown demonstrating the process of making a basket in Tucson, Arizona. She is a San Carlos Apache.

E-4. *What are the principal elements of the Indian Arts and Crafts Act of 1990?*

The Indian Arts and Crafts Act (IACA) is a remarkable piece of legislation, particularly concerning the no-nonsense penalties associated with it. The Act is intended to promote the Native American artwork and handcraft business, reduce foreign and counterfeit product competition, and halt deceptive marketing practices (Indian Arts and Crafts Board 1991a). Specifically, the act declares that, "It is unlawful to offer or display for sale or sell any good...in a manner that falsely suggests it is Indian produced, an Indian product, or the product of a particular Indian or Indian tribe or Indian arts and crafts organization, resident within the United States...." Whoever knowingly violates the prohibition, if an individual, is subject to criminal prosecution and may be fined up to $250,000 for a first offense and jailed for up to five years. For a subsequent offense, the penalties can be up to $1,000,000 and 15 years of incarceration. If a violator is a corporation, the fines may be up to $1,000,000 on the first offense and up to $5,000,000 each time thereafter. The Indian Arts and Crafts Board of the Department of the Interior is authorized to receive relevant complaints and refer them to the FBI for investigation. The Board may also recommend prosecution by the U.S. Department of Justice.

Civil suits may be brought under the Act by the U.S. Attorney General or an Indian tribe on behalf of itself, an individual Indian, or an Indian arts and crafts organization. Civil penalties can include an injunction, or other equitable relief, and the greater of (1) treble damages or (2) $1,000 for each day the violation continues for each aggrieved Indian, tribe, or Native arts and crafts association. Punitive damages and legal costs may also be awarded.

The IACA defines an Indian as an individual who is a member of an Indian tribe or who, if not a member, is certified as an Indian artisan by a tribe. Tribes cannot charge a fee for certification, and they are not required to have an artist certification program. "Tribe" is defined as (1) any tribe, band, nation, Alaska Native village, or other organized group or community which is federally recognized or (2) any Indian group which is formally (legally) recognized by a state.

Regarding the sale of Indian products from Canadian, Mexican, Central American, or South American Native groups, the Indian Arts and Crafts Board now recommends that sellers clearly state that the products are not made by U.S. Indians. The Board also recommends to Indian artists, tribes, museums, and retailers that, before an art work or hand craft is offered or displayed for sale, verification of the maker's tribal membership be furnished or obtained. Copies of tribal documents showing membership, artist enrollment numbers, or written guarantees of intermediate sellers would probably be sufficient to show compliance with the Act in most cases (Indian Arts and Crafts Board 1991b). The Board is now in the process of promulgating specific regulations for implementation of the IACA. The regulations should clarify ambiguities in the act and specify compliance procedures. Completion is anticipated, at least in proposed form, by late 1993 or early 1994 (Andrews 1991).

E-5. *How many Indian languages are there?*

It is believed that about 300 languages were spoken by the Native residents of North America in 1492 when Columbus arrived in the Western Hemisphere (Campbell and Mithun 1979). These ancestral languages have been classified into several major linguistic groups. Though not all experts agree on the classifications, eight language group names have been commonly employed: Algonquian, Athapaskan, Caddoean, Iroquoian, Muskhogean, Penutian, Siouan, and Uto-Aztecan (Bureau of Indian Affairs 1974).

About 250 Native languages are identified with what is now the United States. Many are no longer viable because they are rarely, if ever, spoken. Even so, more than 100 languages are spoken by contemporary Native Americans. In some tribes, however, only a handful of speakers remain. It is estimated that approximately one-third of all Native Americans still speak their languages. Navajo, Iroquois, Inuit (Eskimo), Tohono O'odham, Pima, Apache, and Sioux peoples show the highest percentages of Native speakers (Waldman 1985).

On October 26, 1992, President Bush signed into law a legislative measure that will help counter the loss of Native languages. It authorizes the Administration for Native Americans to make grants to tribal governments and other groups to teach children, train educators and interpreters, compile histories, develop teaching materials, and acquire equipment for language lessons (Indian Country Today, November 5, 1992).

E-6. *Was the speaking of Native languages prohibited historically?*

Yes, but the prohibition was not a legislative or wholesale one. It was generally limited to the religious and government schools attended by Indian children (Deloria 1973). The effects of enforced limitations on language in schools throughout the country, from the 1870s through the 1950s, have been marked. Because so many Indian children attended boarding schools during this era, their young-life experiences provided little opportunity for learning their own languages. They, in turn, often raised children who learned only English.

General enlightenment, increased emphasis on the importance of culture, and increased tribal control over education have brought an end to the language prohibition policies of former times. A highlight of this evolution occurred on October 30, 1990, when Title I of Public Law 101-477 was signed into law as the Native American Languages Act. It declares a United States policy "to preserve, protect, and promote the rights and freedoms of Native Americans to use, practice, and develop Native American languages." This officially reverses the scattered policies of the 19th and 20th centuries that so devastated Native languages.

> *Religious schools established for Aleut people in Alaska, in the 19th century, taught written and spoken Aleut until the last school, at Unalaska, was forcibly closed in 1912 by education officials who opposed the use of Native languages.*
>
> Lantis 1984

E-7. *What religious practices have Indian people generally observed, both before and after Euro-American influence?*

BEFORE

There were at least as many specific religions as independent tribes, bands, clans, villages, and living groups. Nonetheless, all religious activity evolved within a common framework of life processes affected by a familiar natural environment. Ruth Underhill (1957) developed a generalized overview of past Indian religion, based on her extensive research. That overview is summarized here and is supplemented with information from Lamphere (1983) and Lantis (1984). Underhill also gave an excellent, in-depth introduction to traditional Native religion in her 1965 book, *Red Man's Religion: Beliefs and Practices of the Indians North of Mexico.* And, Vecsey (1991) has compiled some useful essays in a timely book on traditional Indian religious issues now being debated in the media and contested in court.

Native Americans' homelands and religions were closely intertwined. The land, the environment, and a strong sense of place all had great religious significance. Essentially everything was tied to the supernatural, which led to a proliferation of religious practices across the continent. Despite their great number, most of the practices come under one or more of six basic areas of supernatural concern.

Universal Force

Native religion was often imbued with the concept that an invisible force pervades the universe. This force could be focused on any special place, being, or object, endowing it with supernatural power. Such words as the Aleut *Agudar*, Lakota *Wakan*, Iroquois *Orenda*, and Algonquian *Manitou* were used to refer to this universal force.

These Piegan Blackfeet are taking part in a Medicine Lodge ceremony. They are Spotted Eagle, Chief Elk, and Bull Child. The whistles they are blowing are made from sacred eagle bones.

Taboo

Certain taboos developed because the focus of power in a being or object could be dangerous to someone who was not in a sacred state. The most widespread taboos pertained to the three "life crises" of birth, puberty, and death. Rituals or techniques of avoidance were used to deal with these uncontrollable events, not because of uncleanliness, but because those in "crisis" were subject to supernatural power. They, or those nearby, needed to do things to keep themselves and others safe. Menstruating women and those giving birth were often secluded, especially among the hunter and gatherer groups. Some form of spiritual purification (e.g., a "sweat") or a period of withdrawal might also be observed by the bereaved, and even by hunters after killing a particular animal such as a whale. This was because the soul of the dead person or special animal might desire company or revenge.

Spirits

All groups believed in spirits and the need to deal with them, one way or another. Besides spirits of the dead–some of whom might end up as individual or group guardians–there were the spirits of plants, animals, places, and natural phenomena. Underhill (1957) wrote:

> To most Indians, there [was] no sharp dividing line between
> these and human beings. The Sioux spoke of all living things as
> the two-leggeds, the four-leggeds, and the wingeds. All these
> had life and must be treated as fellow beings. So must plants and
> Mother Earth who bore them.

Wild things were treated with consideration, and apologies were sometimes made to game after the kill. The hope was that the animal spirits would be appeased and go back to their own villages, later to return in tangible form to again feed the people.

Not all groups identified a high god or supreme spirit. Some who did were the Algonquian ("Great Spirit"), the Creek ("Master of Breath"), and the Lakota ("Creator").

Visions

These took many forms among Native groups. Some visions were sought at puberty, especially among boys, to guide their personal growth and success through life as hunters, warriors, cultivators, or group leaders. A vision quest might be done once, or it might be repeated through life. Seclusion and fasting often played roles, and, perhaps, ordeals of self-inflicted pain and suffering were experienced. Frequently, the vision included an animal guide who might teach a special song, give instructions, or describe a power-giving fetish.

The Shaman

A "medicine man," or shaman, was a top visionary. His, and sometimes her, power frequently came from direct contact with the supernatural. In addition, it might be enhanced by inheritance, or training as an apprentice. A shaman's baseline power could be obtained through quest, ordeal, or unsought dreams. It was the hunter-gatherer groups which had full shamanic belief systems. Their cultural and physical survival depended on a balance of various natural and supernatural forces, of which the shaman was guardian.

Acting as a mediator between the visible and invisible worlds, the shaman's jobs were many. They included foretelling the future, and helping to achieve good hunting, good fishing, a good harvest, success in battle, favorable weather, health, and safe childbirth. Often, the shaman's primary function was curing, frequently by "removal" of some maligning influence in a patient. This might be accomplished through rubbing, blowing, smoking, brushing, singing, art symbolism, the spreading of sacred pollen or meal, and sometimes herbology.

In some societies a distinction was made between a shaman, as a holy man, and as an herbal healer. A shaman, acting as a priest, could direct one or more sacred ceremonies, but someone with only herbal training would not have been qualified to direct these special events.

Communal Ceremony

Groups held ceremonies because they served as a communal appeal to the spirits, asking for their help in achieving some common goals. Typically, such goals included maintaining or increasing necessary plant and animal life, protecting warriors, restoring of health, giving thanks, and securing long life and well-being for individuals and the community. Hunters and food gatherers found it difficult or impossible to participate in large ceremonies during most of the year because there was not enough food available to sustain everyone. On the plains, for example, ceremonies might occur only during such times as an annual buffalo drive. Large ceremonies were most frequently observed by the agriculturists, like those of the pueblo communities, whose food supplies and more sedentary circumstances would support the activity. Some of the practices observed in communal ceremonies included sacred dancing, singing, smoking, drumming, feasting, and making use of holy objects.

AFTER

By various means, Christianity has made enormous inroads into Native society over the last five hundred years. Among some groups, like the Aleut who were thoroughly converted to the Russian Orthodox Church in the 19th century, few if any traditionalists remain. Today, most (but certainly not all) religious Native people practice Christianity, or a combination of it and Native religion. During the past two decades, however, there has been a resurgence of Native interest in traditional religious practices. This has occurred throughout the country and includes groups which had been separated from their religious traditions for many years. Religious freedom is a premier concern among Native Americans today.

E-8. *Is it true that traditional Indian religious ceremonies were outlawed historically?*

Yes. Spanish prohibitions are well known. They began shortly after the arrival of Columbus and coincided with the Spanish Inquisition. Horrible punishments were meted out for "pagan" activities. Those charged were tortured in a number of ways, including slow roasting over a fire or being garroted. The latter was a common practice used by the Spaniards to achieve strangulation by progressively twisting a rope around the neck (Rosenstiel 1983).

Though generally much less severe than the Spanish policy, American colonial policy was also oppressive. As early as 1646, the Massachusetts Bay Colony, following requests by "Apostle" John Eliot, outlawed the practice of Native religion in the special "praying towns" set aside for certain Indian groups. Some sources say violation of the religious practice rule was done "under pain of death"

(Axtell 1988), though others suggest the death penalty was limited to murder, bestiality, and adultery (Spicer 1969).

In 1883, Secretary of the Interior Henry M. Teller (with backing from Christian religious organizations) established what came to be known on Indian reservations as "courts of Indian offenses." Teller's initial goal for the courts, which evolved to cover numerous minor offenses, was to eliminate "heathenish practices" among the Indians. The rules of the courts, published in the 1880s and 1890s, effectively forbade the practice of all public and private religious activities by traditional tribal members on their reservations (Prucha 1990b). Significantly, non-Indians were not subject to prosecution for participating in the same activities.

4. *Offenses.* – For the purpose of these regulations the following shall be deemed to constitute *offenses,* and the judges of the Indian court shall severally have jurisdiction to try and punish for the same when committed within their respective districts.

(a) Dances, etc.–Any Indian who shall engage in the sun dance, scalp dance, or war dance, or any similar feast, so called, shall be deemed guilty of an offense, and upon conviction thereof shall be punished for the offense by the withholding of his rations for not exceeding ten days or by imprisonment for not exceeding ten days; and for any subsequent offense under this clause he shall be punished by withholding his rations for not less than ten nor more than thirty days, or by imprisonment for not less than ten nor more than thirty days....

(c) Practices of medicine men.–Any Indian who shall engage in the practices of so-called medicine men, or who shall resort to any artifice or device to keep the Indians of the reservation from adopting and following civilized habits and pursuits, or shall adopt any means to prevent the attendance of children at school, or shall use any arts of the conjurer to prevent Indians from abandoning their barbarous rights and customs, shall be deemed to be guilty of an offense, and upon conviction thereof, for the first offense shall be imprisoned for not less than ten nor more than thirty days: *Provided,* That for any subsequent conviction for such offense the maximum term of imprisonment shall not exceed six months.

Official antagonism toward Native religion by the federal government continued at least into the 1920s when Commissioner of Indian

Affairs Charles Burke sent his famous letter "To all Indians." He urged them to give up "dances" and "ceremonies" voluntarily or he might be forced to "issue an order against these useless and harmful performances" (Spicer 1969, p. 241). Unofficial antagonism continues today, both directly and indirectly, through adverse legislative, executive, and judicial decisions and actions. This is in spite of the fact that a Congressional resolution on American Indian Religious Freedom was passed in 1978.

E-9. What is the Native American Church?

> [T]he right to free religious expression embodies a precious heritage of our history.
>
> California Supreme Court
> *People v. Woody* 1964, p. 821

The Native American Church (N.A.C.) is a greatly misunderstood religious organization of Indians. Its practices, which are threatened, are among those at the forefront of the current struggle for Indian religious freedom in the United States. The church is numerically important because it has the largest membership of any Indian organization in the country—approximately 250,000 members from more than 50 tribes in the U.S. and Canada. Official membership in the U.S. has been judicially recognized as being "limited to Native American members of federally recognized tribes who have at least 25 percent Native American ancestry" (*Peyote Way Church of God, Inc. v. Thornburgh* 1991). Non-members, both Indian and non-Indian, have sometimes been allowed to participate in peyote rituals by subgroups of the church.

The religion teaches an ethical doctrine very similar to those of the monotheistic religions, and is related to Christianity. However, it has avoided the specific "Christian" label, partly in reaction to the subordinate place so often given to Christian Indian converts in church organization (Underhill 1974). The most notable and controversial aspect of the N.A.C. is its use of the peyote cactus as a sacrament.

Peyote

Stewart (1987) describes peyote as a small, spineless cactus native to the Rio Grande region of south Texas and northeast Mexico. It grows several inches high from a long tap root, sprouting single or multiple fleshy "buttons" of one to two inches across. The buttons contain alkaloid compounds, the most significant of which is mescaline, an hallucinogen. They are extremely bitter. When ingested by chewing or in a tea, peyote frequently causes nausea and sometimes vomiting.

Peyote buttons are harvested by severing them from the tap root, which will continue to produce buttons. After removal, they are dried before consumption. Peyote buttons can produce sensations that include a warm and pleasant euphoria, an agreeable point of view, relaxation, colorful visual distortions, and a sense of timelessness. Non-religious consumption of peyote is considered by N.A.C. members to be a very serious sacrilege (Slotkin 1967). Drug experts, anthropologists, and courts have determined that peyote is not habit-forming and that the peyote religion does indeed have an observed positive moral effect on its Indian members. (See *Peyote Way Church of God v. Thornburgh* 1991; Stewart 1987; Farb 1968; *People v. Woody* 1964; *Toledo v. Nobel-Sysco, Inc.* 1986; Underhill 1965 and 1974.)

Church History

Some people believe the N.A.C. was an offshoot of the "hippie" era of the 1960s. This is completely untrue. However, that view probably arose with publicity surrounding a high degree of non-Indian use of peyote during the era (Brand 1988). The federal government's first prohibition of non-religious use of peyote occurred in 1966.

Peyote use in Mexico as a folk remedy and for religious purposes predates European arrival. References to peyote religion in Spanish records go back to 1560. Also, Spanish attempts to outlaw peyotism because of its competition with Catholicism began at least as early as 1620. Use of peyote by some members of Pueblo tribes in what is now New Mexico was recorded in the 1630s. Therefore, investigation into the origins of modern peyotism among Native Americans discloses a history of centuries (Stewart 1991).

Tribes from the areas which became New Mexico and Texas, who were familiar with peyote from the early 1600s, include the Lipan Apache, Tonkawa, Mescalero Apache, Caddo, Carrizo, and Karankawa. Later, the Comanche, Kiowa, and Kiowa-Apache encountered peyotism as a result of extensive raids made in Mexico. In the mid- and late-1800s, all but the Mescalero were removed by the U.S. to Oklahoma. For 400 years, the various Oklahoma tribes had scattered experiences with the religion. Late in the 1800s, the Plains version of peyotism evolved in Oklahoma. The "new" religion helped tribes cope with loss of their cultures and freedom, maintain a sense of spiritual independence from the ever-present missionaries, and deal with repressive control exercised over them by White society (Farb 1968).

Comanche Chief Quannah Parker and 10 other leading peyotists supported peyotism at the 1907 Oklahoma Constitutional Convention. The state legislature subsequently recognized peyotism as a bona-fide religion in 1908 (Stewart 1987 and 1991). In 1918, the N.A.C. was officially organized in Oklahoma as the corporate form of the peyotist religion. A need to broaden the church arose as the religion spread around the U.S. Another Oklahoma charter established the N.A.C. of the United States in 1950. The name was soon revised to the N.A.C. of North America to accommodate peyotists of Canada. It is now the official primary church of Native peyotists of the continent, many of whom have incorporated local N.A.C. chapters where permitted by law.

Theology

Native American peyotists believe peyote is a sacred and powerful spiritual plant. Even its name, coming from the Aztec word *peyotl*, means "divine messenger." The several forms of the peyote religion combine Indian and Christian elements in varying degrees. In many tribes, the cactus is personified as Peyote Spirit–considered to be God's equivalent for the Indian to His Jesus for the non-Indian. Peyote is seen as a medicine, protector, and teacher. Consuming it in a ritual context allows an individual to commune with God and the spirits and to receive spiritual power, guidance, reproof, and healing. Peyotism teaches brotherly love, obedience to parents, fidelity to spouse, family care, charity, self-support through steady work, and avoidance of alcohol. This way of life is known as the Peyote Road. (See *Toledo v. Nobel-Sysco, Inc.* 1986; Encyclopaedia Britannica 1990; Stewart 1987.)

Ritual

Peyote ceremonies are held on the request of a church member. They may be conducted for healing, to honor a person, to acknowledge a death, to send someone away, to welcome someone home, and for general purposes of worship. The all-night ritual usually begins on a Saturday evening and usually takes place in a teepee around a crescent-shaped earthen altar and a sacred fire. Services are directed by a "Road Man" and include prayer, singing, sacramental eating of peyote, water rites, contemplation, and testimonials. At dawn on Sunday morning, a communion breakfast is eaten. Prayers are then offered, asking God's help for Indians, non-Indians, and all the world, thus ending the meeting (Stewart 1987; Underhill 1965 and 1974).

Legality

Federal legislation outlaws possession and distribution of peyote (21 U.S. Code, Secs. 812, 841, and 844). However, bona-fide religious use of the cactus by members of the N.A.C. is currently exempted from the law (21 Code of Federal Regulations, Sec. 1307.31; *Peyote Way Church of God, Inc. v. Thornburgh* 1991). The federal exemption is legally considered to be political and not racial, based on (1) the "quasi-sovereign" nation status of the tribes to which the church's members belong and (2) the government's objective and responsibility of preserving Native American culture. In the *Peyote Way* case, the court has said that each state has three legal options concerning peyote use. It can forbid anyone to use it, allow use only by members of the N.A.C., or allow all bona-fide religious use of the cactus. The states seem willing to accept only one or the other of the first two options.

E-10. *Is there more tolerance for Native religions today?*

Though it is not universal, the general answer would have to be "yes." A moving example is the "Public Declaration of Apology" made in 1987 to Indian and Eskimo people of the Pacific Northwest by an ecumenical group of Christian religious leaders. (See Appendix 7.) In addition, on October 30, 1991, clergy from Alaska's Roman Catholic, Lutheran, Russian Orthodox, and Presbyterian Churches made public apologies directed to all Alaska Natives. They referred to their churches' actions for the past 200 years by saying:

> We have responded with fear, suspicion, arrogance, hostility, and a patronizing attitude that treats your people like children....
> [We] pray for your forgiveness for our sins against your people.

Associated Press 1991a

Officiating at the special service was Father John Hascall, a Catholic Priest and Ojibwa medicine man from Michigan. Father Hascall was quoted (Associated Press 1991a) as saying to the non-Indian participants, "I don't want you to feel sorry for us. I want you to look at us as Native people, as people of sovereign nations, which we are. As people of high morals. As people of high respect. As people who want to be equal."

Despite these statements and similar apologies, a major need remains to strengthen the American Indian Religious Freedom Act through legislative action. Primary purposes behind changing the act include protecting traditional Native religions and sacred sites. Both are threatened by insensitive or chauvinistic views and thoughtless land development.

E-11. *What is the American Indian Religious Freedom Act?*

The 1978 "Act" is actually a joint resolution by the U.S. Senate and House of Representatives. It expresses the general policy of the U.S. government toward traditional Native American religions and their practice. The resolution's specific purpose, as stated in its legislative history, is "to insure that the policies and procedures of various Federal agencies, as they impact upon the exercise of traditional Indian Religious practices, are brought into compliance with the constitutional injunction that Congress shall make no laws abridging the free exercise of religion." The brief resolution has no enforcement provisions. This deficiency, as well as recent Supreme Court cases which have all but made a mockery of the resolution (e.g., *Lyng v. Northwest Indian Cemetery Protective Association* 1988), have stimulated legislative proposals to strengthen protections for Native religious activity. Reproduced below and on the following page is the full text of the 1978 resolution which remains the *official* but frequently ignored U.S. policy.

Public Law 95–341
95th Congress
Joint Resolution
American Indian Religious Freedom.

Whereas the freedom of religion for all people is an inherent right, fundamental to the democratic structure of the United States and is guaranteed by the First Amendment of the United States Constitution;

Whereas the United States has traditionally rejected the concept of a government denying individuals the right to practice their religion and, as a result, has benefited from a rich variety of religious heritages in this country;

Whereas the religious practices of the American Indian (as well as Native Alaskan and Hawaiian) are an integral part of their culture, tradition and heritage, such practices forming the basis of Indian identity and value systems;

Whereas the traditional American Indian religions, as an integral part of Indian life, are indispensable and irreplaceable;

Whereas the lack of a clear, comprehensive, and consistent Federal policy has often resulted in the abridgment of religious freedom for traditional American Indians;

Whereas such religious infringements result from the lack of knowledge of the insensitive and inflexible enforcement of Federal policies and regulations premised on a variety of laws;

Whereas such laws were designed for such worthwhile purposes as conservation and preservation of natural species and resources but were never intended to relate to Indian religious practices and, therefore, were passed without consideration of their effect on traditional American Indian religions;

Whereas such laws and policies often deny American Indians access to sacred sites required in their religions, including cemeteries;

Whereas such laws at times prohibit the use and possession of sacred objects necessary to the exercise of religious rites and ceremonies;

Whereas traditional American Indian ceremonies have been intruded upon, interfered with, and in a few instances banned; Now, therefore, be it

Resolved by the Senate and House of Representatives of the United States of America in Congress assembled, That henceforth it shall be the policy of the United States to protect and preserve for American Indians their inherent right of freedom to believe, express, and exercise the traditional religions of the American Indian, Eskimo, Aleut, and Native Hawaiians, including but not limited to access to sites, use and possession of sacred objects, and the freedom to worship through ceremonials and traditional rites.

SEC. 2. The President shall direct the various Federal departments, agencies, and other instrumentalities responsible for administering relevant laws to evaluate their policies and procedures in consultation with Native traditional religious leaders in order to determine appropriate changes necessary to protect and preserve Native American religious cultural rights and practices. Twelve months after approval of this resolution, the President shall report back to the Congress the results of his evaluation, including any changes which were made in administrative policies and procedures, and any recommendations he may have for legislative action.

Approved August 11, 1978.

E-12. *What is the Native American Graves Protection and Repatriation Act?*

The Native American Graves Protection and Repatriation Act, or NAGPRA, became law in 1990. It is now the strongest federal legislation pertaining to aboriginal remains and artifacts. The act acknowledges the interests which Native communities, including Native Hawaiians, have in this aspect of their heritage (Price 1991). The act has several significant provisions. All agencies and private museums which receive funding from the federal government have five years to inventory their collections of Native American human remains and related funerary objects. After they have completed their inventories, the agencies and museums are required to notify the tribes where the materials originated, or which are culturally affiliated, or from whose land the materials came. If a tribe requests that remains and objects be returned, that request is to be honored.

The law establishes that Native American tribal groups own or control human remains or cultural items which are discovered on tribal and federal lands. They also have the right to determine the disposition of such discovered remains and items. NAGPRA further

[I]n the summer of 1986. ...a number of Northern Cheyenne Chiefs visited Washington, D.C. During the course of their visit they arranged to tour the Smithsonian Institution's Cheyenne collection at the National Museum of Natural History. "As we were walking out," a Northern Cheyenne woman who worked on Capitol Hill later recalled, "we saw [the] huge ceilings in the room, with row upon row of drawers. Someone remarked there must be a lot of Indian stuff in those drawers. Quite casually, a curator with us said, 'Oh, this is where we keep the skeletal remains,' and he told us how many–18,500. Everyone was shocked." ...This discovery...helped generate a national Indian movement that eventually resulted in...enactment [of] NAGPRA.

Sockbeson 1990, p. 1

In 1868, for example, the Surgeon General of the United States ordered Army personnel to procure as many Indian crania as possible for the Army Medical Museum. Under that order, the heads of more than 4,000 Indians were taken from battlefields, prisoner camps and hospitals, and from fresh graves or burial scaffolds across the country.

Sockbeson 1990, p. 2

The NAGPRA represents a major federal shift away from viewing Native American human remains as "archaeological resources" or "federal property" alone. Instead, the government is slowly beginning to view these remains as Native Americans do–as our ancestors.

Sockbeson 1990, p. 2

prohibits trafficking in aboriginal human remains and cultural items when these materials are obtained in violation of the act's provisions (Price 1991; Sockbeson 1990).

The act does not apply to materials found on private or state land, and the Smithsonian Institution is also exempted from the law. An earlier and separate law, the National Museum of the American Indian Act (1989), specifically addresses the repatriation issue as it pertains to the Smithsonian.

E-13. *What is the Indian Child Welfare Act?*

In 1978, Congress passed two major pieces of legislation to help protect the social and cultural integrity of American Indians. The first was the joint resolution on American Indian Religious Freedom. The second was the Indian Child Welfare Act. In this act, Congress addressed a major concern: that Indian children who had to be placed with foster or adoptive parents often ended up with non-Indian families and were raised outside their Native culture.

Congress declared that part of the federal trust responsibility of the United States is:

> ...to protect the best interests of Indian children and to promote the stability and security of Indian tribes and families by the establishment of minimum federal standards for the removal of Indian children from their families and placement of such children in foster homes...which will reflect the unique values of Indian culture, and by providing for assistance to Indian tribes in the operation of child and family service programs.

The heart of the act has four basic provisions. They include: (1) definitions of tribal and state jurisdictions over child placement, (2) authorization for tribes and states to enter into agreements for the care and custody of Indian children and jurisdiction over child custody proceedings, (3) a provision that full faith and credit be accorded by states to the laws and court decisions of Indian tribes in child placement cases, and (4) a requirement that preference be given to an Indian child's extended family or Indian homes and institutions if a foster home or adoptive placement is necessary (Cohen 1982).

The Indian Child Welfare Act does not cover custody proceedings between parents in connection with divorce. It was specifically designed to protect the integrity of tribes and the heritage of Indian children. The act does this by directly inhibiting the common practice of taking children, who were in troubled homes, from their families and tribes and then raising them as non-Indians (Canby 1981).

F-14. *Where does the word "pow wow" come from and what does it mean?*

"Pow wow" represents the modern spelling of a word derived from the Algonquin-speaking Narragansett tribe of the Rhode Island region. In its original usage, it meant a Native healer or priest. For example, in 1646, the Massachusetts Bay Colony defined "pawwows" as "witches or sorcerers that cure by the help of the devil" (Spicer 1969, p. 174). In 1674, another observer wrote, "Their physicians are Powaws or Indian Priests" (Oxford English Dictionary 1989). Early

Modern pow wows, such as this 1991 inter-tribal gathering in Arizona, provide opportunities for Indians to share their cultural heritage. Visitors are usually welcome to attend such functions.

on, the meaning of pow wow was expanded by non-Indians to include ceremonies in which Indian healers or religious leaders participated. The word was later widely applied and accepted by Indians and non-Indians as a generic term to cover nearly all Indian gatherings involving feasts, councils, or inter-tribal conferences. Today the term is still applied to healers and spiritual leaders, but that meaning is used mostly by some of the eastern tribes. In Indian country, "pow wow" currently means a tribal or inter-tribal dance, fair, rodeo, celebration, or other gathering. These may vary in size from small social functions to the very large "Gathering of Nations" pow wow, which annually draws people to Albuquerque, New Mexico, from throughout the U.S. and Canada. In addition to their recreational value, pow wows are socially significant for individual participants and are important to Indian solidarity, spirituality, cultural identity, and exchange of socio-political information.

E-15. *Why are feathers so important in Native American culture?*
From the Inuit of the Arctic to the Seminoles of the Everglades, feathers have always had highly significant practical and symbolic importance. On the practical side, Hodge (1907) reported many uses that were common in the past. Parkas, for instance, were made from feathered bird skins sewed together by Arctic peoples. Eastern tribes cut bird skins into strips and sewed them into blankets, just as certain western tribes did with rabbit skins. Fans and clothing accessories were made by the Iroquois and other tribes. Captain John Smith, for example, wrote of seeing beautiful cloaks of knotted feathers worn by the Indians of Virginia. For stabilizing the flight of arrows, Native hunters secured either flat or split feathers on the shafts. Among some California tribes, bird scalps were even treated as a form of money. And, the uses of feathers for everyday decoration have been myriad. Simple examples come from the Yupik Inuit, who sewed attractive sprays of down into the seams of garments, and many California tribes which decorated their woven basketry in a similar way. The most striking uses of feathers, however, continue to be in connection with social customs and religious symbolism.

Feathers are tangible symbols of the birds from which they come. And it is birds, unique within creation, which fly among or with supernatural powers or spirits. In the plains states, the Kingfisher often symbolizes the powers of quickness and agility (Capps 1973). In Alaska, the raven is considered a descendant of the creator or "Raven Father" (Royce 1899). In the Southwest, hummingbirds might be entreated to carry messages from human speakers to spirits, while owls may represent spirits of the dead (Ortiz 1983). And everywhere, the revered eagle has extensive spiritual, healing, and magisterial powers (Hodge 1907; O'Brien 1989). The eminence of eagles is not lost on non-Indian culture, either, as the symbol printed on the right rear of every American dollar testifies.

Feathers are often featured prominently in ceremonial clothing such as that worn by a young Indian boy at a recent pow wow in Arizona.

Indians can access the special powers and social symbols associated with birds by acquiring and using the right feathers from the
right birds. Feathers, whether plain or specially notched and painted,
may be used for different purposes. They may be worn in the hair or
atop the head. In the past, wearing feathers in this manner was commonly practiced by many tribes to indicate rank or personal achievement. The headdress of the Plains Indians, with feathers representing
deeds or exploits, is the dominant image the public has of the way
Indians use feathers.

Feathers are very important in ceremonials. For curing ceremonies, bundles of feathers may be brushed over a patient to sweep
away or pull out causes of illness. They may also be used to help a
celebrant "see" more clearly with his or her own mind or spirit. Some
tribes' ceremonials associate feathers with the clothing of supernaturals, or with rain and water. Power in feathers may also be invoked as
a protection or to bring about a desired outcome of events.

For these reasons, and for other aesthetic, ceremonial, and sacred
purposes, many Native Americans routinely place feathers on themselves and on special possessions such as prayer sticks, dance wands,
effigy figures, pipe stems, shields, spears, clubs, rifles, baskets, clothing, drums, and horses. Feathers are thus employed as bridges
between the spirit world and ours. In summary, ceremonial and religious feathers can be described as antennae directed to the cosmos
(Chasing Horse 1991).

Brief, non-technical overviews on the meanings or definitions of
some of the more prominent cultural symbols, items, and terms of
various tribes may be found in *Turtle Island Alphabet* by Hausman
(1992). A much older, but excellent, encyclopedic reference on hundreds of similar topics is the two-volume set by Hodge (1907 and
reprinted in 1975), titled *Handbook of North American Indians North of
Mexico.* Another contemporary work on cultural topics is *Indian
Givers,* by Weatherford (1988).

SECTION F: WARFARE

> *Gone to fight the Indians. Will be back when the war is over.*
> Note tacked on the Washington, D.C., office door of
> Archibald Henderson, Commandant of the Marine Corps,
> in relation to the Creek Indian War of 1836
> Heinl 1962, p. 41

F-1. *Over how many years did the U.S. military engage in armed conflict with Indians, and just how much fighting was there?*

Official U.S. military involvement in warfare against American Indians occurred over a 115-year period, from 1776 to 1891. However, the U.S. Army was involved in a dozen or more police actions relating to Indian tribes between 1891 and 1907.

A review of military records, some of which are incomplete, shows at least 1,470 official incidents of Army action against Indians from 1776 to 1907 (Harlow 1935; Hill 1981; Old Army Press 1979; U.S. Department of the Interior 1894; Webb 1966; Washburn 1988). These actions varied from nonviolent pursuits or minor exchanges of gunfire to large scale battles.

The 1,470 federal incidents do not include independent actions against Indians by the U.S. Navy. This is because the Navy's records pertaining to Indian-related operations are so widely scattered that they are extremely difficult to locate and enumerate. The Navy's actions were not at all numerous when compared with the Army's. Nonetheless, the Navy and the Marine Corps played significant roles in the Creek War of 1836, in multi-year campaigns against the Seminoles in Florida, in efforts to subdue the Puget Sound tribes in Washington, and in making a show of force to coastal Natives in southern Alaska. In addition to supporting land operations involving the Army, the Navy engaged in some of its own such operations and is also known to have shelled Native villages on two, and probably more, occasions (Heinl 1962; Hill 1981; Wrone and Nelson 1973).

The vast majority of military-Indian fighting occurred between 1866 and 1891. Army records for this period show that the Army fought 1,065 combat engagements with Indians during that 25-year

103

period. It was a time of relentless pursuit and conquest by a U.S. military establishment baptized in the Civil War. Federal casualties for the period totaled 948 killed and 1,058 wounded. Indian casualties listed by the Army for the same 25 years are 4,371 killed and 1,279 wounded, with 10,318 captured. Experts caution that the Indian casualty figures may be somewhat exaggerated (Utley 1988). Over the many decades of conflict, far more Indians were killed by disease, despair, and starvation than by bullets.

The last combatant killed in an "Indian war" was Lt. Edward W. Casey, who commanded a troop of Cheyenne scouts recruited in Montana. While on a scouting mission with two of his men in the final days of the so-called "Sioux Ghost Dance War," he was shot by Plenty Horses, a young Lakota warrior. Plenty Horses, a Brulé (Sicangu), had been educated at Carlisle Indian School in Pennsylvania. This incident occurred on January 7, 1891.

Referring to sources like the *New York Times* and *Nation* magazine, Matthiessen (1991) stated that the U.S. Army got directly involved in behind-the-scenes operations for "Wounded Knee II" in 1973. FBI agents, U.S. Marshals, and BIA police besieged lightly armed Indian protesters who had occupied the tiny community of Wounded Knee, South Dakota, on the Pine Ridge Reservation. Military intelligence and counsel, and perhaps weapons and equipment, were provided to the civilian authorities, with unofficial approval reportedly coming all the way from the White House. A lot of ineffective gunfire was exchanged during the 71-day stand-off, but two Indians died and one federal officer was crippled. It is reported that, at one point, the FBI requested the assistance of 2,000 soldiers to seize control of the entire reservation. This would have allowed the FBI to focus on making its desired arrests. The request was wisely refused.

The most recent pitched shootout between a semi-organized group of Native Americans and U.S. federal law enforcement officers occurred in 1975 on the Pine Ridge Reservation. During the brief firefight, one Indian and two FBI agents were killed. As far as is known, the U.S. military had no involvement, even indirectly, with the 1975 incident. (See Matthiessen's detailed but controversial book.)

If all hostile actions involving non-Indians, on one side, and Indian people, on the other, could be counted, they might far exceed the U.S. military numbers given above. As an example of uncounted incidents, during the three decades after gold was discovered in California, mounted militia and private armies were periodically organized to hunt and exterminate entire tribes or bands of Indians. The participants in some of these genocidal expeditions were reimbursed for their expenses with federal funds. In 1894, the U.S. Department of the Interior reported, "It has been estimated that since 1775 more than 5,000 white men, women, and children have been killed in individual [non-military] affairs with Indians, and more than 8,500 Indians [killed]. History, in general, notes but few of these combats" (U.S. Department of the Interior 1894, p. 637).

One cavalry-like action, thought to be the last of its kind in the U.S., occurred in 1911. Mounted troopers of the Nevada State Police tracked down and killed a small band of "free" (i.e., non-reservation) Shoshone who had been accused of the death of a Basque shepherd in the far western part of the state. To this day, a controversy remains as to whether the Indians killed the shepherd, or whether it was done by some of the cattlemen who accused them.

F-2. Was the "Battle of the Little Bighorn" the greatest single military defeat for the United States in the so-called Indian Wars?

No. But it is next in line. As a result of action against a large gathering of Sioux (plus some Cheyenne and Arapaho allies) at the Little Bighorn River in Montana Territory, on June 25, 1876, the U.S. 7th Cavalry lost 289 men killed and 51 wounded out of a total force of about 600 (Graham 1959; Time–Life Books 1990). About 225 of the dead were in the five companies that were directly under the command of Lt. Colonel George Custer. The remainder of the killed, as well as all the wounded, were commanded by Major Reno and Captain Benteen. The latter were surrounded and besieged for a day, several miles from where Custer met his end. Indian dead in the Little Bighorn battle are estimated to have been about 100.

On November 4, 1791, nearly 85 years before the Battle of the Little Bighorn, the greatest single military defeat of U.S. forces by

PHOTO COURTESY OF THE SMITHSONIAN INSTITUTION

Red Horse, a Minneconjou Sioux who participated in the Little Bighorn battle, drew this picture sometime after the engagement.

Native Americans took place. The encounter occurred near what is today the community of Fort Recovery, Ohio, on the upper Wabash River, in the western part of the state. President George Washington had appointed Arthur Saint Clair to command an army that grew to include 625 regulars, 1,675 citizen soldiers called "levies," and 470 militiamen. Their mission was to subdue Indian tribes in the Ohio region. Just before dawn on the 4th, the federal encampment of 2,770 men was attacked by a force of up to 2,000 warriors. This was an inter-tribal army of Miamis, Wyandots, Delawares, Shawnees, Ottawas, Chippewas, Potawatomis, and Kickapoos. Only 1,400 of the disorga-nized U.S. forces were able to engage in the defensive action. Total federal casualties amounted to 632 killed and 264 wounded; much of the army ran off in a panic. Exact Indian casualties are unknown but are thought to have been much less than on the federal side. Little Turtle of the Miami and Tecumseh of the Shawnee were two of the better known Indian participants. The episode, called "Saint Clair's Defeat," stunned the nation and precipitated the very first Congres-sional inquiry into the conduct of the executive branch (Iacopi 1972; Mahon 1988; Webb 1966).

F-3. Were Oklahoma (Indian Territory) tribes involved in the Civil War?

Yes. More than a dozen tribes formally allied themselves, through treaty, with the Confederate States of America. In addition, large and small factions of some of these tribes maintained less formal allegiances to the Union. In fact, there were enough "loyal" Indians from Indian Territory and the neighboring states of Kansas, Missouri, and Arkansas, for the federals to raise an "Indian Brigade" for service in the region. It consisted of perhaps several thousand men.

Indian Territory was mostly a Confederate stronghold and was made part of the Confederate Army's Department of the Trans-Mississippi. Four Indian regiments were raised, with total forces exceeding 5,000 men. In the Indian Territory, these troops engaged in some significant battles against organized federal forces during the early part of the Civil War. Subsequently, most fighting involved inter- and intra-tribal conflict between opposing factions allied with the Union or Confederate causes.

General Robert Edward Lee surrendered his Army of Northern Virginia at Appamattox Courthouse on April 9, 1865. Confederate General Edmund Kirby-Smith surrendered his Trans-Mississippi forces on May 26. However, because of their independent nation status, the Confederate Indian regiments of the Trans-Mississippi held out. The last Confederate general to surrender was Cherokee Brigadier General Stand Watie, who capitulated on June 23. It seems, however, that the distinction of being the last organized regiment of Confederate troops to surrender to Union forces goes to the Chickasaws, who had been under the command of Colonel Tandy Walker (Choctaw) and who formally laid down their arms on July 14, 1865—three full months after Appamattox (Harlow 1935).

F-4. When was the last surrender and who was involved?

The final surrender, which closed out what the federal government has always termed the "Indian wars," took place on January 15, 1891. The surrender specifically ended the two-month-long "Sioux Ghost Dance War," which had become the largest military operation in the

U.S. after the end of the Civil War. It was during the Ghost Dance campaign that the Wounded Knee massacre occurred, on December 29, 1890. Historians report that 200 or more Indian men, women, and children were killed by federal troops at Wounded Knee (Utter 1991).

At the start of the campaign, thousands of Lakota Sioux had been frightened, confused, intimidated, and angered by the deployment of 3,500 federal troops in and around their South Dakota reservations late in November 1890. Government officials had sent troops to suppress the Ghost Dance religion, a theology that swept through the tribes of the West in 1890 and which Indian practitioners had hoped would restore the old life. (See Utley 1963 for an excellent presentation of the story.)

The surrender procession of the Lakota, which included about 4,000 men, women, and children, was described in a publication by Captain W. E. Dougherty, U.S. Army, shortly after the event:

On a hill overlooking Wounded Knee Creek, on the Pine Ridge Indian Reservation in South Dakota, lies a mass grave. It is where the bodies of many Indian men, women, and children were buried by the U.S. military after the infamous "Massacre at Wounded Knee" on December 29, 1890. The site now serves as an Indian cemetery as well as a memorial to those who died in 1890. Photo by Jack Schultz.

> It was a spectacle worth beholding. They moved in two columns up White Clay Creek, one on each side, about 5,500 [sic] people in all, with 7,000 horses, 500 wagons, and about 250 travois, and in such good order that there was not at any point a detention on any account.... The rear and right flank of this mass was covered during the movement by a force of infantry and cavalry deployed in skirmish order, and moved with a precision that was a surprise to all who witnessed it.
>
> Utley 1963, p. 260

Also present and surrounding the Lakota were the Sixth, Seventh, and Ninth Cavalries; the First, Second, and Seventeenth Infantries; and a contingent of cavalry from Fort Leavenworth. Major General Nelson A. Miles was the senior commander of all troops in the region and had been in charge of the Army's Ghost Dance campaign from the beginning. The single formality observed during the surrender took place when Kicking Bear, first cousin to Crazy Horse and a Ghost Dance apostle, laid his rifle at the feet of General Miles.

Kicking Bear, who fought vigorously at the Little Bighorn in 1876, was a Lakota Ghost Dance apostle. He was the last Indian leader to surrender to the U.S. Army, on January 15, 1891.

PHOTO COURTESY OF THE SMITHSONIAN INSTITUTION

SECTION G: LAND, RESOURCES, AND ECONOMICS

G-1. *What is an Indian Reservation?*

A reservation is an area of land "reserved" for an Indian band, village, or tribe (or tribes) to live on and use. Title to the Indian-owned reservation land is held in trust by the United States for the benefit of said Indians (Bureau of Indian Affairs 1968; Cohen 1982). The name "reservation" is taken from the early practice whereby Indian tribes were coerced, enticed, or otherwise persuaded to relinquish, or "cede," the majority of their homelands by treaty to the federal government, while holding back or "reserving" a portion of their original lands for their own use. The practice goes back to at least 1640, when the Mohican chief, Uncas, ceded a large part of the colony of Connecticut and retained a reservation for his tribe (Cohen 1947).

Not all reservations have been created by treaty, however, nor have all been established on tribal homelands. Acts of Congress, executive orders of the President (until prohibited in 1919), and congressionally authorized actions of the Secretary of the Interior have been used in the establishment, expansion, and restoration of Indian reservations (Canby 1981). It was also common for tribes to be removed from ancestral lands and to be placed on reservations entirely outside those lands. That practice began as early as the 1820s. The most well known examples involve the many former reservations of Oklahoma, established for about 40 tribes who were moved there from various parts of the U.S. during the 1800s.

Depending on the federal policies that have affected a particular reservation, some or even most of the land may now be owned *not* by the tribe but by individual Indians or even non-Indians. Lands owned by non-Indians are no longer held in trust by the U.S. They passed out of Indian ownership as a result of the land allotment system established by Congress in 1887 and continued until repeal of the system by the Indian Reorganization Act (1934).

110

G-2. *What are the largest and smallest federal Indian reservations?*

By far, the largest is the Navajo Reservation which covers between 14 and 15 million acres of trust lands in Arizona, Utah, and New Mexico, about 95 percent of which is tribally owned (Bureau of Indian Affairs 1987b). The rest is held under individual Indian allotments. Only about 45 percent of all federal reservations contain land that is wholly owned by the tribes.

Each of 11 additional reservations has more than a million acres of Indian trust lands (Russell 1991). They are listed on the following page, with acreage figures rounded to the nearest 1,000 acres (Bureau of Indian Affairs 1985a).

Many small reservations are found in a number of states, like the rancherias in California. The smallest reservation is probably Sheep Ranch Rancheria, east of Sacramento, which contains slightly more than nine-tenths of one acre. Blue Lake Rancheria, in far northwestern California, comes in a close second and is also less than one acre.

State	Reservation	Acreage
Arizona	Fort Apache	1,665,000
	Hopi	1,561,000
	San Carlos Apache	1,827,000
	Tohono O'odham	
	(Sells Unit)	2,774,000
Montana	Crow	1,516,000
South Dakota	Cheyenne River	1,396,000
	Pine Ridge	1,779,000
Utah	Uintah & Ouray	1,096,000
Washington	Colville	1,063,000
	Yakima	1,130,000
Wyoming	Wind River	1,888,000

G-3. *How many federal and state Indian reservations are there, and where are they located?*

Federal

The number of federal Indian reservations totals about 300, and they are located in 33 states. These reservations include not only areas referred to as "reservations," but also Indian pueblos, rancherias, communities, and colonies where a land base of some size is held in trust by the U.S. or is otherwise protected by the government. Obviously, there are more tribal entities (greater than 500) than reservations. Thus, to be federally recognized does not necessarily mean that a tribe has been able to retain or acquire lands which can be designated as a reservation. Twenty-one of the 24 states west of the Mississippi River have at least one Indian reservation within their borders. The exceptions are: Missouri, Arkansas, and Hawaii. Only 11 of the 26 states east of the Mississippi have one or more federal Indian reservations (Bureau of Indian Affairs 1989a).

California has the highest number of federal reservations—nearly 95—but approximately half of these are small rancherias which range in size from less than one to several hundred acres. In fact, the total acreage of reservation land in the state is just under 450,000 acres –much less than is included in many single reservations in the western states. The highest concentration of Indian reservation trust land is in Arizona, where approximately 27 percent (about 20 million acres) of the state's 73 million acres lies within the boundaries of some 22 reservations (Bureau of Indian Affairs 1985a).

State

According to the Bureau of Indian Affairs (1989a), there are currently 12 small Indian reservations, located in six eastern states, which have been established and administered by agreement between the states and tribes affected. The states and their associated reservations are:

Connecticut	Shagticoke, Paugusett (2), and Paucatuck Pequot
Massachusetts	Nipmuc-Hassanamisco
Michigan	Potawatomi (2)
New York	Poosepatuck and Shinnecock
South Carolina	Catawba
Virginia	Pamunkey and Mattaponi

Federal and state Indian reservation lands are shown in Figure 5. Indian groups which do not have reservations are shown in Figure 6.

G-4. *What is (or was) Indian Territory?*

In the early 1830s, during the administration of President Andrew Jackson, a policy proposal arose to establish an Indian territory in the West (Cohen 1982). The territory was to be formally organized by the U.S. and governed by a confederation of tribes. Several bills, including the "Western Territory" bill of 1834, were introduced in Congress to officially establish this Indian territory. It was to include the land area in all of present-day Kansas, most of Oklahoma, and parts of what became Nebraska, Colorado, and Wyoming. Although no such legislation was ever enacted, and no territorial Indian government was ever established, the name "Indian Territory" came into common use by Congress and others.

Indian Territory steadily diminished in size as new territorial governments were established and states were carved out of it. By the

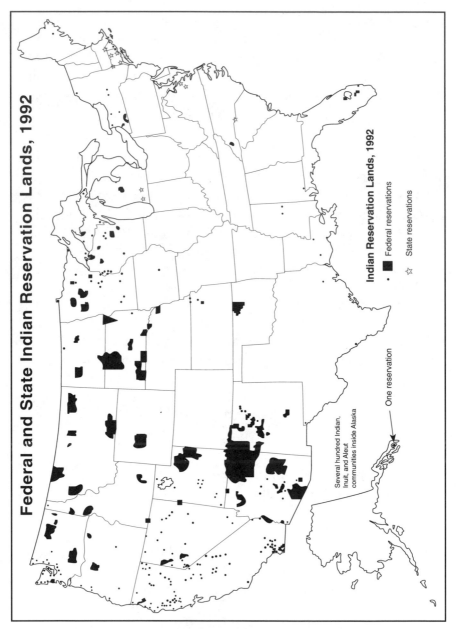

Federal and State Indian Reservation Lands, 1992

Indian Reservation Lands, 1992

■ Federal reservations

☆ State reservations

Several hundred Indian, Inuit, and Aleut communities inside Alaska

One reservation

Figure 5. Federal and state Indian reservations are located as shown. Very small reservations appear as black dots.

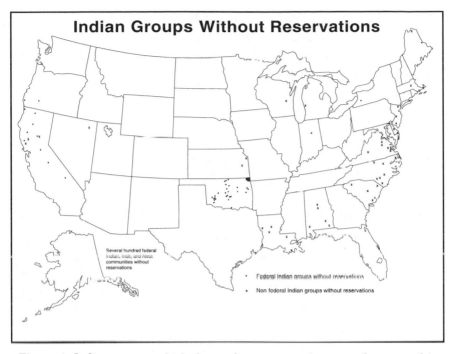

Figure 6. Indian groups which do not have reservations are shown on this map. Some are federally-recognized, others are not.

1870s, Indian Territory was reduced to the size of today's Oklahoma, excluding the panhandle. Many plains tribes were "removed" to western Indian Territory on lands yielded in 1866 by the Five Civilized Tribes, after the Civil War. Congress was pressed by thousands of non-Indians, the railroad interests, and land speculators to open up more of the Indian land to use by non-Indians. They got their way.

In 1890, the Oklahoma Organic Act created Oklahoma Territory out of the western portion of Indian Territory. All that remained of the original Indian Territory was the combined lands of the Five Tribes and the Quapaw Agency tribes. It was an area which included roughly all the land in Oklahoma located south and east of a line running from Bartlesville (in the northeast) to Lawton (in the southwest).

During the succeeding years, Congress passed several laws to make allotments of tribal lands to individual Indians and then sell off the "excess." One such law was the Curtis Act of 1898.

In 1906, the Oklahoma Enabling Act provided for combining Oklahoma Territory and Indian Territory and admitting them as the state of Oklahoma. Statehood was proclaimed in 1907, and Indian Territory ceased to exist.

(Note: Indian Territory differs from "Indian country." See the answer to question H-11, pages 167-170, for information about Indian country.)

G-5. Did the Indians of North America have clear conceptions of land ownership before European contact?

> One does not sell the land upon which the people walk.
>
> Crazy Horse
> Oglala Lakota

Yes, though theirs differed from the European concept. For example, buying and selling land and establishing arbitrary, straight-line, and razor-sharp boundaries were alien ideas.

Land was of primary value in Native American societies. Without a politically defined and controlled land and resource base, survival of tribes or bands was greatly impaired or impossible. That is the reason so many serious conflicts about land and resources occurred, both before and after Europeans arrived in the Western Hemisphere (Arnold 1976).

Considerable variation existed among tribes with respect to their concepts about ownership, but a few general statements can be made. In addition, the resources of a particular land area might often be given higher value than the land itself. First, most land was not individually owned. There were, in some instances, cultivated tracts, fishing sites, and wild seed, fruit, or vegetable patches held by individual families (Ceram 1971). These were, however, often scattered within much larger areas under the communal control or "ownership" of all tribal members.

Another significant aspect of band or tribal ownership was its sometimes exclusive nature. Some tribes held their land for tribal use only–not making it available to other groups for any purpose, including settlement, hunting, gathering, or travel. Bands or tribes usually had clearly identified boundaries that were associated with land features and were known to all groups in the region. To trespass on another tribe's property, in some settings, could be a very risky undertaking, similar to a serious breach of international etiquette. Depending on the attitudes and relative power of the groups involved, and the severity of the trespass, an encroachment might lead to the capture, punishment, or even death of the violators. Further, it might be considered an outright foreign invasion, whether intended or not, and precipitate a war.

Finally, individual tribes' concepts of their land ownership and boundaries were often specific enough that they were used to describe land cessions in treaties and agreements. These boundaries, of course, were subsequently defined by federal surveys that would locate precise land lines. Later, the pre-survey descriptions were sometimes used in establishing judicially recognized Indian land claims for which the U.S. government, and occasionally other interests, owed compensation to various tribes (U.S. Indian Claims Commission 1978). Land and resource issues remain extremely important to Indian people.

G-6. What is the specific meaning of "aboriginal title," and is it relevant today?

> *All...claims of aboriginal title in Alaska...are hereby extinguished.*
> Alaska Native Claims Settlement Act 1971

"Aboriginal title," "original Indian title," or just "Indian title" are three terms applied to a land ownership concept that was attributed to the Native people of the Western Hemisphere by Euro-American governments.

From the beginning, Europeans wanted to determine what kind of Native land rights should be recognized legally. Two very different sides of the debate emerged. One put forth by many was that Indians had no rights after "discovery." They were infidels who stood in the way of much superior civilizations and should be swept away. On top of that, they had no deeds with notary seals and ribbons attesting to their ownership, as the Europeans had.

The preeminent Spanish theologian, Francis de Vitoria, developed an opposite and quite liberal view as early as 1532. He dismissed the hallowed discovery doctrine (see Part I), declaring it applied only to lands not already possessed by other peoples. Furthermore, in his analysis, the Indians "were true owners, both from the public and the private standpoint" (Cohen 1947, p. 45). So powerful were Vitoria's arguments that Pope Paul III incorporated them into a 1537 proclamation addressing Indians' rights to property and freedom from slavery. In response, and for several centuries thereafter, colonial governments vacillated somewhere between Vitoria's precept and the "no rights" contention. Of course, Indian views were never solicited.

For the United States, the issue was settled by the Supreme Court in *Johnson v. McIntosh* (1823). Chief Justice Marshall, writing for the court, chose a compromise position. He embraced the European doctrine of title by discovery, but said it did not completely extinguish all Indian rights. The government held a superior sovereign title to the land, but the Indians retained a right to occupy and use it as they always had, until their right was extinguished through conquest or purchase by the federal government. Therefore, *aboriginal title is an exclusive right of occupancy and use*. It is superior to any claimed right of a state or individual, but it is not an outright and full ownership of the land exclusive of a *federal* interest.

When Indian groups ceded land to the government–which had to be done before their land could legally be taken into possession by the government or anyone else–Indian title to the land was said to be "extinguished." It then became part of the public domain, available for sale or other disposition under the federal land laws. Again, only the federal government could extinguish aboriginal title, and it did so to roughly 2,500,000 square miles of land (Cohen 1947; Alaska Native Claims Settlement Act 1971). This was done through hundreds of treaties and agreements and the expenditure of millions of dollars, in often below-market compensation. (Reservation trust land is not held under the partial ownership doctrine of Indian title. Rather, it is held generally under a full title that is established, sanctioned, and held in trust by the U.S. government.)

The largest extinguishing of aboriginal or Indian title in the U.S. came in 1971 when Alaska Natives ceded their rights to more than 300,000,000 acres of the state to the federal government. This relatively recent action, however, was not the last involving Indian title. Other famous but much smaller claims by several eastern tribes have followed, e.g., Maine Indian Claims Settlement Act (1980) and Mashantucket Pequot Indian Claims Settlement Act (1983). Thus the issue is not yet irrelevant in the U.S. It continues to arise periodically in relation to land claims wherein Indians discover and assert that former tribal lands were taken in ways inconsistent with established federal law. Some members of Congress, like Senator Helms of North Carolina, are trying to change federal law to bar such claims.

The general U.S. idea about aboriginal title has been borrowed by other countries in the Western Hemisphere, like Canada for instance. At this writing, the Canadian government has negotiated an agreement with the Inuit (Eskimos) of the Northwest Territories. Once ratified, the land cession will dwarf even the Alaska claims. Under a tentative agreement announced on December 16, 1991, the 17,500 Inuit involved will give up aboriginal claims to as much as a million square miles of land and sea area. In exchange, they are reportedly to receive outright ownership of 135,000 square miles within a new government territory of 740,000 square miles, to be called "Nunavut." In addition, the Inuit will retain a right to hunt, fish, and trap across all of Nunavut, which is being carved out of the old Northwest Territories (Associated Press 1991d).

Agreement on the Nunavut issue, which has taken 15 years of negotiations, will still leave much to do in the settling of aboriginal land claims in Canada. More than 600 remain (Anquoe 1991a). In the coming decades, more will also be heard about aboriginal rights in Mexico and in Central and South America, especially as the Native people in those areas are able to organize and educate themselves to press their long-dormant claims.

G-7. *What is Indian trust land, how much is there, and is the amount increasing or decreasing?*

Beginning with a simple definition, Indian trust land is Indian-owned land, title to which is held in trust by the United States. What this essentially means is that the "ownership" is divided between the federal government, which holds "bare legal title," and the tribe (or individual Indian) which holds full equitable title (National Congress of American Indians 1976).

The great majority of trust land is reservation land, but not all reservation land is trust land. This is a result of the now defunct reservation allotment policies which functioned in earnest from 1887–1934. Great sell-offs of reservation land to non-Indians resulted. Not all reservations were affected, however. In addition to holding title to trust land, the U.S. government also exercises a significant measure of oversight authority regarding its use and management. During the 19th century, the federal government decided a major part of its government-to-government trust responsibility toward the tribes was to hold their lands in trust. The intended purpose was to prevent "unscrupulous" business and government interests from wrongfully acquiring Indian lands. Trust land has been established in five different ways: (1) by treaties with the U.S. government, (2) by legislative agreements negotiated with tribes, (3) by specific legislative designations, (4) by executive orders of the President, and (5) by administrative land "withdrawals" of the Secretary of the Interior, setting aside public domain lands as reservation lands (Hall 1981).

As already suggested, there are two types of trust land–that owned by individuals and that which is tribally owned. Presently available data indicate that the individually owned total is approximately 10,184,000 acres (Bureau of Indian Affairs 1985a). The tribal total is about 46,000,000 acres, for a grand total of about 56,000,000 acres of trust land (Jones 1991). In general, neither the government nor the Indian owner can sell or otherwise dispose of trust land without consent from the other. The major exception is that Congress can unilaterally take Indian lands for dams, irrigation projects, federal highways, or other "public purposes" under its controversial "plenary," or near absolute, powers over Indian affairs.

Approximately 98 percent of the trust land is in the lower 48 states, but it represents only 2.8 percent of the total land area there. In

Alaska, however, there is a very substantial amount of non-trust, privately held Indian land. Because of the different legal status of nearly all Native lands in that state, particulars about the Alaska situation are discussed in Section M of this book.

Nationwide, the total of Indian trust lands has increased by approximately 3,000,000 acres since 1985 (Jones 1991). This growth has occurred only within the lower 48 states and was accomplished by congressional, Interior Department, or direct tribal acquisitions of lands that were converted to trust status. The "increase," however, has to be put into historical perspective.

In 1887, the year allotment began in earnest–and long after the reservation system had been well established–the total of Indian landholdings was 138,000,000 acres. This represented about seven percent of the area of the lower 48 states. By the end of the allotment period in 1934, however, the area of Indian landholdings had been reduced to 48,000,000 acres (Collier 1934). At the rate of increase that has taken place since 1934 (to the present 56,000,000 acres), it would take another 600 years for the tribes to regain the reservation lands they held in the late-1880s. This is unlikely to happen, of course, because most of their former reservation lands are covered with cities, towns, farms, ranches, military reservations, factories, national parks, national forests, and so on.

G-8. *What significant natural resources do Native American tribal groups have?*

Land

First and foremost among the natural resources controlled by Native Americans is land. Its value is often three-tiered: economic, social, and spiritual. These values can create strongly competing concerns when questions of land and resource development arise. Indian trust lands (56,000,000 acres) and Alaska Native corporation lands (44,000,000 acres) now cover 156,250 square miles of U.S. territory. This amounts to four percent of the nation's total land area of 3,615,210 square miles.

Minerals

Politicians of the 19th century, through their policies, deprived the Indian people of much of their good land and other subsistence resources. Unknowingly, however, they left a number of tribes with non-subsistence resources, such as coal, oil, gas, and uranium, that would become very valuable in the 20th century. For example, in 1988 (the most recent year for which figures were available), Indian trust lands produced $161 million from mineral leases, mostly for oil, gas, and coal. Roughly 10 percent of the nation's total coal reserves and a third of its low-sulfur coal lie beneath Native American soil. Oil is also found in substantial quantities on several reservations and under some Alaska Native corporation lands. And, nearly one-sixth of America's natural gas reserves may lie under Indian land.

In the 48 states, however, only 29 percent of Indians belong to tribes with notable amounts of mineral resources (O'Brien 1989). During the 20th century, periodic mismanagement or corruption within the Bureau of Indian Affairs, as well as within certain state and tribal agencies, has resulted in the cumulative loss of hundreds of millions of dollars in tribal royalty revenues from oil and gas leases (Hall 1981; White 1990; White and Cronon 1988).

Besides the carbon-based minerals, more than half of America's uranium is on Indian land. Other mineral and related resources that are found in varying amounts within one or more Indian reservations or Native communities include gold, silver, copper, molybdenum, zeolite, phosphate, vanadium, sandstone, basalt, shale, sulfur, limestone, chat, lead, zinc, peat, iron, clay, gypsum, volcanic cinders, sand, gravel, and building stone (Washburn 1988).

Timber

About one-fourth of all Indian reservation lands, or nearly 13 million acres, have some kind of forest cover. Almost a third of the forest land is considered to be of "commercial" quality, which means it is theoretically capable of growing timber at a volume that can be harvested for a profit on a renewable basis (Bureau of Indian Affairs 1992a). In recent years, nearly 60 tribes obtained 25 to 100 percent of their non-federal revenues from timber operations (Hall 1981), and as many as 130 tribes belong to the "Tribal Timber Consortium" (O'Brien 1989).

Timber mismanagement has plagued BIA-directed forestry programs, where "getting the cut out" has sometimes taken precedence over long-term protection of ecosystems. Similar problems affect the national forests. Many Indians and non-Indians, who now see that forests are more than mere sources of timber and other commodities, are pressing the issue of forest conservation with their leaders and government agencies.

Water

Water is the most critical resource in the western states, and that is where most Indian reservations are located. Therefore, intense competition and conflicts over water are found between tribes and non-Indian interests. The issue frequently centers on the fact that Indians legally "have" the water, or rights thereto, and some other individual, group, agency, corporation, or local government "wants" it.

Reservation Indians and tribes have well established rights to large but not yet fully quantified amounts of water. These rights are based on the doctrine of reserved water rights, first acknowledged in

PHOTO COURTESY OF EASTERN WASHINGTON STATE HISTORICAL SOCIETY

In the West, as elsewhere, Indian rights to fisheries and water resources have been the focus of intense controversy over the years. Natives in the Northwest, for example, have fished the Columbia River system for centuries, but the development of hydroelectric power, along with fishing competition from non-Indians, created conflicts. Photo circa 1930s.

the famous Supreme Court case of *Winters v. United States* (1908) and later affirmed and clarified in the equally important case of *Arizona v. California* (1963). The concept behind the doctrine is that the establishment of Indian reservations meant not only that the land was "reserved" but also that the right to sufficient water to fulfill the purposes of the reservation was also reserved. In other words, the government could not put Indians on reservations and leave them without rights to sufficient amounts of water to maintain and later develop their reservations and resources (Cohen 1982).

As tribes continue to hold and use their water rights, while population and development pressures in the West further strain the already over-extended water resources, conflict with competing interests will increase. Precisely how the problems will ultimately be resolved, if they ever are, is unclear. But what *is* clear is that the roles of the tribes in brokering and adjudicating western water rights will continue to grow in importance.

G-9. *How important are Native American hunting and fishing rights, and what are some of the major controversies pertaining to those rights?*

When Europeans arrived in the southern and eastern part of the continent in the late 15th century, and in Alaska in the mid-18th century, hunting, fishing, and related activities were absolutely vital to tribal life. Understandably, preservation of the rights to continue pursuing such activities became central topics in peace negotiations and land cessions, and were directly or indirectly guaranteed through treaties, agreements, legislation, or executive actions. As the 20th century changes to the 21st, these very same rights continue to have critical importance to hundreds of Native communities–for both cultural and economic reasons.

In Alaska, where no official treaties were entered into by the U.S. and Native people, hunting and fishing rights are part of the overarching issue of "subsistence." The subsistence issue, because it relates specifically to Alaska, is discussed in Section M of this book.

To say that the controversies surrounding tribal hunting and fishing rights in the lower 48 states can be complicated and intense is putting it mildly. Some conflicts in the Northwest and Great Lakes regions, for example, have led to vigilantism and violence. The following discussion mentions the major controversies and gives general answers to the basic jurisdictional questions which are at their foundation. Information is taken from Canby (1981), Cohen (1982), Getches, Rosenfelt, and Wilkinson (1979), and O'Brien (1989).

Four themes are commonly heard from opponents of Indian treaty hunting and fishing rights: (1) they are unfair to non-Indians, (2) they are basically illegal, (3) they interfere with the hunting and fishing regulatory function of a state, and (4) they are contrary to conservation goals. On the unfairness claim, things may seem unfair to non-Indian hunting and fishing interests when a local tribe has equal or "superior" rights to their own. But, such a view is taken out of context. The Indian tribes in the lower 48 states gave up 98 percent of the land area through treaties and agreements with the colonial, state, and federal governments. Retaining two percent of the land base and some locally or regionally significant hunting and fishing rights does not appear to the tribes, Congress, or the courts as an unfair trade. However, to the non-Indian who is subject to state laws and game limits, it might naturally seem unfair. Nonetheless, controversies over the issue of Indian rights cannot be divorced from their historical and legal contexts.

Five essential points need to be emphasized before moving on to the regulatory and conservation questions. First, it is well settled in the law that establishment of a federal reservation includes a right of Indians to hunt and fish on their reservation, free of state interference.

Second, when some of the tribes gave up lands, they retained the rights to continue hunting and fishing on all or parts of their former homelands. These rights were retained through both explicit and implicit language in the treaties. Such rights can be likened to easements. Many Washington state tribes, several Chippewa tribes, the Crow Tribe, the Navajo, the Southern Cheyenne, and a few other groups retained off-reservation rights. These and the on-reservation rights are part of the "reserved rights doctrine" mentioned elsewhere with regard to Indian water rights. The doctrine is tied to the well-founded legal concept that, when Indian land rights were reserved, other associated rights (e.g., hunting, fishing, trapping, gathering of plant materials, water use, etc.) were reserved for the tribes' continued cultural and economic well-being.

A third point is that, under its plenary (near absolute) power over Indian affairs regarding federally recognized tribes, Congress, and not the states, has the ultimate authority to regulate all aspects of Indian hunting and fishing pertaining to reserved rights. It has rarely exercised this authority, however, leaving most regulatory responsibility to the tribes.

Fourth, on a few former reservations where the U.S. "terminated" the tribes' federal status and extinguished their aboriginal title to the reservations, Indian hunting and fishing rights continue to be in effect unless specifically extinguished by Congressional action.

Finally, in the absence of acknowledged treaty rights, Indians outside of legally defined "Indian country" are subject to the same laws as everyone else.

Tribal authority over on-reservation hunting and fishing

When no federal law exists to the contrary, tribes can regulate the hunting and fishing of Indians and non-Indians on Indian-owned land. To do so, tribes must establish comprehensive hunting and fishing codes for management, licensing, and enforcement purposes. Many have done so. As part of their regulatory authority, tribes can bring *criminal* charges in tribal court against Indians who violate tribal game laws, but not against non-Indians. However, tribes can impose *civil* penalties for game and fish violations by non-Indians. These penalties might include fines, equipment confiscation (questionable), or ejection from the reservation. Tribes may also request federal prosecution of non-Indians for violating federal trespass laws.

State authority over on-reservation hunting and fishing

States may regulate on-reservation hunting and fishing in two circumstances. First, if no federal or tribal regulatory program has been established for Indian-owned reservation lands, the state may step in and fill the regulatory void. The state, however, may not authorize non-Indians to hunt and fish on Indian-owned reservation lands without the affected tribe's permission. Second, states can allow and regulate non-Indian hunting and fishing on non-Indian land that is within the exterior boundaries of a reservation, whether or not the affected tribe agrees. That is, unless the conduct of non-Indians threatens or has some direct effect on the political integrity, economic security, or health and welfare of the tribe.

Tribal authority over off-reservation hunting and fishing

The several tribes that retained off-reservation hunting and fishing rights in their treaties have the authority to regulate their members in this off-reservation activity. Unless Congress changes existing law, the states affected cannot prohibit the tribes from exercising their treaty rights and cannot require tribal members to buy state game licenses. Furthermore, neither the state nor a private landowner can prevent tribal access to reserved sites. Tribal rights predate non-Indian acquisition of the land and are legally "attached" to it in the form of a treaty easement.

State authority over off-reservation hunting and fishing

There are two exceptions to exclusive tribal regulation of off-reservation hunting and fishing allowed by treaty. Tribes have a responsibility to conserve off reservation fish and wildlife. If they do not, and conservation requires action, the federal courts will allow states to impose regulations. Also, at least one state court has successfully held that an Indian violating tribal game and fish laws at an off-reservation site could be arrested and prosecuted by the state because he had (1) also violated state law and (2) stepped beyond his tribally protected rights.

Conservation

The opposition argument that Indian treaty hunting and fishing causes much greater pressure on game and fish populations than is caused by other pressures—like loss of habitat, poor logging practices, general environmental degradation, or fishing and hunting by non-Indian interests—is not supported by the evidence. Where conservation becomes an issue, either the tribes or the federal government, or both, are obliged to take remedial action. If they fail to do so, and if a state can show a "necessity for conservation," the state may proceed to take appropriate and non-discriminatory regulatory action to address identified problems.

G-10. *What does "environmental racism" mean and how much of a concern is it in Indian country?*

"Environmental racism" was coined by the Reverend Benjamin Chavis, Jr., executive director of the Commission of Racial Justice of the United Church of Christ (Associated Press 1991c). In 1987, Dr. Chavis first used the term in describing results of a study done by his commission that found a very strong correlation between race and the selection of sites for hazardous industries and waste disposal facilities. Environmental racism is generally defined as racial discrimination in environmental policy making, regulation enforcement, and waste facility siting, and also includes the exclusion of people of color from the decision-making process as well as from leadership positions in the environmental movement. It is very much an issue in Indian country.

In recent years, waste disposal agencies and companies have increased their contracting efforts in Indian country to try to entice tribes to take advantage of potentially profitable agreements. As an example, the federal government's chief nuclear waste negotiator has made a point of attending meetings of the National Congress of American Indians. He has offered money and assistance programs to those tribes who would allow development of nuclear waste sites on tribal lands (Workman 1991).

While a few tribes, or factions within the tribes, are actively courting government agencies and private companies to consider tribal lands for profitable waste disposal projects of different kinds, others are adamantly opposed. Several of the concerns beyond the waste disposal issue include water quality and quantity issues, the environmental effects of oil and gas development, health and environmental damage caused by uranium mining, and the effects of ongoing air and ground training and testing by the military services.

In October 1991, the first "National People of Color Environmental Leadership Summit" was held in Washington, D.C. The 600 participants included Native Americans, African Americans, Hispanic Americans, Pacific Islanders, Canadians, Mexicans, and Central and South Americans. Speakers like Wilma Mankiller, principal chief of the Cherokee Nation of Oklahoma, called for such things as (1) an end to the myth that people of color are not involved in the environmental movement, (2) education of Indian people on the dangers of economic development projects that involve hazardous wastes, and (3) environmental justice for all people (Tallman 1991).

G-11. *How do Native Americans earn a living?*

> *The mind of mainstream America bears its Native citizens back ceaselessly into the past. Whereas many feel that economic progress is fine for every other ethnic group (thinking the quicker the better) too many of us non-Indians prefer our Natives as living museum pieces, in the saddle or the dugout, living out some storybook version of "natural" subsistence. In this view, economic progress is corrupted into a fall from aboriginal grace.*
>
> White 1990, p. 276

Native Americans earn their livelihoods in as many and varied ways as do other people. For example, there are Native American teachers, loggers, physicians, soldiers, carpenters, factory workers, ranchers, cooks, corporate executives, rodeo cowboys, secretaries, farmers, radio announcers, accountants, dentists, engineers, commercial fishermen, homemakers, legislators, foresters, veterinarians, musicians, actors, salespeople, janitors, lawyers, truckers, authors, bureaucrats, service station attendants, police officers, and psychologists. The list goes on. It also includes some individuals and groups in Alaska who rely on subsistence hunting, fishing, and even occasional whaling for much of their livelihoods. Some tribal members are eligible for per capita payments from tribal resource, business, or investment income, or corporate investments, trust accounts, and judgments awarded by the Indian Claims Commission and the Court of Claims.

Unemployment on reservations ranges from a low of 0 to 1 percent to a high of about 90 percent (Bureau of Indian Affairs 1989b). In a 1986 BIA study, it was found that 41 percent of Indians on reservations lived below the poverty line. On average, a reservation Indian family lives on 40 percent of the income of a non-Indian family in the U.S. (O'Brien 1989).

The motion picture industry is one area in which some Native Americans have been able to obtain employment. For example, Nathan Chasing Horse (right) played the role of "Smiles a Lot" in *Dances With Wolves.* He and his father, Joseph Chasing Horse, are Sicangu (Brulé) Lakota from the Rosebud Reservation in South Dakota.

Many Indians make all or part of their living by selling arts and crafts. Authentically-made items are given a certain degree of protection under the Indian Arts and Crafts Act. Phil Garcia, a Laguna Pueblo carver displays some of the tools of his trade.

There is one occupation in which Native Americans can work and others cannot. That is the production of authentic arts and crafts items. It is a violation of federal law for non-Natives to willfully offer for sale or display imitation "Indian" arts and crafts, while representing them as authentic. Some Indians and Alaska Natives make their entire livings from arts and crafts, while many thousands supplement their incomes in this way. Annual retail sales of Native arts and crafts total several hundred million dollars, but non-Native interests currently control most of the retail market (Andrews 1991).

Wilson Hunter, a Navajo, is Chief of Interpretation at Canyon de Chelly National Monument, on the Navajo Reservation in Arizona. He is shown here (left) while on a tour of the Monument in 1992. As an employee of the National Park Service, Wilson has developed a national reputation for his ability to interpret the natural and cultural heritage of Canyon de Chelly to its thousands of annual visitors.

G-12. *May Indians qualify for the major social services and assistance programs offered by non-BIA agencies?*

Generally, yes. But an overview and comparison of relevant Bureau of Indian Affairs and other programs (like that given in Cohen 1982) can clarify the sometimes confusing aspects of this issue.

BIA programs

The BIA has had programs to assist needy Indians since the 19th century. Until 1944, however, general assistance funds for the needy were routed through Indian agents on behalf of eligible Indian people. In that year, BIA welfare payments were authorized to be paid directly to individuals who were eligible for them. Until 1977, the BIA generally refused to make payments to Indians in need who lived outside the boundaries of a reservation. The exceptions were in parts of Alaska and Oklahoma. Some difficulties arose because many potentially eligible Indians lived *just outside* reservations. Today, needy Indians who live on "or near" a reservation may apply for general assistance from the BIA. Title 25 of the Code of Federal Regulations, Sec. 20.20, specifically defines the important term "near a reservation." The BIA's general assistance and child welfare programs are designed to provide social service assistance to needy Native Americans who do not receive similar benefits from state or federal programs. The federal government's position is that the overall Social Security program (discussed below), and not the BIA, has the *primary* responsibility for providing financial support for economically disadvantaged Native Americans.

Social Security programs

Indians and Alaska Natives who have worked under and contributed to the Social Security system have the same coverage as other people. This includes the "old age" benefits, for those 65 and over, that most people think of when social security is mentioned. The Social Security Act, however, also provides both federal and state financial assistance, administered in large part by the states and their subdivisions, to impoverished United States citizens. Under various programs, the act authorizes welfare payments to the poor and direct aid to disadvantaged senior citizens, dependent children, and disabled citizens. Native Americans in need, like other citizens and state residents, may qualify for benefits under the Social Security Act. According to the BIA, general assistance is not available to Indians receiving social security benefits.

USDA programs

The Department of Agriculture's food stamp program aims to help economically disadvantaged or low income households, including those of Native Americans, obtain a nutritious diet. Uniform eligibility requirements are established by the USDA. The overriding rule states that food stamps are for "those households whose incomes and other financial resources...are determined to be a substantial limiting factor in permitting them to obtain a more nutritious diet" (7 USC, Sec. 2014(a)). States normally administer the food stamp program. However, a tribal government may administer the program on its reservation if the Secretary of Agriculture determines that the state government is not doing an adequate job. Surplus food commodities that the USDA stores and then distributes to communities around the country, to prevent waste, are also available to Indian communities.

Tribal programs

On a few reservations which have substantial resources, there are tribal social service programs funded through the tribes' own finances. The increase in tribal gaming enterprises over the past decade, for example, has expanded several tribes' abilities to fund some of their own social service programs.

Other assistance programs

During 1990 and 1991, Roger Walke of the Congressional Research Service, Library of Congress, compiled a 331-page report for the Senate Select Committee on Indian Affairs titled *Federal Programs of Assistance to Native Americans* (102nd Congress, 1st Session, S. Prt. [sic] 102-162). It provides basic information on all government programs that specifically serve or are of particular interest to American Indians, Alaska Natives, and Native Hawaiians. This very important report, with a publication date of December 1991, is for sale by the Superintendent of Documents, U.S. Government Printing Office, Washington, D.C. 20402; phone (202) 783-3238.

G-13. *How does the gaming issue fit into the tribal economic picture?*

Only since the early 1980s has gaming (the "politically correct" term for gambling) become a significant economic activity in Indian country. Revenues derived from gaming by non-Indians, on Indian land, now supplement tribal government incomes on a number of reservations throughout the U.S. Headlines are also being made as federal, tribal, and state governments argue, in the courts and in the press, over who is going to regulate what in tribal gaming enterprises. Gaming is, by far, the most politically charged economic issue in Indian country during this final decade of the 20th century.

Background of the issue

In 1979, the Seminole Tribe of Florida was the first tribe to enter into the bingo gaming industry in a major way (Sokolow 1990). By 1982, their bingo operation was annually netting $2.7 million. This, and a few other success stories around the country, caused many additional tribes (and the Reagan administration) to encourage more gaming enterprises on reservations to stimulate economic development. Economic self-sufficiency was a cornerstone of the administration's Indian policy. Gaming enterprises were seen by many, then as now, as a quick fix for the difficult economic conditions on numerous reservations with limited resources.

Immediately upon the expansion of gaming in Indian country, conflicts arose among federal, state, and tribal governments as to what was legal and what was not—and who had jurisdiction. What resulted from the conflict was the Indian Gaming Regulatory Act (IGRA) of 1988. The meaning and application of this act is now the focus of most of the conflict over Indian gaming.

The stated multiple purposes of the act are: (1) to provide a legislative basis for the operation and regulation of gaming by Indian tribes; (2) to establish a National Indian Gaming Commission as a federal agency to meet congressional concerns and protect gaming as a means of generating tribal revenue; (3) to promote economic development, self-sufficiency, and strong tribal governments; (4) to shield tribes from organized crime; and (5) to assure fairness to operators and players.

Three classes of gaming and related jurisdiction are treated by the IGRA. Class I includes social, traditional games in connection with tribal ceremonies, pow wows, or celebrations. These are under the exclusive jurisdiction of the Indian tribes.

Class II gaming includes such things as bingo, lotto, pull tabs, punch boards, tip jars, and certain card games. Excluded from this class are baccarat, chemin de fer, blackjack, all slot machines, and all electromechanical facsimiles of any game of chance, such as video poker and video bingo. The IGRA permits Class II gaming on Indian lands if the gaming is located in a state which allows it for any purpose, by any person or entity. Only five states (Arkansas, Hawaii, Indiana, Mississippi, and Utah) criminally prohibit all types of gaming, including bingo. The tribes involved and the National Indian Gaming Commission share regulatory jurisdiction over Class II gaming activities.

Class III includes all gaming that is not covered in Classes I and II, i.e., the usual casino games of baccarat, blackjack, roulette, and craps, as well as slot machines, video poker, horse and dog racing, etc. Before Class III games can be offered legally, a tribe and the state involved must first negotiate a tribal-state regulatory compact. It must then be approved by the Secretary of the Interior.

Much of the current news about the Indian gaming issue involves the topic of state-tribal compacts. Some states have been almost immovable in their attitudes toward negotiating compacts. According to many tribes, the states have not engaged in "good faith" negotiations as the IGRA requires. Some tribes are taking their complaints to federal court. For example, in June 1991, a federal district court in

This newspaper advertisement for an Indian casino operation in Sault Ste. Marie, Michigan, appeared in January 1993.

Wisconsin ruled that Wisconsin must negotiate *any* form of Class III gaming with a tribe if state law permits at least *some* form of Class III gaming. This critical decision has been appealed, and the appeals court's decision will have far-reaching consequences.

As of December 1992, 160 tribes (about half the number in the lower 48 states) were involved in Class II or III gaming of some kind (Gamerman 1992; Dvorchak 1992). Just under 30 had compacts with a state. As the tribes, states, and federal government continue to wrangle over regulation of Indian gaming enterprises, the tribes involved hope to preserve gaming as a source of revenue. This, after all, was one of the major purposes of Congress in passing the IGRA.

Estimates of *gross* revenues from Indian gaming for 1992 reached as high as several billion dollars. Even if *net* returns were on the low end of a reasonable 10 to 15 percent, the $300 million would be more than 20 times the amount appropriated directly for the BIA economic development program in fiscal year 1991. Obviously, Indian gaming will continue to play a major role in tribal economies.

The debate

A number of quotations from selected news stories and a key congressional document are presented here to demonstrate the character and gravity of the wide-ranging and very serious gaming debate.

> Just when Indians find something that works, the feds [and states] ride in and say "whoa."...The tribes got into gaming as a way to make up for federal revenues lost under the Reagan administration. They were encouraged...for the money it would bring. They use the money for things like schools, home rehabilitation services, and emergency assistance programs.
>
> Editorial, *Arizona Daily Star*
> January 4, 1992

> They shouldn't be able to have some sort of safe harbor for illegal activities on reservations.... There's a lot of illegal things they could do to make money. They could sell drugs and make a lot of money. But it's illegal.... That [gambling] generally attracts a negative element to the places that have it.
>
> Grant Woods, Arizona Attorney General
> January 22, 1992
>
> *[Note: Arizona has four lotto drawings per week as well as horse and dog racing.]*

> The Mille Lacs band of Chippewa plans to parlay casino profits into $20 million in construction projects that would include a school, health clinic, day-care unit, and water system.
>
> *Lakota Times*, Associated Press article
> January 21, 1992

> I am writing in regard to the No. 1 issue in Indian country.... Our tribe has been in a tumult because of the issue of gambling. It has brought out the worst in people. Such as power hungry leaders who have sold themselves out to greed.... As a tribal leader, I have never been bothered so much in my life by people who want to invest in our tribe—for gambling.
>
> Wallace Wells, Jr.
> Crow Creek Sioux Tribe
> Letter to *Lakota Times*
> January 21, 1992

We were told...[by our ancestors]...that gambling would destroy us. ...Today I see our [Indian] nations forfeiting our sovereignty to hang on to the right to gamble. It is short term. ...[It] will dry up. ...We were told to make decisions for the seventh generation to come. Gaming will not last into the seventh generation.

> Oren Lyons
> Onondaga Elder
> *Lakota Times*
> August 26, 1992

The perception in the media and elsewhere that Indian gaming operations are rife with serious criminality does not stand up under close examination.

> Paul Maloney
> U.S. Department of Justice
> Associated Press
> December 11, 1992

Twelve California tribes have requested compact negotiations with the state for large-scale casino operations. The rush of letters sent to Governor Pete Wilson's office comes on the heels of state police raids and seizures of nearly 300 gambling machines October 30 at casinos on three San Diego County reservations.... The Sycuan, Barona, and Viejas reservations have filed suit for damages and return of the machines, asserting lack of jurisdiction.

> Bunty Anquoe
> Reporter for *Lakota Times*
> November 20, 1991

We should be candid about gambling. This issue is not about crime control, morality, or economic fairness. Lotteries and other forms of gambling abound in many States, charities, and church organizations nationwide. It would be hypocritical indeed to impose on Indian people more stringent moral standards than those by which the rest of our citizens choose to live. Moreover, Indian tribes may have a competitive economic advantage because, rightly or wrongly, many states have chosen not to allow the same types of gaming in which tribes are empowered to engage. Ironically, the strongest opponents of tribal authority over gaming on Indian lands are from States whose liberal gaming policies would allow them to compete on an equal basis with the tribes.

Senator Daniel Evans
Indian Affairs Committee
Senate Report No. 100-446, 1988

[S]ome members of Congress, including myself, have stated that they would rather see Tribes involved in other revenue raising activities. We must ask ourselves, however, if we have provided Tribes with sufficient opportunities to generate non-gaming revenues and thereby allow Tribes to increase their economic self-sufficiency. The answer is a resounding no. We have not done enough. Once this gaming debate is over, I challenge those involved in this debate to devote their energies toward increasing long-term economic development opportunities for Indian tribes.

Senator John McCain, Vice Chairman
Indian Affairs Committee
Senate Report No. 100-446, 1988

For further information on the gaming issue, contact the National Indian Gaming Commission by phoning (202) 632-7003, and the National Indian Gaming Association, at 1 (800) 325-3557. In addition, a monthly trade magazine of the Indian gaming industry, *Indian Gaming*, is published by the Public Gaming Research Institute, 15825 Shady Grove Road, Suite 130, Rockville, MD 20850; phone (301) 330-7600.

G-14. *What can be said about the state of the economy in Indian country?*

Only general statements can be made because of the great diversity, nationwide, in the economic circumstances of tribes and individual Native Americans. Indian country, like everywhere else, is affected by changing national economic trends.

Starting with perhaps the most successful situation, there seems to be at least one tribe in the country in which everyone is doing exceedingly well, financially. It is the tiny Cabazon Tribe of Indio,

California. The 30-plus members have a 1,700-acre reservation located 20 miles east of Palm Springs on a creosote-flats desert. When the author first visited there in 1970, some of the people were living under relatively poor conditions. Now, with a few highly controversial non-Indian business managers (who are government-wise and extremely effective at what they do), each tribal member is reported to have an annual income of perhaps $500,000 or more. This is derived from several hundred million dollars' worth of development that has been taking place on the reservation since the early 1980s. It includes gaming enterprises, a 1,300-unit housing project for non-Indians, a Canadian-backed electrical power plant, and possible military hardware and international trade projects (Littman 1991).

In contrast to the Indians of the Cabazon Reservation, thousands of individual Native people, from Florida to Alaska and Maine to California, are mired in poverty. White (1990) reports that approximately 25 percent of *all* Native Americans live below the poverty line, and one in seven lives on less than $2,500 a year. The situation is generally worse on reservations, where about 40 percent of Indians live below the poverty line (O'Brien 1989). More than half of the Native population resides in and around urban areas, and perhaps a quarter of these Americans are unemployed and impoverished.

On the brighter side, a number of Indian tribes and communities have businesses and resource-based enterprises—like electronics plants, fishing interests, cattle ranches, casinos, oil and gas wells, coal mines, resorts, retail outlets, waste disposal businesses, industrial parks, or sawmills—that generate steady and respectable returns. These now include the Passamaquoddies of Maine, the Mississippi Band of Choctaws, various Native corporations in Alaska, the Ak-Chin Community near Phoenix, the Confederated Tribes of the Warm Springs Reservation of Oregon, the Navajo Nation, the Cherokee Nation of Oklahoma, the Pascua Yaqui Tribe near Tucson, the Mescalero Apache Tribe of New Mexico, the Oneidas of New York, and many others. But even among these comparatively successful tribal groups and communities, there are often unemployment rates of 20 to 50 percent or higher. The point is that, although numerous tribes' businesses may be successful, this does not necessarily mean those businesses create nearly enough job opportunities for all or even a majority of the members of the tribe.

Most reservation tribes (this excludes Alaska Natives) have no substantial formal economy of their own to generate operating capital. Their revenues are derived primarily from outside the reservations. An average reservation tribe obtains 30 percent of its revenue from tribal businesses, taxes, investments, etc., or from annuities relating to former land sales or court-awarded judgments on property claims. The remaining 70 percent of tribal income enters the reservation as federal program dollars. These federal funds, in combination with tribal monies, are important not only to tribes but to local off-reservation communities which provide goods and services to the tribes and their members. Thus, federal Indian programs, tribal enterprises, and off-reservation activities constitute the major interacting elements of the economy in Indian country (O'Brien 1989).

On the issue of unemployment, while the nation as a whole is concerned with a current unemployment rate of 7 percent–going as high as 9 percent in several states–the numbers in Indian communities are so much higher as to be shocking. The most recent labor force statistics available from the Bureau of Indian Affairs (1989b) show the nationwide unemployment rate for the one million Native Americans counted in the BIA's service population has been at 48 percent. It is common to find individual Native community unemployment rates that go to 50 or 80 percent. Even Alaska Natives, with their many successful corporate businesses, have had a recent unemployment rate of 57 percent. But, the highest unemployment rate in the country, in 1989, was reported for the Rosebud Reservation in South Dakota, where an incredible 93 percent of the work force was unemployed. About 90 percent of these people were looking for work, which shows the rather poor opportunities for employment on that particular reservation in 1989. As bad as all of these statistics may seem, they are still better than they used to be decades ago.

What is being done about the problem? Plenty, but it is not always effective. Roughly three billion dollars a year are pumped through various federal programs devoted to Native Americans. More than a billion dollars a year goes into the Bureau of Indian Affairs alone. But, as much as a third of it is absorbed into the agency before it gets out to any reservation. According to Arizona Senator John McCain, Vice Chairman of the Select Committee on Indian Affairs, only 12 cents of every dollar appropriated for Indian programs ever reaches a Native American. It is also important to note that federal and tribal jobs, most with relatively good salaries, account for almost half of Native American incomes. This leaves little incentive for change in the bureaucratic system. But change is occurring and has been since the 1970s. Furthermore, it seems to be developing an accelerating pace for the 1990s (White 1990).

Policy failures, corruption, bureaucratic incompetence, and politics have gone far toward holding Native Americans back economically since the U.S. became a nation. The many, well-educated Native people of today, however, are very familiar with the laws, economics, and government bureaucracies that so thoroughly affect their lives. They and fellow Indians and Alaska Natives appear to be moving in a determined way to take control of their economic destiny. This process is a palpable happening. It may take years for some communities, or generations for others, but it is an ongoing trend.

The worst thing that non-Indian America can do is to presume–as it has so often done in the past, with such disastrous results–that it knows what is "right" for Native Americans. As Wilma Mankiller, principal Chief of the Oklahoma Cherokee Nation, has stated on this subject, "The best solutions to our problems are within our own communities" (White 1990, p. 275).

All who are concerned should also remember that tribal business and other economic development are not panaceas for the various problems facing Native America. Native culture and the hundreds of Indian nations are not so simplistic as that. Better business and job opportunities, however, will go a long way toward improving economic self-determination, to which Native Americans seem to be firmly dedicated.

SECTION H: LEGAL STATUS AND TRIBAL SELF-GOVERNMENT

H-1. *Are Indians wards of the federal government?*

No. The Government is not the guardian of individual Indians. It is, however, the trustee of certain kinds of Indian property. Such "trust" property is most frequently associated, in one way or another, with current and former reservation lands and resources and with proceeds derived therefrom. The government only holds property in trust for federally recognized tribes. This property may be tribal or individual, depending on the circumstances.

Consider a general comparison of what is trust property and what is not. Navajo reservation land, for example, is held in trust by the United States. Therefore, major decisions involving reservation land require approval by the Bureau of Indian Affairs. In contrast, a home lot purchased by a Navajo Indian in the far-away city of Phoenix is not trust property. It is entirely private property, the same as for any non-Indian. It would be purchased with private—not tribal—resources, and it would be done without government involvement.

From the early 1800s to the early 1900s, reservation Indians were often referred to and often treated as wards by the three branches of the federal government. Frequently, the term "wards" was employed to mean non-citizen Indians. This situation began to be corrected with policy changes in the 1920s and 1930s which resulted from passage of the Indian Citizenship Act (1924) and the Indian Reorganization Act (1934). The latter act ended the destructive land allotment system which had begun in earnest in 1887. Allotment had progressively dismantled numerous reservations and forced the affected tribes into a more dependent or ward-like status. The self-determination policies of the '20s and '30s, fortunately, began to reverse that trend. To assure that there will be no turning back, additional reforms have been adopted. They were rightfully demanded by Native Americans and their supporters in the 1960s and later years .

> *The Wyandot Indians, having become sufficiently advanced in civilization, and being desirous of becoming citizens...are hereby declared to be citizens of the United States.*
>
> Treaty with the Wyandots
> 1855

H-2. *Are Indians U.S. citizens?*

Yes. Indians born in the U.S., or born of citizens who are outside the country at the time of birth, are American citizens. They are also citizens of their states of residence. In addition, most Indians are also citizens, or members, of federally recognized Indian tribes, which are political bodies that exercise substantial powers of self-government. In the 19th century, the prevalent opinion was that an Indian could not be both a tribal member and a U.S. citizen. This notion has long since been refuted by federal law. Therefore, Indian citizenship is not in any way inconsistent with tribal membership (Cohen 1982).

The road to citizenship was long and bumpy. A few early treaties offered citizenship options, e.g., the Treaty with the Cherokees (1817), the Wyandot treaty quoted above, and the Treaty with the Senecas, et al. (1867). Individual Indians were required to make a choice between (1) staying with their tribes which were being removed to a distant part of the country or (2) severing their tribal ties and remaining behind to accept citizenship and a small land allotment.

Besides treaties, roughly a dozen congressional acts have directly addressed the Indian citizenship issue in some way. The General Allotment Act of 1887 was one of the most significant. It conferred citizenship on Indians who were born within the U.S. and to whom the government made individual land allotments, of usually 80 to 160 acres, from tribal reservation lands. Another significant act, passed in 1888, declared that, "Every Indian woman...who may hereafter be married to any citizen of the United States is hereby declared to become by such marriage a citizen of the United States" (25 U.S. Code, Sec. 182). This piecemeal process of selectively conferring citizenship on the U.S. Indian population came to an end in 1924 with passage of the one-sentence law titled The Indian Citizenship Act. It reads: "[A]ll non-citizen Indians born within the territorial limits of the United States...are hereby declared to be citizens of the United

States...." At the time the act was passed, perhaps one third of the U.S. Indian population did not have citizenship.

As with much Indian legislation, many non-Indians still questioned the effect of the Citizenship Act, suggesting that it did not apply to Indians born after passage of the act on June 24, 1924, or to Alaska Natives. Subsequent amendments contained clarifying language granting citizenship "at birth" and including Alaska Natives. (See 8 U.S. Code, Sec. 1401.)

In 1983, Congress enacted what will probably be the last Indian citizenship legislation ever passed in this country. The act involved a band of Kickapoo whose ancestors had fled the central plains in the 1800s to live in isolation along the Texas-Mexico border area. For over a century, these Indians and their descendants moved back and forth between Mexico and the U.S., with no citizenship status in either country. The Texas Band of Kickapoo Act (1983) established federal recognition of the tribe, provided for the acquisition of a small reservation near Eagle Pass, Texas, and authorized tribal members to "apply for United States citizenship" within a five-year period after passage of the act.

A few of the more traditional Indians, retaining views consistent with pre-1924 law, do not regard themselves as American citizens, but as citizens only of their own tribes (Deloria and Lytle 1983). In addition, a few tribes issue passports. Traditional leaders of the Hopi Nation and the Iroquois League, for example, have traveled to international meetings using only passports issued by tribal governments (O'Brien 1989). Historically, in the late-1700s and early 1800s, federal law required U.S. citizens traveling in Indian country to have passports.

H-3. *Can Native Americans vote and hold public office?*

Voting Rights

The general right to vote comes with citizenship and state residency. Therefore, Native Americans have the same rights to vote in federal, state, and local elections as do other U.S. citizens. But, getting the vote in *every* state was a long time in coming.

Even after the Indian Citizenship Act of 1924, a number of states continued to prohibit Indians from voting. The states' legal arguments were (1) that Indians were "under guardianship" and therefore not competent to vote or (2) Indians were not residents of the states in which they lived if they resided on reservations. These arguments were progressively invalidated in each of the holdout states over the four decades following enactment of the citizenship law.

The last states to fully extend voting rights to Indians were Arizona (1948), Maine (1954), Utah (1956), and New Mexico (1962). Two of the most instructive court cases on the issue were Arizona's *Harrison et al. v. Laveen* (1948) and New Mexico's *Montoya v. Bolack* (1962). Indian voting rights cases that have arisen since 1962 have generally involved local issues such as county residency and school district expenditures (e.g., *Little Thunder et al. v. State of South Dakota* 1975 and *Prince v. Board of Education* 1975, respectively).

Public Office

Besides being able to serve in tribal government, Native Americans have the same rights as other citizens to hold public office at all levels of government, whether elected or appointed. Nationwide, Native people now hold municipal, county, state, and national office.

The highest elected office ever held by an Indian in the U.S. was the vice presidency. Charles Curtis was a quarter-blood Kaw from Kansas who became an attorney and had a remarkable political career. He served as a Republican county attorney, U.S. Representative, U.S. Senator and majority leader, and finally vice president under Herbert Hoover. Often referred to as an example of Indian achievement, he was very much an assimilationist. His major Indian policies were vigorously opposed by many tribes (Harlow 1935). Even among his own tribe, some considered Curtis as something other than a supporter of Indian causes (Heat-Moon 1991).

A few other Indians have been elected to Congress over the past century, but Native Americans have always been underrepresented.

The only Indian serving in Congress, as this book goes to press, is Ben Nighthorse Campbell. He became a member of the House of Representatives from Colorado in 1986 and was elected to the U.S. Senate in November 1992. Senator Campbell is an enrolled member of the Northern Cheyenne Tribe of Montana.

Ben Nighthorse Campbell, U.S. Senator from Colorado.

Also, during the 1992 campaign, Ms. Ada Deer, a Menominee and widely respected Indian rights advocate from Wisconsin, ran unsuccessfully for the House of Representatives. And, Oklahoma State Senator Enoch Haney, a Seminole, entered the race for U.S. Senator from Oklahoma. He also was unsuccessful in his election bid. It is obvious that more Indian interest and activity in the national political scene will develop over the coming decade.

The box on the next page lists those American Indians who have served in the United States Congress. The information is from the Congressional Research Service.

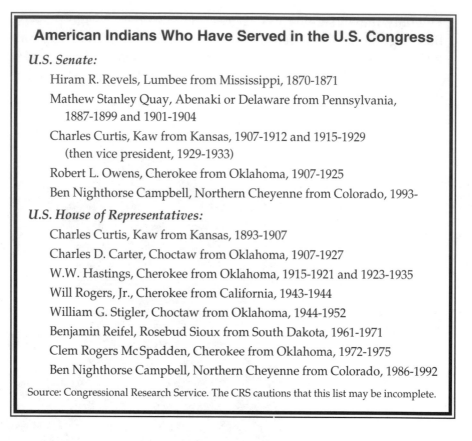

American Indians Who Have Served in the U.S. Congress

U.S. Senate:

    Hiram R. Revels, Lumbee from Mississippi, 1870-1871

    Mathew Stanley Quay, Abenaki or Delaware from Pennsylvania,
       1887-1899 and 1901-1904

    Charles Curtis, Kaw from Kansas, 1907-1912 and 1915-1929
       (then vice president, 1929-1933)

    Robert L. Owens, Cherokee from Oklahoma, 1907-1925

    Ben Nighthorse Campbell, Northern Cheyenne from Colorado, 1993-

U.S. House of Representatives:

    Charles Curtis, Kaw from Kansas, 1893-1907

    Charles D. Carter, Choctaw from Oklahoma, 1907-1927

    W.W. Hastings, Cherokee from Oklahoma, 1915-1921 and 1923-1935

    Will Rogers, Jr., Cherokee from California, 1943-1944

    William G. Stigler, Choctaw from Oklahoma, 1944-1952

    Benjamin Reifel, Rosebud Sioux from South Dakota, 1961-1971

    Clem Rogers McSpadden, Cherokee from Oklahoma, 1972-1975

    Ben Nighthorse Campbell, Northern Cheyenne from Colorado, 1986-1992

Source: Congressional Research Service. The CRS cautions that this list may be incomplete.

H-4. *Do Indians pay taxes?*

Yes. Depending on specific residency and employment circumstances, and also the legal status of specific property, individual
Indians are subject to most, and frequently all, of the same tax laws
and liabilities that non-Indians are. Various income, estate, gift, sales,
employment, property, business, and excise taxes are levied against
Indians, just as they are against non-Indians. In the limited situations
where taxation exceptions exist, they relate to (1) the retained sovereignty of tribes over their members and territory and (2) the trust status of some Indian property.

    Several basic tenets apply to the general subject of Indian taxa-
tion. First, tribes have the power to lay and collect certain taxes from

Indians and non-Indians within reservation boundaries. States, however, generally lack jurisdiction to tax Indians within tribal lands unless they have specific federal authorization. Also, federal trust status over certain Indian property inside and outside reservations precludes some state taxes. The federal government, on the other hand, has broad authority under existing law to tax Indians. Treaties and federal statutes, however, have been interpreted to exempt Indians and tribes from a number of the tax scenarios the government could devise, beyond those already in place. The major reasoning behind tribal exemptions is expressed by the maxim, "With the power to tax comes the power to destroy." The federal government is legally and morally bound to see that the tribes are not taxed out of political existence (Cohen 1982).

Seven general exceptions to taxation pertain to Indians (Bureau of Indian Affairs 1991a; Cohen 1982). Listed below, they deal with government activity, trust property, and transactions that occur within reservations. Recall from earlier in Part II that less than half of the Indian population resides within reservations.

1. Federal income tax provisions do not apply to the income of tribal governments, just as they do not apply to the states and other units of government.
2. Federal income taxes are not levied against that portion of an individual Indian's income that is derived from trust land, legal title to which is held by the U.S., or other trust property.
3. State income taxes are not assessed against the income of tribal governments.
4. State income taxes are not assessed against an individual Indian's income that is earned on a reservation.
5. State income taxes are not assessed against an individual Indian's trust property income.
6. State sales taxes are not paid by Indians for transactions they enter on their reservations.
7. Local property taxes are not paid on tribal trust land or individually owned trust land.

Here is a caveat regarding Indian taxation. Beyond the issue of trust property, what the rule of law is today may not be the rule tomorrow. Indian taxation topics seem to be among those fluid issues, changing with the times and the mood of the U.S. Supreme Court–

which is now almost hostile to Indian cases. The complexity of Indian taxation issues always requires a cautious approach because minor variations in the facts from case to case can have major consequences.

H-5. *Why are Indian tribes and their members treated differently from other citizens by the federal government, and what is the "trust relationship" that influences the federal treatment?*

> *[T]ribes remain quasi-sovereign nations which, by government structure, culture, and source of sovereignty, are in many ways foreign to the constitutional institutions of the federal and state governments.*
>
> U.S. Supreme Court
> *Santa Clara Pueblo v. Martinez* 1978

At its inception, the United States recognized the power and influence of the Indian nations within its territory. It, therefore, negotiated treaties and passed laws which acknowledged the special rights and responsibilities of Indian tribes and their members, apart and distinct from other American residents and citizens (Kickingbird and Kickingbird 1977). The tribes were treated as separate political entities and their members were not U.S. citizens. The lack of citizenship has been changed but the tribes remain separate political entities with limited powers of self-government.

Some form of special federal relationship was implicit in the decision, made after the Revolutionary War, to keep Indian affairs in the hands of the federal government. This was justified as a means of protecting the tribes from the states and unscrupulous citizens, thereby avoiding Indian wars (Canby 1981). An early foundation for federal over state authority appears in Article IX of the Articles of Confederation (ratified in 1781). It declares "The United States in congress assembled shall have the sole and exclusive right and power of...regulating the trade and managing all affairs with the Indians...." This concept was carried over to Article I, Section 8, Clause 3 of the Constitution when the latter superceded the Articles in 1789. It reads:

"The Congress shall have power...to regulate commerce with foreign nations, the several states, and with the Indian tribes...." The meaning attributed to "commerce," of course, is extremely broad. In summary, the doctrine that Indian affairs are subject to control by the federal government and not the states (except in specific instances approved by Congress) is based on the general constitutional powers which empower Congress to (1) ratify treaties, (2) regulate commerce with the Indian tribes, (3) admit new states, (4) administer federal property, and (5) enact legislation in pursuance of these enumerated powers (*Martinez v. Southern Ute Tribe* 1957).

The "trust relationship" portion of the question can be understood more easily by considering the following quotation from law professor William Canby (1981, p. 32).

> Much of American Indian Law revolves around the special [trust] relationship between the federal government and the tribes. Yet it is very difficult to mark the boundaries of this relationship, and even more difficult to assess its legal consequences. At its broadest, the relationship includes the mixture of legal duties, moral obligations, understandings and expectancies that have arisen from the entire course of dealing between the federal government and the tribes. In its narrowest and most concrete sense, the relationship approximates that of trustee and beneficiary, with the trustee (the United States) subject in some degree to legally enforceable responsibilities.

The United States government "has charged itself with moral obligations of the highest responsibility and trust" toward the Indian tribes (*Seminole Nation v. United States* 1946). This trust responsibility was first formally addressed by the Supreme Court in *Cherokee Nation v. Georgia* (1831). Chief Justice Marshall found that, under U.S. dominion, tribes were no longer foreign nations. He determined that they constituted "distinct political" communities "that may, more correctly...be denominated domestic dependent nations" whose "relation to the United States resembles that of a ward to his guardian."

Some might assume Marshall's statement to mean that individual Indians are "wards" of the government, in conflict with the answer to question H-1. A clear reading shows that he wrote about Indian *tribes* or "nations," not individual Indians. So, the Indian tribe-to-U.S. trust relationship is one of government-to-government which "resembles" that of ward to guardian. *Protection* of the tribes as political entities is the key (Hall 1981; United Effort Trust 1979).

The American Indian Policy Review Commission (1977, p. 130) outlined the modern concept of the trust relationship, or responsibility, in its final report to the Congress.

> The scope of the trust responsibility extends beyond real or personal property which is held in trust. The U.S. has the obligation to provide services, and to take other appropriate action necessary to protect tribal self-government. The doctrine may also include a duty to provide a level of services equal to those services provided by the states to their citizens [e.g., educational, social, and medical]. These conclusions flow from the basic notion that the trust responsibility is a general obligation which is not limited to specific provision in treaties, executive orders, or statutes; once the trust has been assumed, administrative action is governed by the same high duty which is imposed on a private trustee.

The government-to-government relationship of American Indian tribes and the United States is a truly unique one in the world system of governments. It is inexorably tied to the uninvited extension of U.S. dominion over all ancestral lands of the formerly independent tribes, bands, and similar groups of Native Americans. The "different" treatment of Indians that is referred to on occasion is actually a different legal, not racial, treatment of the tribes and their members. It is based on the tribes' continuing political existence as "Quasi-Sovereign Domestic Dependent Nations" (Bush 1991), and the U.S. responsibility to those nations.

As additional questions and answers in this section indicate, this does not leave Indian people immune from the general rights and responsibilities of other citizens. It does, however, affect some of those rights and responsibilities. It is not unlike the way being a citizen of Arizona, Alaska, American Samoa, or Guam would have varying effects due to different laws, regulations, rules, and government services applicable to residents of these respective American states and territories. (See the following questions on self-determination and sovereignty.

H-6. *What different criminal jurisdiction can be applicable to Indians?*

This and the following question on civil jurisdiction are among the toughest of all to answer. Often referred to as a jurisdictional maze, questions arising from jurisdictional disputes among the federal government, tribes, and states are the most complex in the field of Indian law. Many jurisdictional questions remain unsettled, and mildly different facts between cases can have substantial effects on jurisdiction. Basic precepts, however, have developed over the years and serve as guidelines to relevant questions. These precepts are summarized in a table, at the end of this answer, following several paragraphs which are necessary to understand the table. The reader is cautioned that the text and table are not definitive. They should be considered introductory in nature and as basic examples of complexity.

It is necessary to understand the definitions of "Indian" and "Indian country" before it is possible to understand the topic of criminal (or civil) jurisdiction. The answer to "Who is an Indian?" will vary according to applicable statutes, court rulings, and tribal membership requirements and records. (See the shaded box below as well as the answer to question A-1.) "Indian country," on the other hand, is legally defined as: (a) land within the exterior boundaries of a federal Indian reservation, (b) land outside reservation boundaries that is owned by Indians and held in trust or restricted status by the federal government, and (c) all other lands set aside by whatever means for the residence of tribal Indians under federal protection, e.g.,

> *For the purpose of criminal jurisdiction, an Indian is a person who has some ethnic connection and some degree of Indian blood. The definition of "Indian" varies according to the statutes, case laws, and administrative enactments that have formulated different definitions. Often, the definition of Indian appears in the individual constitution [or] legal codes of a tribe. In general, however, certain considerations are relevant in order to be considered an Indian. These include: an individual's residence, the particular law involved, a person's degree of Indian blood, tribal enrollment, and an individual's opinion as to his own status.*
>
> Flowers 1983, p. 5

"dependent Indian communities" (Cohen 1982). Tribal jurisdiction is largely restricted to Indian country, and Indian country is where most jurisdictional disputes originate. (See the answer to question H-11 for non-legal definitions of Indian country.)

At the time of early European contact, Native American tribes, bands, and clans had exclusive "jurisdiction," in fact and theory, over all people in their territory (Canby 1981). This gradually changed as the power of the Euro-American governments grew and their populations expanded. By the height of the reservation period, in the early-1880s, U.S. law enforcement policy for Indian country had evolved to where federal officers and courts had exclusive jurisdiction over non-Indian and interracial crimes. In other words, the jurisdiction applied to federal criminal offenses involving only non-Indians or where both Indians and non-Indians were involved. The General Crimes Act (now codified as 18 U.S. Code, Sec. 1152) embodied the early 1880s policy for Indian country. At the same time, Indian-to-Indian crime was still left to tribal jurisdiction. Congress began to change this in 1885, however, by passing the Major Crimes Act which significantly reduced the tribes' sovereign authority over law enforcement regarding their members or other Indians.

The early version of the act specified only seven crimes, but today's Major Crimes Act includes 14 offenses. Such offenses are often subjected to federal jurisdiction only. Their investigation is handled by the FBI and is prosecuted by the U.S. Department of Justice. The list of crimes which follows is quoted from the Major Crimes Act (18 U.S. Code, Sec. 1153). It is self-explanatory.

> Any Indian who commits against the person or property of another Indian or another person any of the following offenses, namely, murder, manslaughter, kidnaping, rape, carnal knowledge of a female, not his wife, who has not attained the age of 16 years, assault with intent to commit murder, assault with a dangerous weapon, assault resulting in serious bodily injury, arson, burglary, robbery, and larceny within the Indian country, shall be subject to the same laws and penalties as all other persons committing any of the above offenses, within the exclusive jurisdiction of the United States.

Another of the many incursions into tribal criminal jurisdiction resulted from the Supreme Court's 20th century application of the

Assimilative Crimes Act to Indian country (*Williams v. United States* 1946). The act, first passed in 1825 and periodically amended (18 U.S. Code, Sec. 13), borrows state-defined crimes not otherwise covered by federal law (such as the Major Crimes Act) and incorporates them into federal law applicable to "federal enclaves." Before the court's 1946 ruling, "enclaves" did not include Indian country, but it did include areas like post offices, national parks, and military reservations. The act's practical function is to allow the federal government to apply minor state criminal laws to Indian country and the other enclaves (Deloria and Lytle 1983). It is effectively limited to crimes that involve non-Indians, or both Indians and non-Indians, and reads "whoever...is guilty of an act or omission which, although not made punishable by an act of Congress, would be punishable if committed or omitted within the jurisdiction of the State...in which such place [e.g., Indian country] is situated,...shall be guilty of a like offense and subject to like punishment."

A significant change in jurisdiction in parts of Indian country developed in 1953 with passage of Public Law 280. This law, a child of the "termination" era, gave six states mandatory and substantial criminal and civil jurisdiction over Indian country within their borders. The key criminal provision gave those states power to enforce the great majority of their regular criminal laws inside Indian country, just as they had been doing elsewhere. The "mandatory" states were Alaska (added in 1958, except for Metlakatla Reservation), California, Minnesota (except Red Lake Reservation), Nebraska, Oregon (except Warm Springs Reservation), and Wisconsin (Canby 1981). When Public Law 280 was applied to these states, the General Crimes Act and the Indian Major Crimes Act, specifically, and the Assimilative Crimes Act, by default, no longer applied to Indian country within the states—except for the reservations just named.

Other federal statutes have granted a few states certain criminal jurisdiction in Indian country, but none has been so broadly applicable as Public Law 280. Even so, Public Law 280 does not grant unlimited jurisdiction. Limitations on state criminal as well as civil jurisdiction continue in such areas as water rights, taxation of trust property, regulatory control over trust property, regulatory control over tribal activity otherwise protected by treaty or statute, and federally protected hunting, trapping, and fishing rights.

From the outset, Public Law 280 was criticized by tribes and states. The latter resented being directed to provide new law enforcement services with no financial assistance, and tribes resented state jurisdiction being forced upon them without their consent. This joint dissent stimulated later amendments to the act which now allow states to retrocede, or transfer back, jurisdiction to the federal government. A number of retrocessions have occurred since the 1960s, usually on a piecemeal or reservation-by-reservation basis.

The 1953 version of Public Law 280 also permitted other states, beyond the original six, to acquire similar jurisdiction in Indian country. The choice was theirs and it did not require tribal approval. (The law was amended in 1968 to require tribal consent.) Ten states opted to accept some degree of Public Law 280 jurisdiction. They were Arizona, Florida, Idaho, Iowa, Montana, Nevada, North Dakota, South Dakota, Utah, and Washington. The authority they assumed varied from limited jurisdiction over things like air and water pollution only (Arizona), to slightly greater jurisdiction over criminal offenses and civil causes of action arising on highways (South Dakota), to full Public Law 280 jurisdiction (Florida). Some of these 10 states have now returned at least part of their jurisdiction to the federal government (Cohen 1982).

Several authors have devised useful tables to simplify understanding of criminal jurisdiction in Indian country. The one by Deloria and Lytle (1983, p. 179), shown on the next page in slightly modified form, follows introductory remarks by the authors:

> The jurisdictional maze that has clouded the Indian system of justice has confused layperson, lawyer, judge, and bureaucrat alike. The basic question to be resolved is which level of government assumes jurisdiction over criminal offenses in Indian country…. The answer to this question revolves around the interrelationship of three factors: (a) the location where the crime is committed, (b) the particular statute that has been violated, and (c) the type of persons involved in the crime (Indian/non-Indian).

GUIDELINES FOR CRIMINAL JURISDICTION

Location Where Crime Committed	*Federal Jurisdiction*	*State Jurisdiction*	*Tribal Jurisdiction*
I. Outside Indian Country			
A. Federal Law Involved	Yes	No	No
B. State Law Involved	No	Yes	No
C. Tribal Law involved	No	No	Maybe
II. Inside Indian Country (in P.L. 280 state, or one given similar jurisdiction)	No	Yes	No
III. Inside Indian Country (no P.L. 280 or similar jurisdiction)			
A. Crimes by Indian v. Indian			
1. Major Crimes Act crimes	Yes	No	No[a]
2. Other crimes	No	No	Yes
B. Crimes by Indian v. non-Indian			
1. Major Crimes Act crimes	Yes	No	No[a]
2. General Crimes Act	Yes	No	Yes[b]
3. Assimilative Crimes Act	Yes	No	Yes
C. Crimes by non-Indian v. Indian			
1. General Crimes Act crimes	Yes	No	No
2. Assimilative Crimes Act	Yes	No	No
D. Crimes by non-Indian v. same	Yes	Yes	No
E. Victimless and consensual crimes			
1. Crimes by Indians	No	No	Yes
2. Crimes by non-Indians		Yes[c]	
a. General Crimes Act	Yes	Yes[a]	No
b. Assimilative Crimes Act	Yes	Yes[a]	No

[a] The law is unsettled in this area.

[b] If there has been prior punishment by tribal court, or if tribal jurisdiction is otherwise established by treaty or statute, federal jurisdiction under General Crimes Act is withheld.

[c] Some statutes permit concurrent jurisdiction.

Source: Deloria and Lytle (1983, p. 179, citing Getches, Rosenfelt, and Wilkinson 1979). Table is for basic reference only.

H-7. What different civil jurisdiction can be applicable to Indians?

[Author's note: The answer to the preceding question on criminal jurisdiction contains information necessary to the understanding of the answer which follows.]

Civil jurisdiction involves private rights, as opposed to the public wrongs which are covered by criminal law. Everyday civil issues include lawsuits and other legal actions pertaining to topics like auto accidents, child custody, probate, and divorce or other domestic relations. For the great majority of Americans the rules of law governing civil matters are those developed by the states. For Native Americans, however, very different jurisdictional rules can apply (Canby 1981; Getches, Rosenfelt, and Wilkinson 1979).

In some ways, questions of civil jurisdiction, as applied to Indians and their property, are more complicated than those which relate to criminal jurisdiction. A major reason is that the federal government has not played as large a role in this arena as it has in criminal law. With a lesser federal role, the laws of several hundred tribes and the different states add a special complexity to civil jurisdiction.

A table summarizing answers to civil jurisdiction questions is shown on the following page. It relates only to those states where civil jurisdiction under Public Law 280 is *not* in effect. As the table makes plain, answers to questions on civil jurisdiction in "non–280" states turn on such issues as (a) who initiates an action (Indian or non-Indian plaintiff), (b) who is defending an action (Indian or non-Indian defendant), (c) the geographic origin of a claim (inside or outside Indian country), (d) the nature of a claim, (e) the nature of property at issue, and (f) the locations of the legal domiciles of the parties involved (inside or outside Indian country). Information in the table is from Canby (1981). As with the previous table, the reader is cautioned that this table should be considered as being representative but not definitive for all cases.

Although Public Law 280 conferred both criminal and civil jurisdiction on the six "mandatory" states, and allowed options for the same jurisdiction in others, the criminal law provisions were clearly the most important to Congress. Civil jurisdiction, it appears, was added as an afterthought, but a powerful one where applicable (Goldberg 1975). The civil section of the statute reads:

GUIDELINES FOR CIVIL JURISDICTION
(STATES OUTSIDE PUBLIC LAW 280)

I. General Civil Litigation

Plaintiff	Defendant	Origin of Claim	Jurisdiction
Indian	Indian	Indian country	Tribal (exclusive)
		Not Indian country	Tribal or state (concurrent)
Non-Indian	Indian	Indian country	Tribal (exclusive)
		Not Indian country	State; possibly tribal (concurrent)
Indian	Non-Indian	Indian country	Tribal, if tribe's code allows; State (concurrent)
Non-Indian	Non-Indian	Anywhere	State (exclusive)

II. Divorce

Plaintiff	Defendant	Domicile of Parties	Jurisdiction
Indian	Indian	Indian country	Tribal (exclusive)
		Not Indian country	State; Tribal, if tribe's code allows (concurrent)
Non-Indian	Indian	Indian country	State (probable); Tribal (concurrent)
		Not Indian country	State (exclusive)
Indian	Non-Indian	Indian country	Tribal (exclusive)
		Not Indian country	State (exclusive)
Non-Indian	Non-Indian	Anywhere	State (exclusive)

III. Adoption and Child Custody (Not Divorce Custody)
[Indian Child Welfare Act applies (25 U.S. Code, Sec 1911)]

Proceeding	Domicile or Residence of Child	Jurisdiction
Adoption and all non-divorce custody	Indian country	Tribal (exclusive)
Adoption or adoptive placement	Not Indian country	Tribal; State (concurrent)
Foster care or termination of parental rights	Not Indian country	Tribal preferred; State (concurrent)

IV. Probate

Decedent	Decedent's Domicile	Property	Jurisdiction
Indian	Indian country	Trust assets	Federal (exclusive)
		Land outside Indian country	State (exclusive)
		Movables	Tribal (primary)
	Not Indian country	Trust assets	Federal (exclusive)
		Land outside Indian country	State (exclusive)
		Movables	State (primary); possibly tribal (concurrent)
Non-Indian	Anywhere	All assets	State (exclusive)

Source: Canby (1981, p. 153-154). Under section "I", wherever state jurisdiction is shown, federal jurisdiction may be acquired if "a federal question" or "diversity of citizenship" (parties from different states) are involved. For the latter, the controversy must exceed $10,000. Where the subject matter of a section "I" claim particularly affects Indian interests, state jurisdiction may be precluded.

Each of the States…listed…shall have jurisdiction over civil causes of action between Indians or to which Indians are parties
which arise in the areas of Indian country listed…to the same
extent that such State…has jurisdiction over other civil causes of
action, and those civil laws of such state…that are of general
application to private persons or private property shall have the
same force and effect within such Indian country as they have
elsewhere in the State…[28 U.S. Code, Sec. 1369(a)].

In the several states where Public Law 280 is in effect, a number
of tribal jurisdictions would no longer apply. As stated in the answer
to the criminal jurisdiction question, however, state civil authority
under Public Law 280 is excluded from encumbering trust property
or interfering with treaty rights.

H-8. What is tribal sovereignty?

> **Sovereign:** *A person, body, or state in which independent and supreme authority is vested.*
>
> **Sovereign People:** *The political body, consisting of the entire number of citizens and qualified electors, who, in their collective capacity, possess the powers of sovereignty and exercise them through their chosen representatives.*
>
> Black's Law Dictionary 1990
>
> *Sovereignty is the supreme power from which all specific political powers are derived.*
>
> Kickingbird et al. 1977, p. 1

Sovereignty is a word of many meanings. At the most basic level, the
term refers to the inherent right or power to govern. Within the
Europe of old, this right was vested in monarchs and was considered
to be God-given. Under the U.S. constitutional system, the right is
inherent in the people and is exercised through their representative
local, state, and federal governments. This is somewhat comparable
to the inherent sovereignty of Indian people in the tribal context
(Canby 1981; Deloria and Lytle 1983).

When Europeans arrived in the hemisphere, the hundreds of Indian groups were sovereign by nature and necessity. They conducted their own affairs and depended on no outside source of power–from Europeans or others–to legitimize their acts of government. Most Indians east of the Rockies had some form of tribal organization. Perhaps the largest and most sophisticated was the Iroquois League, which had a population of up to 17,000. The Five Civilized Tribes of the Southeast organized governments based on cities. The majority of the plains Indians, like the Sioux and Cheyenne, established the tribal organizations that have become so familiar to non-Indians. The Pueblos of the Southwest lived in tightly organized villages governed by theocracies. Weaker, less centralized tribal organizations existed throughout the rest of the Southwest, California, and the Northwest Coast, where family groups and clans tended to be the principal political units. Similarly, there was usually little in the way of political organization in the Great Basin, Arctic, and Sub-Arctic regions beyond the family group or clan (Canby 1981; Cohen 1982).

Contact with Euro-Americans irrevocably changed the original nature of tribal governments. Some of their traditional aspects, like the general council, continue to survive, but most tribes have adopted written constitutions and legal codes. Primary laws are now made through tribal councils, and violations or internal conflicts are resolved in tribal courts (Cohen 1982).

As declared by Congress, the Executive, and the Supreme Court, the present rights of tribes to govern their members and remaining territories derive from a sovereignty that pre-dates European arrival. It was a sovereignty that once made them fully independent nations. That sovereignty has been limited, but never abolished, by the tribes' inclusion within the territorial boundaries of the United States. The three fundamental principles behind contemporary tribal powers are:

> (1) An Indian tribe possesses, in the first instance, all the powers of any sovereign state. (2) Conquest renders the tribe subject to the legislative power of the United States and, in substance, terminates the external powers of sovereignty of the tribe, e.g., its power to enter into treaties [or go to war] with foreign nations, but does not by itself affect the internal sovereignty of the tribe, i.e., its powers of local self-government. (3) These [internal] powers are subject to qualification by treaties and by express legislation of Congress, but [unless expressly qualified] full powers of internal sovereignty are vested in the Indian tribes and in their duly constituted organs of government.
>
> Felix Cohen, quoted *In*
> Getches, Rosenfelt, and Wilkinson 1979, p. 254

Therefore, the principal attributes of tribal sovereignty today can be generally summarized as follows: (1) Indian tribes possess inherent governmental power over all internal affairs, (2) the states are precluded from interfering with the tribes' self-government, and (3) Congress has plenary (i.e., near absolute) power to limit tribal sovereignty and thereby limit the first two attributes (Canby 1981).

This power of Congress regarding the Indian tribes is extensive, and pledges by the U.S. can be eradicated even without consent of the tribes (Getches, Rosenfelt, and Wilkinson 1979). Congress can unilaterally abrogate treaty promises, alter tribal powers of self-government, extinguish aboriginal and trust title to land, and even end the special political and trust relationships between the tribes and the federal government (*United States v. Wheeler* 1978). However, the federal policy of tribal self-determination, with its beginnings in the 1930s and a renewal in the 1970s, has created opportunities for tribes to retain their limited sovereignty and to overcome some of the restraints arbitrarily or improperly placed on that sovereignty over the past 150 years. Still, it seems an inter-governmental tension may always be present and the tribes' sovereignty may always be in a state of challenge from various quarters.

> *A number of Indian people argue that tribal sovereignty remains total, even today—that Indian nations have never been conquered and that all federal or state laws limiting tribal sovereignty are illegal. The federal government's familiar argument is that Indian tribes today are quasi-sovereigns, or domestic dependent nations.*
>
> O'Brien 1989

H-9. What have been the general characteristics of traditional tribal governments?

> *Historically, only a few tribes had formal governments or written laws. There were exceptions, such as the Iroquois Confederacy.... But most Indian societies were oral cultures, a tradition that has by no means disappeared. This does not mean that "law" was absent.... Clearly understood rules developed by consensus and were strengthened by the tribes' pantheism which blended religion into all aspects of Indian life. The result was a "complex and smooth-working social organization of the tribes which functioned without need for written laws or the paraphernalia of European Civilization"* (W. Washburn, The Indian in America 40, 1975).
>
> Getches, Rosenfelt, and Wilkinson 1979, p. 300

When Europeans first arrived, there were perhaps 600 tribal entities in what is now the U.S. These Native people had many complex and pervasive forms of government and social control, on both large and small scales. On the large scale, the most highly developed tribal government was that of the powerful Iroquois League of the near Northeast. Even before Columbus sailed, the Iroquois had a constitution in the form of the Ne Gayaneshagowa, or Great Binding Law. The constitution was embodied in the symbolized writing of sacred

wampum belts made of patterned sea shell beads. Specialized pat-
terns were read aloud at ceremonies as a recitation of the Great Law,
which was acknowledged as the instrument of Iroquois nationality.
Their government provided for such sophisticated procedures as tribal confirmation of council representatives, initiative, recall, referen-
dum, equal suffrage, a system of checks and balances, and specific
delegations of wartime and peacetime responsibilities to tribes of the
League. Other large Indian confederacies, like the Creeks of the
Southeast, also developed extensive and complex governments
(Deloria and Lytle 1983; Kickingbird, et al. 1977).

Less sophisticated but socially pervasive governments were
found among Native peoples in areas like the Great Basin deserts and
the Arctic. Environmental limitations in such areas prevented the
coming together of substantial numbers of people in organized living
groups. This, in turn, reduced the need for highly developed governments. Relying on less formal traditions, mores, and social pressures
was better suited to the needs of family and clan living. For basic
government, a small group might have met daily to discuss matters
of general importance. Leadership naturally fell to elders who were
respected for their wisdom (O'Brien 1989). Despite the contrast with
tribes like the Iroquois, there were still important characteristics common to the small and grander forms of Native government.

An idea like separation of church and state would have been
inconceivable to *all* traditional governments. They made little distinction between the political and the religious. All aspects of life were
inextricably bound together. Political and religious power were often
the same. Government actions were pursued with spiritual guidance
and were oriented toward combined spiritual and political fulfill-
ment (O'Brien 1989).

At the base of individual and tribal life was the belief that a spirit
force resided within every natural being. The concept of "beings"
who peopled the tribe's world included the land, plants, animals, and
humans. Native people were not superior to the natural world but
were an integral part of it. Therefore, it was incumbent upon their
combined religious and political governments to strive for harmony
among the many elements of life important to their specific tribal
groups. The tribe was primary and individuals secondary (O'Brien
1989; Underhill 1965).

Power to govern came from the community and flowed upwards. Rights of birth, so important to European rulers, were generally insignificant–with some exceptions. The great tribal leaders, who sometimes served only during times of special need or crisis, were those who proved themselves by deed and ability, and who demonstrated an overriding concern for the welfare of the community. They lacked dictatorial power; therefore, they depended on their persuasive and other abilities–and the respect of the people–to achieve governmental goals. Powers of persuasion were often of paramount importance, for tribes generally made decisions based not on mere majority rule but on consensus. Dissension and disharmony within the tribe, and spiritual or physical imbalance with the living environment, were things to be avoided. Thus, unusually broad concepts of balance and harmony, with a strong religious foundation, were the common primary tenets of Native government (O'Brien 1989; Owen, Deetz, and Fisher 1967).

H-10. *What are the characteristics of modern tribal governments?*

> [T]here are two important changes that time has brought on the form and nature of tribal governments. First, whereas the traditional form functioned primarily as an adjudicatory body settling disputes within the tribes, today tribal bodies have become legislative in their outlook and bureaucratic in their operations…. Second, tribal governments have taken on the cloak of Anglo-American institutional forms. The structures, the functions, the technologies, the politics, and even the goals of the [non-Indian] community are in many ways displacing the traditional ways of the Indians. The unanswered question…is how much of the traditional Indian culture and values can survive if tribal government continues to develop along these lines.
>
> Deloria and Lytle 1983, p. 109

The dwindling number of traditional Native governments which survived into the 1800s were almost totally disrupted by the end of the century. The principal causes were (1) contact with European culture, (2) removal and placement of tribes within confining reservations, and (3) establishment of the powerful Indian agent system by the federal government. Only a few groups, most notably the Pueblos, escaped this political fate and have been able to continue their traditional governments largely intact to the present.

Federal erosion of tribal organization was at its peak during the land allotment period (1887–1934), when official policy was to destroy Indian tribalism (Canby 1981). But a dramatic policy change came in 1934 with passage of the Indian Reorganization Act (IRA). The act was purposely designed to help re-establish self-government and restore to tribes sufficient powers to represent tribal interests in a variety of political and economic circumstances. Much of the bureaucratic stranglehold and paternalism of the Bureau of Indian Affairs was reduced. However, the majority of the new governments that emerged under the act (181 of 258 tribes voted to accept reorganization) became constitutional governments organized on a legalistic European model. The two main reasons for this were (1) by the 1930s, most of the tribes' traditional governments and customs had been dormant too long or were too badly eroded to resurrect in short order and (2) all tribal governments that were developed under the IRA had to be approved by the Secretary of the Interior. So, the change wrought in the 1930s was positive but it was not a panacea. The decades since passage of the IRA have seen the continuation and evolution of a variety of governments (Deloria and Lytle 1983).

Quoting the National American Indian Court Judges Association, Deloria and Lytle list the categories of government into which most tribes fall:

> *Representative:* Here the tribe elects a governing body that operates under a constitution which the tribal members have approved [e.g., Jicarilla Apache of New Mexico].
>
> *Representative/Traditional Combination:* Under this system, governmental officials are elected by tribal members, but some governmental positions are reserved for traditional leaders by virtue of their traditional lineage. The officials operate under a written constitution voted on by the tribal members [e.g., Warm Springs Tribes of Oregon].
>
> *General Council:* The tribal membership adopts bylaws which govern and control the tribal officers, but these tribal officials have no

substantive authority. When a substantive issue arises, officers call a General Council meeting of the tribe and the members vote on the issue [e.g., Crow Tribe of Montana].

Theocracy: Both the civil leaders and officers of the tribe are selected by the religious leaders. This is the most traditional form of tribal government [e.g., the Pueblos of New Mexico].

To this contemporary list must be added the ongoing Iroquois government mentioned above, the town corporation government of several eastern tribes under state rather than federal supervision, and the Alaska Native corporations for villages and regions. The latter are technically not governments but, with passage of the Alaska Native Claims Settlement Act in 1971, they supplanted most existing Native governments by assuming control over management of finances, lands, and resources.

The many–and complicated–activities of today's tribal governments include defining conditions of membership, regulating domestic relations of members, prescribing rules of inheritance for reservation property not in trust status, levying taxes, regulating property under tribal jurisdiction, controlling conduct of members by tribal ordinance, administering justice, conducting elections, developing tribal health and education programs, managing tribal economic enterprises, managing natural resources, and maintaining inter-governmental relations at the federal, state, and local levels (American Indian Lawyer Training Program 1988; Bureau of Indian Affairs 1991a).

Reflecting on the opening quotation, scattered but dedicated attempts are now being made in Alaska and the lower 48 states to restore more traditional ways into tribal governments.

H-11. *What is Indian country?*

The term "Indian country" has been around for more than two hundred years. It originated in popular designations for lands beyond the frontier that were mostly unknown and inhabited by Native peoples who were deemed "uncivilized" (Deloria and Lytle 1983). The term has developed to the point where it is now commonly heard in three contexts–legal, socio-political, and military.

Legal

This first definition is the most important and complex. Whether an area is legally classified as Indian country is the basic question in legal jurisdiction issues involving federal Indian law. The term denotes those geographic areas in which tribal and federal laws normally apply and state laws do not (Getches, Rosenfelt, and Wilkinson 1979). (See Figures 7 and 8.) The statutory definition of Indian country that is relevant today was enacted by Congress in 1948 as part of a criminal statute (18 U.S. Code, Sec. 1151). The U.S. Supreme Court, however, has found that it also applies to questions involving civil jurisdiction. The definition reads:

> [T]he term "Indian country,"...means (a) all land within the limits of any reservation under the jurisdiction of the United States government,...(b) all dependent Indian communities within the borders of the United States,...and (c) all Indian allotments, the Indian titles to which have not been extinguished....

Subsection (a) refers to *all* territory within the exterior boundaries of a designated Indian reservation, whether a parcel in question is Indian-owned or not, e.g., the Navajo Indian Reservation. Subsection (b) refers to reasonably defined areas occupied by dependent Indian communities that are federally recognized, e.g., the Reno, Nevada, Indian Colony. Subsection (c) deals with individual Indian land allotments still held in trust by the U.S., whether the allotments are in or outside a reservation, e.g., Indian-owned land originally acquired under the homestead laws and held in trust by the U.S. (Cohen 1982).

A significant development regarding legal application of the term "Indian country" arose on January 13, 1992. On that date, the U.S. Ninth Circuit Court of Appeals ruled, in *Native Village of Tyonek v. Puckett et al.*, that the geographic area of the Alaska Native Village of Tyonek–which is privately owned by the village corporation and is, therefore, not a reservation or trust land–was indeed part of Indian country. Heretofore, most similarly situated villages were presumed by many observers to be outside the legal definition of Indian country. Citing various relevant precedents, the court stated that Indian country includes any unceded lands *owned* or occupied by an Indian nation or tribe. As to whether or not the village corporation qualified as being a "tribe," in the legal sense, with certain retained rights of sovereignty, the court also stated, "We have previously held that

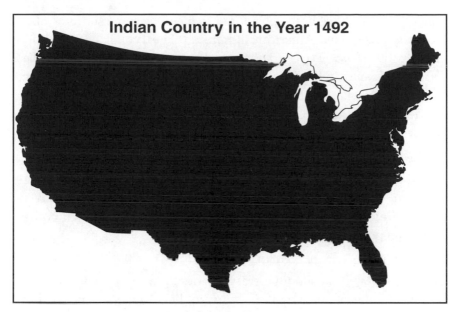

Figure 7. When Columbus landed in the Western Hemisphere, all the land of what is today the United States was "Indian country."

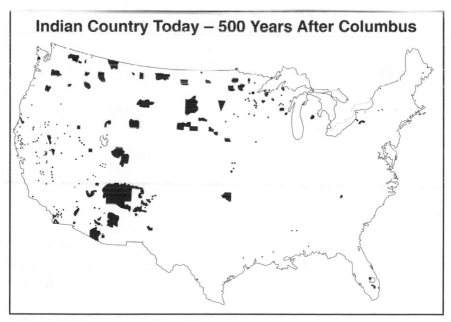

Figure 8. The shaded areas on this map represent all that is left of Indian country today in the lower 48 states. It represents less than three percent of the total land area.

Alaska Natives have been considered to have the same status as other federally recognized American Indians...." The Tyonek case and others (e.g., *Oklahoma Tax Commission v. Citizen Band Potawatomi Indian Tribe of Oklahoma* 1991; *Alyeska v. Kluti Kaah*, U.S. District Court for the District of Alaska, January 17, 1992) are helping clarify and enhance the definition of Indian country and the associated meaning of sovereignty in Alaska and elsewhere—but not without controversy.

Socio-political

In this context, Indian country is the Indian equivalent of terms like "African American community," "Hispanic community," "Jewish community," etc., and is frequently used to refer to the national Native American population.

Military

Indian country is a colloquialism, considered inappropriate by many, that has long been used by U.S. Army soldiers to mean "enemy territory." It was very commonly heard in Viet Nam and was sometimes invoked in the war with Iraq.

H-12. *What is the meaning and derivation of the term "Indian self-determination?"*

> *Self-determination: Decision-making control over one's own affairs and the policies that affect one's life.*
>
> O'Brien 1989, p. 319

"Self-determination" is a catch-all term that covers a variety of concepts including tribal restoration, self-government, cultural renewal, reservation resource development, self-sufficiency, control over education, and equal or controlling input into all policies and programs arising from the Native American-federal government trust relationship (Waldman 1985).

The present movement toward heightened self-determination had its recent beginnings in the early 1960s with the growth of pan-Indian organizations that demanded meaningful control of programs affecting the Indian community (Kelly 1988). There had been an earlier start toward self-determination, however, in the era surrounding the Indian Reorganization Act (IRA) of 1934. (Discussed in Part III of this book.)

By the 1920s, the growth of the administrative power of the Bureau of Indian Affairs had effectively destroyed most pre-existing forms of tribal government. The agency had evolved into the role of colonial administrator and directed programs and services on reservations under a policy which later became known as "paternalism." A dictionary-like definition of paternalism would be "a policy or practice of treating or governing a people in a fatherly manner, especially by providing for their presumed needs without giving them representation or responsibility."

In the early 1930s, the power brokers in Washington had to admit that paternalism was doing a great disservice to Native American tribes and their people. The response at the congressional level was the IRA, which was referred to as the Indian "New Deal" by the Roosevelt administration. Revolutionary for its time, the IRA fell far short of the current policy of "Indian self-determination without termination." It nonetheless provided a number of opportunities for renewed tribal self-government and the exercise of certain dormant powers of sovereignty.

But, the momentum that began in the 1930s dwindled into the unconscionable termination era of the 1950s, which sought to terminate entirely the federal recognition—or government-to-government relationship—of the Indian tribes through legislative and administrative fiat. Scores of Indian tribes and communities were "terminated" and a renewed paternalism took hold over the rest of Indian country.

The turn-about started in the 1960s and got an official boost in 1970 from Richard Nixon in his July 8th congressional "Message from the President of the United States Transmitting Recommendations for Indian Policy."

> It is long past time that the Indian policies of the Federal government began to recognize and build upon the capacities and insights of the Indian people. Both as a matter of Justice and as a matter of enlightened social policy, we must begin to act on the basis of what the Indians themselves have long been telling us. The time has come to break decisively with the past and to create

the conditions for a new era in which the Indian future is determined by Indian acts and Indian decisions.

Congress subsequently debated and eventually passed the Indian Self-Determination and Education Assistance Act of 1975. This act authorizes federal agencies to contract with and make grants directly to Indian tribal governments for federal services, much like it does with state and local governments. The legislative logic is that the tribes know best their own problems and can better allocate their resources and energies in the necessary direction, compared with decisions made by distant federal bureaucrats (Deloria and Lytle 1984). The broader effect of the act is that it has set the statutory climate for the rejuvenation of tribal governments by admitting, rejecting, and countering yesteryear's paternalistic policies.

> [T]he prolonged Federal domination of Indian service programs has served to retard rather than enhance the progress of Indian people and their communities by depriving Indians of the full opportunity to develop leadership skills crucial to the realization of self-government, and has denied to the Indian people an effective voice in the planning and implementation of programs for the benefit of Indians which are responsive to the true needs of Indian communities... (Sec. 2 (2) (1).).

> The Congress declares its commitment to the maintenance of the Federal Government's unique and continuing relationship with and responsibility to the Indian people through the establishment of a meaningful Indian self-determination policy which will permit an orderly transition from Federal domination of programs for and services to Indians to effective and meaningful participation by the Indian people in the planning, conduct, and administration of these programs and services...(Sec. 3. (b).).

SECTION I: THE BUREAU OF INDIAN AFFAIRS

I-1. *What are the administrative roots, current mission, objectives, and program responsibilities of the Bureau of Indian Affairs?*

Roots

In August 1786, the Secretary of War was placed in charge of Indian affairs by Congress (Horsman 1988). General authority over Indian matters, though shared on specific issues with other involved agencies, remained with the War Department for decades. However, there was little in the way of a formalized administrative structure for Indian matters most of that time.

In 1824, Secretary of War John C. Calhoun created a Bureau of Indian Affairs (BIA) in the War Department and assigned a superintendent and two clerks to operate the fledgling agency. The duties of these employees included administering appropriations for treaty annuities, approving expense vouchers, managing funds used to "civilize" the Indians, managing official correspondence regarding Indian affairs, and deciding on trespass, damage, and other claims arising between Indians and non-Indians (Taylor 1984).

Eight years after the founding actions of Secretary of War Calhoun, an act of Congress officially authorized an Office of Indian Affairs within the War Department. In 1849, the Office of Indian Affairs was transferred to the newly created Department of the Interior, where it obtained bureau status and where it has remained for nearly 150 years.

Mission

The BIA's mission and policy responsibilities, as defined by Congress and the Executive, have evolved since the 1820s from removal of eastern tribes to the West, to reservation confinement, to land allotment and assimilation, to termination, and finally to tribal self-government and self-determination. The current basic mission of the BIA is (1) to act as the principal agent of the United States in carrying on the government-to-government relationship that exists between the United States and federally-recognized Indian tribes and (2) to carry out the

173

responsibilities of the United States as trustee for property it holds in trust for federally-recognized tribes and individual Indians (Bureau of Indian Affairs 1987a).

Objectives

The primary objectives of the BIA are to (1) encourage and assist Indian and Alaska Native people to manage their own affairs (under the trust relationship with the federal government), (2) help them facilitate full development of their human and natural resource potentials, (3) mobilize all public and private aids to the advancement of Indians and Alaska Natives, and (4) utilize the skills and capabilities of these people in the direction and management of programs established for their benefit (United States Government Manual 1990).

Responsibilities

The BIA is the largest and most complex bureau in the Department of the Interior. Its general administrative responsibilities are numerous and varied. They include: a 40,000-student education program, a 50,000-client social services program, law enforcement, mining and mineral leasing, forestry, agriculture and irrigation programs, power systems development and management, road construction and maintenance of a 20,000-mile road system, and management of a combined trust fund valued at $2 billion. The agency's service population includes about 950,000 individuals who are members of some 300 tribes and 200 Alaska Native villages and corporations (Bureau of Indian Affairs 1992b).

I-2. How is the BIA administered?

It is an agency run by Indians. Of the approximately 12,900 Bureau employees, 84% are Native Americans (Simmons 1992). This is not a recent phenomenon. Indians have made up the majority of personnel in the BIA at least since 1950 (Taylor 1984). The high percentage of Native employees holds true for the Washington office and the 12 BIA regions or "areas." The area offices, and the smaller "agency" offices within the areas, have the majority of the BIA's direct contact with the tribes and often pride themselves on the high percentage of

Native people hired at all levels. The Juneau Area office in Alaska, for example, reports that 95% of the BIA's Alaska employees are American Indian and Alaska Native (Tundra Times 1991). Also, the top administrators in the Bureau's Washington, D.C., headquarters are American Indian.

The most significant factor contributing to the high percentage of BIA Indian employees is an employment preference for qualified Indians and Alaska Natives that was established by Congress in the Indian Reorganization Act of 1934. It was administratively expanded in the early 1970s by the Secretary of the Interior. Questioned by some, this preference has been declared by the Supreme Court as being a political and not a racial policy under the broad constitutional authority of Congress over Indian affairs (*Morton v. Mancari* 1974).

1.3. *Where are the BIA's major administrative offices, and how many Native Americans are directly affected by programs administered by the BIA?*

The latter portion of the question is answered first. Although the Census Bureau reported an Indian population of nearly two million in 1990, the BIA estimates that its "service population" is approximately 950,000 individual Indians and Alaska Natives (Bureau of Indian Affairs 1991a). These are Native Americans who have ongoing relations with the agency, either through social service, education, trust property, or related programs. They are also people who meet the agency's general qualifying criteria of living on or near a reservation, being a member (or descendant of a member) of a federally recognized tribe, and having a Native blood quantum of one-fourth or more (Bureau of Indian Affairs 1989b).

The BIA has one national office, a dozen geographic area offices, and 109 agency and special offices distributed throughout the 12 geographic areas. (See Figure 9.) The mailing addresses and main telephone numbers for the national and area offices are given below. (For correspondence, insert "Bureau of Indian Affairs" as a second line for each area address.)

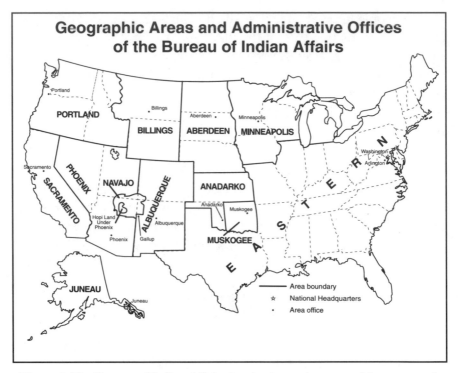

Figure 9. The Bureau of Indian Affairs has twelve main geographic areas, each of which has an office to serve Native Americans in that region. National headquarters is in Washington, D.C. (After Nash 1988.)

Deputy Commissioner
Bureau of Indian Affairs
1849 C Street, N.W.
Washington, DC 20240
(202) 208-3711

Aberdeen Area Director
115 4th Ave. S.E.
Aberdeen, SD 57401
(605) 226-7343

Albuquerque Area Director
P.O. Box 26567
Albuquerque, NM 87125-6567
(505) 766-3171

Anadarko Area Director
WCD Office Complex
P.O. Box 368
Anadarko, OK 73005
(405) 247-6673

Minneapolis Area Director
331 S. Second Ave.
Minneapolis, MN 55401
(612) 373-1000

Muskogee Area Director
Old Federal Building
Muskogee, OK 74401
(918) 687-2296

Navajo Area Director
P.O. Box 1060
Gallup, NM 87305
(505) 863-8200

Billings Area Director
316 North 26th Street
Billings, MT 59101
(406) 657-6315

Eastern Area Director
3701 N. Fairfax Drive
Suite 260
Arlington, VA 22203
(703) 235-2571

Juneau Area Director
P.O. Box 3-8000
Juneau, AK 99802
(907) 586-7177

Phoenix Area Director
P.O. Box 10
Phoenix, AZ 85001-0010
(602) 379-6600

Portland Area Director
911 N.E. 11th Avenue
Portland, OR 97232-4169
(503) 231-6700

Sacramento Area Director
Federal Building
2800 Cottage Way
Sacramento, CA 95825-1884
(916) 978-4691

I-4. What is the BIA's annual budget for its various programs?

Throughout the lean, eight-year period of the Reagan era in the 1980s, the Bureau's annual budget averaged about one billion dollars. In 1987, for example, the amount was 1.02 billion (Bureau of Indian Affairs 1987b). With a change in administrations, the budget began to increase substantially in important areas like education. Data provided by the BIA in 1992, outlining its fiscal year appropriations, show an annual appropriation of somewhat more than 1.5 billion dollars. (See table on next page.) Another half-billion dollars were appropriated for "permanent" expenditures and trusts, i.e., financial obligations of the government that are theoretically not subject to the annual roller coaster ride of fiscal year appropriations. Annual appropriations, and not permanents and trusts, are the key indicators of BIA budget direction which, lately, has been down. (For updated information about the budget, phone the Public Information Office, Bureau of Indian Affairs, Washington, D.C., at 202-208-3711.)

BUDGET FOR THE BUREAU OF INDIAN AFFAIRS
APPROPRIATIONS FOR 1992 & ESTIMATES FOR 1993

	FY 1992 Enacted	FY 1993 Estimate	Change from FY 1992
	(amounts in thousands of dollars)		
Appropriations:			
Operations of Indian Programs	1,220,503	1,208,459	- 12,044
Construction	203,477	129,615	- 73,862
Misc. Payments to Indians	87,617	31,709	- 55,908
Indian Direct Loan Program Acct.	4,008	0	- 4,008
Indian Guaranteed Loan Prog. Acct.	9,412	9,770	+ 358
Technical Asst. of Indian Enterprises	987	2,987	+ 2,000
Navajo Rehabilitation Trust Fund	3,950	0	- 3,950
Subtotal, Appropriations	1,529,954	1,382,540	- 147,414
Permanents and Trusts:			
Misc. Permanent Appropriations	71,136	59,518	- 11,618
White Earth Settlement Fund	11,000	12,000	+ 1,000
Misc. Payments to Indians (Perm.)	35,000	0	- 35,000
Indian Loan Guar. & Insur. Fund	11,000	11,000	0
Cooperative Fund (Papago)	701	619	- 82
Operation & Maintenance of Quarters	6,000	6,000	0
Misc. Trust Funds	392,425	411,124	+ 18,699
Subtotal, Permanents and Trusts	527,262	500,261	- 27,001
TOTAL, BUREAU OF INDIAN AFFAIRS	2,057,216	1,882,801	- 174,415

The Bureau of Indian Affairs (BIA), acting as agent of the U.S. Government, carries out most Federal responsibilities for American Indian Tribes and Alaska Native Groups. The budget places BIA's emphasis on four areas of responsibility: (a) to recognize and preserve the inherent rights of tribal self-government, to strengthen tribal capacity to govern, and to provide resources for tribal government programs; (b) to fulfill and carry out the Federal Government's trust obligations to American Indian Tribes; (c) to improve Indian education; and (d) to emphasize management improvement activities that will strengthen the Bureau's ability to serve Indian people.

Source: Bureau of Indian Affairs, Washington Office (budget mimeograph).

I-5. *What are the most frequent complaints about the BIA?*

> To us, the situation with the bureau is often that "we can't live
> with it and we can't live without it."
>
> Phillip Martin 1984, Chief
> Mississippi Band of Choctaw Indians

Complaints about the BIA are legion. They vary from time to time, depending upon the politics of the day, and they come from all quarters – including individuals, tribes, the public, Congress, and the Executive. Whenever anything goes wrong concerning any Indian or Alaska Native issue, there is a good probability that finger-pointing will begin or end with the BIA, whether or not the agency is ultimately at fault.

Sometimes the agency escapes unscathed, however, as when Congress, the White House, interest groups, land owners, state government, and the Passamaquoddy tribe took the initiative in hammering out a solution to the Maine land claims issue of the 1970s. In 1972, the tribe claimed two-thirds of the state, based on a land cession made in 1791 which was in violation of the 1790 Non-intercourse Act. In 1980, through the Maine Indian Claims Settlement Act, the tribe gave up its legal claims to most of the state in exchange for retained rights to 120,000 acres and a $40 million settlement (White 1990). The BIA officially entered the arena only *after* the settlement act was passed and then only to comply with the provisions in the act which required BIA administration.

Several selected newspaper headlines and column quotes follow. They give the general flavor of some of the major complaints surfacing (or resurfacing) in the 1990s. There is no intention here to apologize for administrative shortcomings which do arise within the BIA. Nevertheless, it is important to remember that *Congress*, and not the BIA, is ultimately and constitutionally responsible for *all* the federal government's Indian affairs policies and programs.

BIA Blames Sloppy Bookkeeping For $23.8 Million In Lost Equipment

WASHINGTON — The federal Bureau of Indian Affairs can't find $23.8 million in equipment it is supposed to own and has over-estimated the value of other machinery by $536 million, officials say…. BIA spokesman Carl Shaw said the audit does not show any intentional wrongdoing, just sloppy accounting … (Associated Press 1991b).

Probe Blames Government For Deficient Indian Schools

WASHINGTON—The government has managed its Indian schools so poorly that students score well below their grade level on standardized tests, an Interior Department investigation concludes.

Only two schools run by the Bureau of Indian Affairs performed at the national median, the Department's Inspector General said in a recent report…(Associated Press 1991f).

BIA Mismanagement Blasted

WASHINGTON—Calling Bureau of Indian Affairs management of the $2 billion Indian trust fund "a continuing crisis" and "a national disgrace," a House committee is urging greater tribal control in trust fund administration…(Anquoe 1992a).

Brown Defends Budget

WASHINGTON—The House Subcommittee on Interior Appropriations chastised Bureau of Indian Affairs officials [e.g., Dr. Eddie Brown, Assistant Secretary for Indian Affairs] for proposed 1993 budget cuts in Indian programs.

"This administration doesn't like Indians, does it?" charged Rep. Sidney Yates, D–Ill., subcommittee chairman, during the April 2 hearing…(Anquoe 1992b).

SECTION J: HEALTH

J-1. What are the goals, structure, and function of the Indian Health Service?

The primary federal health resource for Native Americans is the Indian Health Service (IHS). It is located within the U.S. Public Health Service which is part of the Department of Health and Human Services. With a current annual budget of more than $1.5 billion, the IHS developed out of very meager beginnings in 1954. At that time, Congress transferred the badly ailing Indian health program out of the BIA and into the Public Health Service. Improvement of the amount and quality of medical service available to Native Americans was the reason behind the transfer, and it worked. But, as with the BIA, the IHS has had its share of problems regarding waste, mismanagement, and fraud.

Goals and objectives

The Indian Health Care Improvement Act of 1976, as amended, establishes two broad goals for the IHS. They are (a) to raise the health status of American Indians and Alaska Natives to the highest possible level and (b) to encourage the maximum participation of Indians in the planning and management of IHS services. This second goal is an extension of self-determination policies.

The IHS has three objectives, also grounded in the 1976 legislation. Rhoades, Reyes, and Buzzard 1987 (p. 353-354) list them as:

1. To assure Indian people access to high-quality, comprehensive health services appropriate to their needs.
2. To assist Indian tribes and Alaska Native corporations to develop their capacity to staff and manage health programs and provide these tribal organizations with the opportunity to assume operational authority for IHS programs serving their communities.
3. To act as advocate for the Indian people in health-related matters and help them gain access to other Federal, State, and local programs to which they are entitled.

Service operations

A decentralized agency, the IHS is comprised of 12 geographic "area offices" which administer programs officially covering 34 states. The

181

area offices, cities where headquartered, and the states covered by each are as follows (Indian Health Service 1991a).

Area	Headquarters	States Covered
Aberdeen	Aberdeen, SD	IA, NE, ND, SD
Alaska	Anchorage, AK	AK
Albuquerque	Albuquerque, NM	NM, CO, TX (part)
Bemidji	Bemidji, MN	MI, MN, WI
Billings	Billings, MT	MT, WY
California	Sacramento, CA	CA
Nashville	Nashville, TN	AL, CT, FL, LA, MA, ME, MS, NC, NY, PA, RI, TN, TX (part)
Navajo	Window Rock, AZ	AZ (northeast), parts of UT, CO, NM
Oklahoma City	Oklahoma City, OK	OK, KS, TX (part)
Phoenix	Phoenix, AZ	AZ (most), UT (most), NV
Portland	Portland, OR	ID, OR, WA
Tucson	Tucson, AZ	AZ (south central)

The areas are subdivided into approximately 136 geographic "service units." These are the basic health care administration units which the IHS serves within each of the 12 geographic areas. Seventy-eight of the service units are operated by the IHS and 58 are operated by tribes. In the lower 48 states, the service units are usually centered around one or more Indian reservations, pueblos, rancherias, colonies, or former reservations. In Alaska they are centered around population concentrations. Both urban and rural programs are included. Service units function like county and city health departments, answering to area offices much like such departments would answer to states.

IHS operations are managed locally by the service units. Within each unit are a number of individual bases of operation. Typically, they are small hospitals or health centers with a number of clinics. An IHS policy of seeking community input into identification of needs and delivery of services affects how these bases of operation function. Individual patient care and community health are their points of focus (Indian Health Service 1988, 1991c).

The San Xavier Health Clinic, near Tucson, Arizona, serves some of the more than 20,000 Indians who live in the Tucson metropolitan area.

In the opening years of the 1990s, the IHS has a service population of just under 1.2 million. This number is expected to increase to 1.4 million by the year 2000 (Indian Health Service 1991b). The various health services available are classified as preventive, curative, rehabilitative, and environmental, e.g., safe drinking water and sanitation. Added to "traditional" physician-patient encounters, there are emergency services, mental health programs, community outreach programs, and additional support services. These are provided through three modes of delivery–direct, tribal, and contract. Clinical services at facilities operated directly by the IHS, or through IHS agreements with tribes, are often the only sources of care reasonably available to many Indian people. When additional care is needed, or in areas beyond the normal reach of IHS and tribal programs, contract services are often relied on. As the name suggests, contract care is purchased through contracts with community hospitals and private practitioners (Rhoades, Reyes, and Buzzard 1987).

The IHS does not pay for all health care needs of its service population, but it does cover about 70 percent. The other 30 percent is covered by additional sources, including the same types of entitlement programs, or insurance, available to non-Indian citizens. When adequate IHS services are available, the agency prefers that program beneficiaries use IHS staff and facilities first. If additional care is needed, then a patient may be authorized by the IHS to use an outside health care facility or private practitioner contracted by the IHS. For more than 30 years, IHS policy has been that the agency should be the payor of last resort when contract health care is obtained. In other words, for contract care, applicable federal, state, local, or private health payment programs, which Indian patients are otherwise entitled to, should be the primary payors (U.S. Public Health Service 1991, Sec. 36.61). There is occasional conflict over this rule. It usually comes from non-IHS health care providers who feel that the IHS should pay most or all coverage in all cases.

Staff

The IHS has about 14,000 employees, of whom 65% are Native Americans. This relatively high percentage of Native employees is attributable to an Indian hiring preference comparable to that of the BIA. In recent years, the IHS has been authorized to fill medical staff positions for approximately 850 physicians, 100 physician assistants, 2,400 nurses, 350 pharmacists, 300 dentists, 60 optometrists, 45 physical therapists, 7 nutritionists, 80 dieticians, and 285 medical technologists. Vacancy rates of from three to 15 percent, high turnover among physicians, and serious regional staff shortages present significant challenges to the Service's health care effort (Indian Health Service 1988 and 1992a).

A major support program, begun in 1968, is the one involving community health representatives (CHRs). They are Native paraprofessional health care providers who are selected, employed, and supervised by their tribes and communities. Their services include home visits, hospitalization follow-up, medication monitoring, health promotion, and disease prevention, incorporating traditional Native concepts whenever appropriate. About 1,400 CHRs work in Indian communities throughout the 12 IHS areas.

In 1991, when the Bush administration proposed cuts in health programs, the IHS director told Congress that the agency actually needed to double the number of physicians it employs. The director also stated that the number of health care workers in the agency is inadequate. He declared that, if improvements are not made, the IHS cannot reach its immediate goal of providing the level of health care for Native Americans that is normally available to the general public (Hazard 1991). By 1993, not much has changed.

Eligibility

IHS regulatory "principles" describe persons for whom the agency provides health care services (U.S. Public Health Service 1991). These include "Indians" (which incorporates Alaska Natives) who (a) are bona fide members of federally recognized tribes, bands, nations, villages, communities, organized groups, or Alaska Native Corporations and (b) reside in a geographically designated Health Service Delivery Area. Beneficiaries also include minor children who are not directly eligible but who have at least one parent who is.

Non-Indian women who are pregnant with an eligible Indian's child are also eligible, but only during the pregnancy and for about six weeks after birth. Non-Indian members of an eligible Indian's household may be eligible for service if it is necessary to control an acute infectious disease or other immediate public health hazard. Public Health Service and other federal beneficiaries may also be eligible under certain circumstances.

Ineligible non-Indians may receive emergency treatment on a fee-for-service basis. Also, on reservations or in remote settings where tribes will approve it, non-Indians living in an IHS area may receive medical services if (a) they pay for them and (b) providing the service does not interfere with delivery of services to Indian beneficiaries.

Facilities

The IHS system has 50 hospitals and 450 outpatient facilities. Among the outpatient facilities, health centers offer the most service and clinics generally the least. Operational control between the IHS and Indian tribes or other groups breaks down in the following manner (Indian Health Service 1991a).

Type of Facility	IHS	Tribal
Hospital	43	7
Outpatient		
Health Centers	66	89
School Health Centers	4	3
Health Stations	51	64
Alaska Village Clinics	–	173

Headquarters location and telephone number
Indian Health Service
U.S. Public Health Service
5600 Fishers Lane
Rockville, Maryland 20857
(301) 443-1087

FEDERAL INDIAN HEALTH PROGRAM – A BRIEF HISTORY

Federal health services for Indians began in the early nineteenth century when Army physicians took steps to curb smallpox and other contagious diseases among tribes living in the vicinity of military posts. Treaties committing the federal government to provide health services to Indians were introduced in 1832 when members of the Winnebago Tribe were promised physician care as partial payment for rights and property ceded to the U.S. government. Transfer of the Bureau of Indian Affairs (BIA) from the War Department to the Department of the Interior in 1849 extended physician services to Indians by emphasizing non-military aspects of Indian administration and developing a corps of civilian field employees. The first federal hospital built to care for Indian people was constructed in the 1880s in Oklahoma. Nurses were added to the staff in the 1890s. Professional medical supervision of health activities for Indians began in 1908 with the establishment of the BIA position of Chief Medical Supervisor. Dental services began in 1913. Pharmacy services were organized in 1953. In 1955, responsibility for American Indian and Alaska Native health was transferred from the Department of the Interior's BIA to the Public Health Service (PHS) within the Department of Health, Education and Welfare (currently the Department of Health and Human Services). On January 4, 1988, the Indian Health Service was elevated to agency status and became the seventh agency in the PHS.

Indian Health Service 1992a

J-2. *What are the major health-related statistics for the Indian population, and how do they compare with those for the general population?*

In 1991, the Indian Health Service published *Trends in Indian Health.* Most of the limited information presented below came from that relatively comprehensive document. The remainder was taken from the IHS companion document, *Regional Differences in Indian Health.* The agency used a number of sources for its data. Some are from the 1980 census and others are from compilations done in the late-1980s and 1990. Readers requiring specifics on the sources and limitations of the data should review the two publications listed. They may be available in a local library or they can be requested from the IHS. Year of collection and general population comparisons are provided with the statistics. Also, when the Indian population is referred to, it does not include all Indians and Alaska Natives counted in the nationwide census. It does include the approximately 1.2 million Native people in the 12 IHS service areas described in the previous answer.

Only national rates for the combined service areas are presented in the table on the following page. Rates for individual areas vary considerably. For example, the accident mortality rate given in the table, for Indians as a whole, is 80.8 per 100,000 population. The rate for the Oklahoma Area, however, is 44.8 (the lowest of all 12 areas); but it is 219.9 for the Tucson Area (the highest of all 12 areas).

Summarizing the table, the Indian birth rate is nearly twice that of the national average, and infant survival is slightly better than in the general population. An Indian child, however, is likely to have a life span several years shorter than the national average. Also, he or she is more likely than someone in the general population to suffer and die from a variety of causes, including all types of accidents (2.3 times as likely), liver disease (3.4 times), diabetes (2.6 times), pneumonia and influenza (1.3 times), suicide (1.3 times), homicide (1.6 times), and tuberculosis (5 times).

Does this mean that the IHS has not been doing the improved job which Congress expected when it transferred Indian health care responsibility from the BIA to the Public Health Service in 1954? No. Although there is room for improvement, the IHS has not been treading water since the 1950s. Past efforts have brought about some remarkable changes. Ongoing programs exist to further reduce the

MAJOR INDIAN HEALTH STATISTICS

	Indian*	U.S., All Races
Birth Rate (1987) (per 1,000 people)	27.5	15.7
Infant Mortality (1987) (per 1,000 live births)	9.7	10.1
Life Expectancy at Birth (1988) (in years)	72.0 (male, 67.1) (female, 75.1)	75.0 (male, 70.7) (female, 78.1)
Leading Causes of Death (1988) (age-adjusted, per 100,000 people)		
All causes	574.3	535.5
Major cardiovascular disease	172.5	206.6
Disease of the heart	138.1	166.3
Cerebrovascular disease	26.4	29.7
Atherosclerosis	3.0	3.4
Malignant neoplasms	91.3	132.7
Accidents	80.8	35.0
Motor vehicle	44.7	19.7
All other	36.1	15.3
Chronic liver disease and cirrhosis	30.4	9.0
Diabetes mellitus	25.8	10.1
Pneumonia and Influenza	18.7	14.2
Suicide	14.5	11.4
Homicide	14.1	9.0
Chronic obstructive pulmonary diseases	13.8	19.4
Tuberculosis, all forms	2.5	0.5

*The term "Indian" includes Alaska Natives.

disparities in statistics shown in the table. Such programs include the upgrading of equipment and facilities, more training of staff, recruitment of career staff, awareness and prevention of injury, treatment of substance abuse, nutrition counseling, mental health counseling, expanded dental services, upgrading of water and sanitation facilities, and so on. Budget limitations, staff shortages, and staff turnover, however, seem to be significant perennial problems.

**MAJOR PROGRAM ACCOMPLISHMENTS
SINCE IHS STARTED IN 1955**

	Percent Decrease in Mortality Rate
Infant	85
Maternal	91
Pneumonia and influenza	71
Tuberculosis	96
Gastrointestinal disease	86
Congenital malformations	57
Accidents	56

	Percent Increase in Services Provided
Hospital admissions	105
Outpatient visits	989
Dental services	1,212

J-3. *How serious is alcoholism among Native Americans?*

Indian drinking is a particularly sensitive issue because it is also a major theme in anti-Indian prejudice and stereotyping. However, alcoholism and its effects are too important to be ignored, whether they involve [non-Indians] or Indians.

Price 1978, p. 188

There is a tremendous pressure in this country to conform. And when a group like the Indian doesn't, there's a sense of failure. Wouldn't it be nice if [non-Indians] were right that Indian alcoholism is a genetic weakness? This ignores their tremendous cultural depression over many, many years. Their alcohol problems are huge. But the reasons are so perplexing. You hear...the sadness.

Dale Walker, M.D., Cherokee, *In* Gibbons 1992, p. 34

Alcoholism, a world-wide plague, is indeed a major problem in many Indian communities. As with non-Indians, the causes are numerous and varied. Dr. Walker's quotation refers to one of the most common.

The most serious statistic kept on the topic of alcoholism by the Indian Health Service (IHS) is the alcoholism *mortality* rate. Among the population served by the IHS (slightly more than one million Native people in 33 states), the alcoholism mortality rate is 33.9 per 100,000 population. This is about 5.3 times the rate for the general U.S. population, but it is still 38 percent lower than it was a decade earlier (Indian Health Service 1991c). There are, however, marked regional differences in alcoholism mortality rates in Indian country. They range from a low of 9.5 per 100,000, in the Oklahoma Area of the IHS, to a high of 69.9 in the Aberdeen Area (Indian Health Service 1991a). Alcohol is also implicated in three-fourths of all traumatic Native American deaths. (See the answer to question J-1 for a delineation of IHS "areas.")

Fetal Alcohol Syndrome, or FAS, is another major alcohol-related concern. This term describes the damage some unborn children can

Alcohol Before Columbus

Prior to European contact, Native use of alcoholic beverages was concentrated in areas of intensive agriculture in Mexico and Central and South America. Such beverages were also made and consumed in the American Southwest, in the area of the Carolinas, and around the Chesapeake Bay region. Alcoholic drinks were most often made by fermenting maize or tapioca, but in northern Mexico and parts of the Southwest U.S., wines were also produced from agave, dasylirion, saguaro and pitahaya cacti, and mesquite or screwbean. In the eastern U.S., Native people made a persimmon wine.

Price 1978; Waldman 1985

In much of the Southwest, among the Zunis, Yuman groups, and Apaches, as well as in the Southeast, alcohol use was mostly non-religious. The Tohono O'odham and Pimas of the Southwest, however, believed that intake of alcoholic beverages could bring rain. For the Aztecs, intoxication served to induce meditation and prophecy. But, public drunkenness was taboo and, in some instances, could be punished by death.

Waldman 1985

suffer when their mothers consume alcohol during pregnancy. In the bloodstream, alcohol can be toxic to the fetus. It depends on the stage of pregnancy and how much is consumed. Damage can range from subtle to severe–causing clumsiness, behavioral problems, stunted growth, disfigurement, and mental retardation (Steinmetz 1992). Specific data on FAS among Indian people are not readily available, but the incidence is relatively high. The rate for the general population is a little higher than 1 per 100,000 births. Some Indian communities may have a rate of 6 per 100,000 births, or greater (Stillman 1991).

Even though the alcoholism *rate* among the Native population as a whole is comparatively high, the fact remains that a relatively small minority of Native Americans are alcoholics. The very complex problem of alcoholism (or other substance abuse) among Indians or non-Indians goes well beyond simple comparisons of cold statistics. It also goes beyond the narrow confines of this book.

J-4. *Is AIDS a major concern in Indian country?*

Spread the News – Not the Disease. AIDS Kills Indians Too.
                                                          AIDS Awareness Poster
                                         Inter Tribal Council of Arizona, Inc. 1993

It is my fear and my belief that AIDS and HIV infection present an unprecedented threat to the future of all Native Americans.
                                                          Josiah Moore, Chairman
                                                    Tohono O'odham Nation, 1991

This is not a disease that only happens somewhere else, that only happens to someone else.
                                                          Daris Hayes
                                                    Lakota man with AIDS, 1991

How we respond to AIDS will tell a lot about us as a people.
                                                          Carole LaFavor
                                                    Ojibwa woman with AIDS, 1991

AIDS is obviously very much a concern in Indian country. AIDS experts consider many Indian people to be at high risk of HIV infections because of "unsafe" sex habits, alcohol use and related poor judgment, IV drug use, and the inter-migration between urban centers and Indian country (Erikson 1991). Statistics on the rate of HIV infection and full-blown AIDS among Native people have, in the past, been sketchy and confusing. One reason is that people being tested by doctors and laboratories generally have not been asked if they are Native American. Reporting techniques are now improving.

The federal Centers for Disease Control is currently maintaining separate records on AIDS with regard to Native Americans. At the beginning of the 4th quarter of 1992, the figures stood as shown in the box on the next page.

Education and the halting of destructive or high risk behaviors are the keys to controlling the AIDS epidemic. Only these actions can reduce the rates or probabilities of infection. There is something that everyone should remember, however. Whenever AIDS or any other tragedy strikes someone, society's ever-important statistics—so coveted by the media, medical experts, and politicians—all go to a 100% reality for the victim. He or she is more than a number.

To obtain additional information, contact the National AIDS Information Hotline at 1-800-342-AIDS, or the Indian AIDS Hotline at 1-800-283-2437.

AIDS STATISTICS FOR NATIVE AMERICANS — 1992

Total number of AIDS cases   416
(No firm numbers exist for those who may be HIV positive.)

Usual number of new cases reported per month in 1992   10–15

Breakdown of reported cases by sex of adult patient
       Cases among females   58
       Cases among males   346

Number of those affected who are children   12

Probable means of infection among the 416 reported cases:
       Sex between gay men   55%
       IV drug use   18%
       Sex with men who inject drugs   14%
       Hemophiliac blood transfusions   2%
       Heterosexual sex or sex with bisexuals   4%
       Receipt of blood transfusions or blood products   2%
       Unknown   5%

NOTE: These data are from the Centers for Disease Control and are current through September 1992.

SECTION K: EDUCATION

The quotation which follows is a reply from Conassatego, of the Iroquois League, to an offer from the Virginia Legislature, in 1744, inviting the Iroquois to send six youths to be educated at the College of William and Mary, in Williamsburg (from O'Brien 1989, p. 239).

We know you highly esteem the kind of Learning taught in these colleges, and the maintenance of our young men, while with you, would be very expensive to you. We are convinced, therefore, that you mean to do us Good by your proposal; and we thank you heartily. But you who are so wise must know that different Nations have different conceptions of things; and you will not therefore take it amiss, if our Ideas of this kind of education happen not to be the same with yours. We have had some experience of it. Several of our young People were formerly brought up in the colleges of the Northern Provinces; they were instructed in all your Sciences; but, when they came back to us, they were bad Runners, ignorant of every means of living in the woods, unable to bear either cold or hunger, knew neither how to build a Cabin, take a deer, or kill an enemy, spoke our language imperfectly, were ther[e]fore neither fit for Hunters, Warriors, nor Counsellors; they were totally good for nothing. We are however not the less obliged for your kind offer, tho' we decline accepting it; and to show our grateful Sense of it, if the Gentlemen of Virginia shall send us a Dozen of their Sons, we will take care of their Education, instruct them in all we know, and make Men of them.

K-1. What is the general history of education programs for American Indians?

The hundreds of tribes, bands, clans, and extended family groups of Native Americans which inhabited North America in the late 15th century had their own forms and concepts of education. These "systems" had evolved with their cultures over the millennia. The broad focus of pre-European education was to facilitate a child's acquisition of environmental and cultural knowledge necessary to (1) survive in

194

a subsistence lifestyle and (2) contribute meaningfully to the overall socio-economic welfare of the group (Bureau of Indian Affairs 1988). The 1490s, however, marked the beginning of the end of an epoch of complete Indian self-determination in the education of their children.

The first time Indian education was formally addressed by a European colonial government was in 1512 in the Laws of Burgos. This was a legal code developed by the Spanish government whereby the Indians under Spanish rule were to have impressed upon them the virtues of Christianity and civilization (Williams 1990). Not many Indians were formally educated under these early laws—only a few Indian leaders' sons, who were entrusted to Franciscan missionaries for four years, received formal training. By and large, the Laws of Burgos functioned to legitimize forced labor and assimilation. In 1568, however, the Jesuits began the long history of non-Indian education of Indian children when they established a school in Havana, Cuba (O'Brien 1989). The purpose of this school, like nearly all of the others for hundreds of years to come, was to "civilize" the Indians. This meant conversion to Christianity, learning reading and writing, developing agricultural and other skills, and adopting "white" values. These included individualism (versus tribalism), materialism, competitiveness, and conquest of the natural world.

British colonial education of Indians took numerous forms. At the simplest level, colonists took Indian children into their homes and educated them in the ways of Euro-American civilization. At the more sophisticated level, small schools were established for basic Indian education. In 1619, for instance, the first British Indian school was established by the Virginia Company near present-day Richmond. More advanced schools were later developed for the "more promising," or better assimilated, students. The College of William and Mary, chartered in 1693, was partly dedicated to Indian education. Dartmouth College in New Hampshire was also established originally to educate Indians. And still other colonial institutions, such as Harvard and the College of New Jersey, provided for Indian education, as did religious organizations (Szasz and Ryan 1988).

The federal government made its first appropriation for Indian education in 1776, when the Continental Congress provided for a minister, a blacksmith, and two teachers to live among some of the Indians in New York. For decades, sporadic, and not very substantive, attempts to address Indian education were made by the federal government through different treaties, executive orders, and limited legislation. At the same time, religious groups increased their efforts in this area by establishing hundreds of missionary schools and several academies. A few of the Indian tribes, most notably the Cherokees, developed flourishing school systems of their own in the late 18th and early 19th centuries, based to a large degree on the Euro-American models of the time (Harlow 1935; Szasz and Ryan 1988).

In 1860, the BIA opened its first Indian school, on the Yakima Reservation in the state of Washington. By the turn of the century, the BIA was operating 147 reservation day schools, 81 reservation boarding schools, and 25 off-reservation boarding schools for Indians in various parts of the country as a part of the government's trust responsibility. The most famous of the boarding schools was Carlisle, in Pennsylvania, the first off-reservation government boarding school. It was established in 1879 by Henry Pratt, a Civil War veteran, whose goal was complete assimilation. "Kill the Indian and save the man" was his motto. Regimentation, reading, writing, arithmetic, the manual trades, and home economics were drilled into the students until the school closed in 1918 (Bureau of Indian Affairs 1988; O'Brien 1989; Szasz and Ryan 1988).

While the mission schools declined in influence, from the 1870s through the 1890s, "contract" schools developed. The government employed religious denominations by contract to run part of its expanding network of schools. Before the practice was ended in 1897, Catholic and Protestant denominations had operated as many as 60 of the government Indian schools.

From the turn of the century through the 1920s, the government's poorly funded and woefully inadequate Indian education system was focused solely on assimilation. This involved federal schools as well as state schools paid by the government. A new attitude toward cultural pluralism, and increased awareness of the bleak conditions at most Indian schools, led to passage of the Johnson-O'Malley Act in 1934. The act, as amended in 1936, permitted the government to contract with states, territories, corporations, private institutions, agencies, and political subdivisions to provide education and other services (Cohen 1982). Despite this act, thirty years later Indian education remained far below national standards. In Alaska, the U.S. Office of Education controlled the education of Alaska Natives from 1887 until the BIA took over in 1931 (Szasz and Ryan 1988).

In 1969, the Special Senate Subcommittee on Indian Education published a report titled *Indian Education: A National Tragedy—A National Challenge.* The upshot of this report, numerous other studies, and contemporary tribal input was that there was a need for cultural relevance and that Indians must be given greater control over the education of their children. Congress soon passed the Indian Education Act of 1972. This legislation established funding for special bilingual and bicultural programs, culturally relevant teaching materials, proper training and hiring of counselors, and establishment of an Office of Indian Education in the U.S. Department of Education. Most importantly, the act required participation of Native Americans in the planning of all relevant educational projects (Cohen 1982; O'Brien 1989).

In 1975, the Indian Self-Determination and Education Assistance Act provided for and encouraged the contracting out of BIA education functions to Indian tribes themselves. The long-term goal of the act is the assumption of managerial and policy-making responsibilities by the tribes for their own affairs. More than 50 tribes have taken over the operation of their own schools under contract with the BIA, affecting about 75 institutions and 30 percent of the total enrollment in BIA-funded schools. The great majority of other Indian students attend BIA-run or regular public schools (Bureau of Indian Affairs 1988, 1991a, and 1991b; O'Brien 1989).

Indian education has improved remarkably in the past two decades. This has come about through periodic increases in funding, updating of legislation, greater cultural relevance, and expanding tribal involvement. Much remains to be accomplished, however. Ongoing problems include deterioration of BIA facilities, poor program management in some areas, higher than average dropout rates, and substandard student achievement in various locales. Despite these problems, there are bright spots which bode well for the future betterment of the tribes and their members. Increased Native emphasis on, involvement in, improvement of, and control over education will continue to be major contributors to the improving situation. Education's influence goes far beyond the classroom and the tribes recognize this increasingly.

K-2. *What are the basic data on federal Indian education facilities and programs?*

Bureau of Indian Affairs

In the early 1990s, the BIA is funding 180 education facilities. These include 48 day schools, 39 on-reservation boarding schools, five off-reservation boarding schools, and eight Bureau-operated dormitories which enable Indian students to attend public schools. In addition, under the provisions of the Indian Self-Determination Act of 1975, the BIA has contracted with various tribes to operate more than 60 day schools, 11 on-reservation boarding schools, one off-reservation boarding school, and six dormitories. Enrollment in all of the schools and dormitories exceeds 40,000, or roughly 10 percent of the total Indian student population. The rest of the student population attends regular public, private, or parochial schools.

The BIA also provides support funding to many public school districts around the country, under the Johnson-O'Malley Act of 1934. Such financial support is designed to aid in the educational needs of more than 225,000 eligible Indian students who attend public school. Under its handicapped children program, the Bureau also provides financial support for the educational costs of 200 to 300 children in at least 28 different institutions (Bureau of Indian Affairs 1988 and 1990).

Two post secondary schools are operated by the BIA. Haskell Indian Junior College, in Lawrence, Kansas, has an enrollment of about 800 students; and Southwestern Indian Polytechnic Institute, in Albuquerque, New Mexico, has more than 400 students.

Approximately 15,000 Indian students receive scholarships under BIA programs to attend colleges and universities each year. Between 400 and 500 of these students are in law school and other graduate programs. Altogether, it is estimated that 70,000 Indian students are attending college. Those who do not obtain BIA assistance are eligible to apply for other assistance programs, just as similarly situated non-Indian students can. The BIA also provides funding for the operation of 22 tribally controlled community colleges which have a combined enrollment of more than 7,000 students. Navajo Community College, on the Navajo Reservation in Arizona, and Sinte Gleska (Spotted Tail) University, on the Rosebud Reservation in South Dakota, are two of the better-known of these institutions.

U.S. Department of Education

The Office of Indian Education (OIE), in the U.S. Department of Education, oversees programs and funding to provide educational opportunities for Indian children and adults, and to address culturally related academic needs of Indian children. Grants to local education agencies supplement services to about 380,000 American Indian and Alaska Native students and also assist in the establishment or operation of Indian controlled schools on or near reservations. "Special programs" grants are also available for (1) planning, pilot, and demonstration programs, (2) educational services, (3) personnel development, (4) student fellowships, (5) gifted and talented programs, and (6) Indian education technical assistance centers. There is also an OIE educational services program which provides grants for adult education (Office of Indian Education 1991).

Indian Health Service

Pursuant to the Indian Health Care Improvement Act of 1976, as amended, and relevant regulations (U.S. Public Health Service 1991), the IHS makes scholarships and grants available to recruit and educate eligible Indians in various health care professions. The purpose of the overall program is to encourage Indians and Alaska Natives to enter the health professions and insure the availability of Native health professionals to serve Native people.

K-3. *How do tribes integrate traditional Indian philosophy with Western educational systems?*

Particular methods vary with different tribes, reservations, institutions, and settings. A good example of one of the better-developed approaches comes from Navajo Community College in Arizona, as described below by McNeley (1990).

> The traditional *Diné* (Navajo) philosophy of learning is embedded in oral traditions accounting for the creation and evolution of the Navajo world. This philosophy is based upon a view of man in nature–of the Navajo people deriving the powers of life,

thought, speech and motion from the forces underlying the workings of the natural world. Knowledge is identified with the cardinal directions. The values and other principles by which people live are identified with dawn and the east; knowledge for making a living, with daylight and the south; planning for social well-being is identified with evening twilight and the west; contentment and reverence for all life, with darkness and the north. Knowledge from all of these sources is essential for a balanced life. The goal of life is to live in harmony with others in society and in nature—a condition called *hozho*—resulting from balancing the four categories of knowledge.

Herbert John Benally's paper describing this *"Diné* philosophy of learning" (1987) challenges educators with the revolutionary proposal that, instead of attempting to fit Navajo knowledge into a Western conceptual organization—an approach which has heretofore characterized Navajo bicultural education—Western knowledge must be fit into the traditional Navajo organization of knowledge referred to above. It will no longer suffice, in this view, to merge bits of the Navajo world view into existing courses of the standard curriculum, fragmented as the latter usually is along lines defined by the academic disciplines which have evolved in the Western world. Rather, the subject matter of Western education must now be accommodated to the traditional Navajo view that all knowledge must be integrated so as to promote the development of harmonious relationships of the individual with his social and natural environment.

...The object of learning as well as of life generally is "a state of being and a society called *hozho,* a state of much good in terms of peace, happiness and plenty" (Benally 1987). The philosophy also provides a set of guiding principles for a program of general education for attaining this shared goal of the Navajo community. The categories of knowledge identified with the cardinal directions are the basis for this program of general education. An adequate general education, in this view:

> *...requires balancing all four categories of Navajo knowledge so that the individual will have sound beliefs and values to make the best possible decisions, will possess skill to provide the best living for the family and provide good leadership to the family and community, and will have a reverence for the earth and for all living things... (Benally 1987).*

The *Diné* philosophy of education, in addition to establishing a clear purpose and guiding principles for general education, also provides an epistemology which eminently facilitates "seeing the connectedness of things," by conceptually placing the individual "at the focus where the four great branches of Navajo knowledge meet to produce the desired condition, *hozho...*" (Benally 1987). It expresses the concept that all of these aspects of knowledge are relevant to all courses and programs of study: "Each course and program at NCC will reflect the thematic areas of the *Diné* philosophy of learning..." (Navajo Community College Presidential Task Force). For example, the course Principles of Economics, if taught in accordance with this philosophy, would place economics in the context of broader life values, would show its relevance to making a livelihood, would relate it to social well-being, and would consider issues of economic impacts on the natural environment. The student educated in accordance with the traditional philosophy would emerge from such a course with enhanced knowledge and understanding of the economic system and of its relevance to the overall goal of *hozho....*

...Certainly, there are universally important aspects of higher education that must not be omitted even from unique programs, including the mastery of communication and numerical skills as well as scientific and technological literacy. Similarly, there are "ways of knowing" which should be encouraged across the curriculum including the processes of inquiry, historical consciousness, the experience of diverse cultures, the exploration of values, and, the processes involved in studying a subject in depth.

...[Nonetheless,] at the local level, pedagogical approaches ...need to be better adapted to Navajo styles of learning. Becktell (1986) argues that even more important than incorporating Navajo content in the curriculum is the need for educators "to understand the Navajo style of learning and develop teaching strategies that address that style." Reservation instructors typically base their teaching methods on the Anglo style of learning in which the learner is expected to act before competency is achieved. One is to "learn by doing." This approach, however, causes major problems for the Navajo student who generally learns by observation and by internal thought until he or she feels competent to act overtly:

> *The Navajo seem uncomfortable when they are expected or asked to perform before they feel mentally prepared for the performance.... This...causes stress in the Navajo learner and sets in motion the endless cycle of premature performance, sense of failure, no confidence, poor performance.... (Becktell 1986).*

Becktell recommends that teachers of Navajo students adopt teaching strategies that are better attuned to Navajo learning styles including greater use of example and metaphor, increased opportunity for learning by observation, and greater opportunities for self-discovery and self-correction. She cites the need for a "handbook of teaching strategies" for Navajo teachers.

...[T]raditional Navajo thought provides the philosophical basis for a potentially effective way of addressing many concerns expressed nationally about American...education. It provides a culturally-focussed purpose for Navajo education which relates well to concern for student character and moral development as well as establishing principles for a program of general education which, if implemented, will provide for integration of the curriculum. The traditional Navajo philosophy of education... provides us with a useful tool for addressing urgent educational concerns....

SECTION L: OTHER AGENCIES AND NATIONAL INDIAN ORGANIZATIONS

L-1. What other government agencies, besides the BIA and IHS, are specifically organized for purposes relating to Native Americans?

Within the U.S. government, scores of agencies have what are called "Indian desks." These are not full-fledged agencies; rather they are usually small administrative units consisting of one or several employees who deal with Indian issues and programs that are peripheral to the overall mission of the larger agency. Walke (1991) presents a good source list of agencies with Indian desks. There are, however, several additional federal as well as state agencies with missions that are specifically related to Native issues. They are described briefly below, in alphabetical order.

Administration for Native Americans

The Administration for Native Americans (ANA) is located within the U.S. Department of Health and Human Services. The mission of the ANA is to promote social and economic self-sufficiency for American Indians, Alaska Natives, Native Hawaiians, and Native American Pacific Islanders (American Samoa Natives, indigenous peoples of Guam, and Natives of the Commonwealth of the Northern Marianas Islands and the Republic of Palau). The agency's activities include provision of financial assistance grants, technical assistance and training, research, demonstrations, and pilot projects (Administration for Native Americans 1991b). The agency can be contacted as follows:

> Department of Health and Human Services
> Administration for Children and Families
> Administration for Native Americans
> 200 Independence Avenue, S.W. — 344F
> Washington, DC 20201-0001
> Phone (202) 245-7727

Indian Arts and Crafts Board

Congress established the Indian Arts and Crafts Board (IACB) in 1935 as an independent agency located within the U.S. Department of the

Interior. The Board serves the Indian, Eskimo, and Aleut communities, and the general public, as an informational, promotional, and advisory clearinghouse for all matters pertaining to the development of authentic Native arts and crafts of the U.S.

The IACB administers the Southern Plains Indian Museum in Anadarko, Oklahoma, the Sioux Indian Museum in Rapid City, South Dakota, and the Museum of the Plains Indian in Browning, Montana.

Misrepresentation or imitation of Native American arts and crafts is a major concern of the Board. Besides providing consumer information about how to avoid these problems, the Board has a responsibility to refer reported cases to proper federal and state law enforcement agencies (Andrews 1991).

The IACB can be contacted as follows:

> Indian Arts and Crafts Board
> Room 4004
> U.S. Department of the Interior
> Washington, DC 20240
> Phone (202) 343-2773

National Indian Policy Center

The National Indian Policy Center (NIPC) is located at George Washington University. It was authorized on a temporary basis by congressional initiative in May 1990 (P.L. 101-301, 104 Stat. 211). Not an "agency" in the normal sense, the NIPC has been aptly described as a "think tank" for Indian policy analysis and development. It attempts to bring together the best minds in Indian country. Since the Center began, it has been conducting a feasibility study aimed at developing the purpose, mission, structure, and function of an institution which would carry out research and analysis of Native issues. In particular, the emphasis would be placed on social, economic, and legal policy issues. The objective of this process was to present a final report which could be used by the 102nd Congress in developing more substantial authorizing legislation (National Indian Policy Center 1991; Parker 1992). The report was presented to Congress in June 1992 and was being reviewed by the Senate Select Committee on Indian Affairs when this book went to press (National Indian Policy Center 1992).

Seven task forces were organized by the NIPC, and their purpose was to focus on major Indian policy issues. These included education, economic development, health and human services, natural resource management and environmental protection, law and administration of justice, tribal governance, and cultural rights and resources. The efforts of these task forces–along with multi-tribal meetings and consultations, regional and national conferences, and distribution of information–are aimed at improving Indian and Alaska Native policy at all levels of government.

The Center can be contacted as follows:

> National Indian Policy Center
> The George Washington University
> 2136 Pennsylvania Avenue, N.W.
> Washington, DC 20052
> Phone (202) 676-4401

National Indian Gaming Commission

The National Indian Gaming Commission (NIGC) is a federal regulatory agency, within the Department of the Interior, established by Congress through the Indian Gaming Regulatory Act (IGRA) of 1988. Among the Commission's various and complicated powers and responsibilities are the promulgation of federal regulations for the Indian gaming industry, consistent with the mandates of the IGRA. Some final regulations have been published and several proposed regulations are under consideration as this book goes to press. For further information on the complex and controversial nature of this new agency and its mission, one should refer to the IGRA and proposed regulations which are available from the NIGC.

The NIGC can be contacted as follows:

> National Indian Gaming Commission
> Suite 250
> 1850 M Street, N.W.
> Washington, DC 20035
> Phone (202) 632-7003

Office of Indian Education

The Office of Indian Education (OIE), in the U.S. Department of Education, was created under the Indian Education Act of 1972. The OIE oversees funding distribution for special programs designed to provide educational opportunities for Indian children and adults and to address culturally related academic needs of Indian children. (See Section K of this book, on Education.)

The OIE can be contacted as follows:
> Office of Indian Education
> U.S. Department of Education
> Room 2177
> 400 Maryland Avenue, S.W.
> Washington, DC 20202-6335
> Phone (202) 401-1887

Congressional Committees

The U.S. Senate and House committees which deal directly with Indian affairs and policy development are exceptionally important and powerful government entities, although they are not "agencies" as such. The committees may be contacted as follows:

> Senate Select Committee on Indian Affairs
> Room SH 838
> Hart Senate Office Building
> Washington, DC 20510
> Phone (202) 224-2251

> Subcommittee on Native American Affairs
> Committee on Natural Resources
> 1522 Longworth House Office Building
> Washington, DC 20515
> Phone (202) 226-7393

State Indian Commissions

At least 40 states have some form of commission, agency, or office of Indian Affairs (Giago 1991d). Missions and activities vary, but those of the Arizona Commission on Indian Affairs (1991) are typical.

> MISSION AND PURPOSE. [T]he mission of the Arizona Commission on Indian Affairs is "to cooperate with and support State and Federal Agencies in Assisting Indian Tribes in developing mutual goals, in designing projects for these goals and in implementing their plans." In this liaison capacity the Commission on Indian Affairs gathers data and facilitates the exchange of information needed by Tribal, State, and Federal Agencies; assists the state in its responsibilities to Indians and Tribes of this State by making recommendations to the governor and the Legislature; confers and coordinates Indian needs and goals with various Government Officials; works for greater understanding and improved relationships between Indians and Non-

Indians by creating an awareness of the legal, social and economic needs of Indians in this State; promotes increased participation by Indians in local and State affairs; and assists Tribal groups in developing increasingly effective methods of self-government.

See Appendix 8 for a listing of the Indian commissions in the various states.

L-2. *What are the major national Indian organizations?*

More than 150 national associations, societies, and organizations of all kinds are active in Indian affairs. Perhaps the best general source for basic information about these organizations, and about various other relevant subjects, is Klein's 1990 *Reference Encyclopedia of the American Indian*. Another good source is *The American Indian and the Media* (Giago 1991d). Listed and described below are some of the more notable and active of the national Indian organizations.

American Indian Anti-Defamation Council

In November 1991, Russell Means, Chairman and Chief Executive Officer of the American Indian Anti-Defamation Council (AIADC), announced the opening of the Council's national office in Denver, Colorado. The AIADC's mission is:

> ...the establishment and operation of a national and international network of education and communication dedicated to the protection, enhancement, and prosperity of the indigenous peoples (American Indians) of the Western Hemisphere. Toward that end, the Council will actively work for the elimination of prejudice, racism, and racial discrimination directed at American Indians, and will actively oppose any human rights and civil rights violations against American Indians. This work will confront anti-Indian racism in the form of sports team mascots, anti-Indian holidays—such as Columbus Day—and other representations in the public realm that demean and defame American Indian people...(American Indian Anti-Defamation Council 1991).

Activities of the AIADC include monitoring of the film, television, and print media–the specific purpose being to insure a positive public image for American Indians, and to advise the media on matters of importance to Indian people. The Council also strives to remind the public of positive contributions of Native Americans to the world, to review educational curricula, and to provide indigenous perspectives on education. Further, it monitors racially motivated acts of "violence" against Indian people, including physical violence as well as what it considers to be economic, social, and political forms of violence. Indian self-determination and economic and political freedom are on-going goals of the AIADC.

For additional information, contact:

>American Indian Anti-Defamation Council
>215 West Fifth Avenue
>Denver, Colorado 80204
>(303) 892-7011

American Indian Movement

The story of the American Indian Movement is one that deals with an evolution of events. In July 1968, Clyde Bellecourt, Eddie Benton Bonai, George Mitchell, and Dennis Banks founded an organization known as "Concerned Indian Americans" in Minneapolis. Because of the acronym CIA, the name was quickly changed to American Indian Movement (AIM). Russell Means later became a prominent member of the organization (American Indian Movement 1991).

The original purpose of AIM was to assist Indians in urban ghettos who had been displaced by the government's programs of termination and relocation. These programs had effectively forced thousands of Indians from their reservations to unfamiliar and hostile urban environments.

One of the earliest and most successful of AIM's projects was the establishment, in 1972, of a "survival school" in Minneapolis. The concept of a survival school, which spread to other regions of the country, was an attempt to help Indian youths adjust to non-Indian society without losing what was most valuable from their own culture.

AIM's goals have developed over time and now encompass the entire spectrum of Native concerns. They include such topics as economic independence, religious freedom, treaty rights, sovereignty, self-determination, cultural revitalization, environmental protection, land and resource management, education, racism, and fair administration of justice.

AIM and its members have been involved in numerous and highly publicized protests and related activities since its founding. It was one of the groups involved in the occupation of Alcatraz Island (1969–1971), the occupation of Mount Rushmore (1970 and 1971), the march on Washington and occupation of the BIA office (1972), the occupation of Wounded Knee (1973), and the controversial firefight between AIM members and federal officers that resulted in the deaths of two FBI agents and one Indian man (1975).

By the late-1970s, with many of its leaders in exile or prison, considerable pressure from law enforcement agencies, and dissension among members, the national leadership disbanded. Attempts were being made in 1992 to reform a national AIM council, while state and regional AIM organizations have, since the start, maintained active roles in a wide range of Native issues. The well known Minnesota chapter, for example, continues to operate Heart of the Earth Survival School (phone 612-331-8862) and remains actively involved in local, state, regional, and national projects.

For additional information, contact:

American Indian Movement
2300 Cedar Ave. South
Minneapolis, Minnesota 55404
(612) 724-3129

– or –

American Indian Movement
2940 16th St., Suite 104
San Francisco, California 94103
(415) 552-1992

Association on American Indian Affairs

The Association on American Indian Affairs (AAIA), founded in 1922, is a non-profit corporation with 15,000 Indian and non-Indian members and more than 40,000 contributors (Association on American Indian Affairs 1991 and 1992). The Association is organized as an advocacy group for American Indians and Alaska Natives. It prides itself on working closely with Native Americans to deal with issues that *they* identify as being of greatest urgency. These often include issues for which there is no other aid available.

The AAIA works to perpetuate the well-being of Native people through efforts that (1) help sustain cultures and languages, (2) protect sovereign, constitutional, legal, religious, and human rights, (3) protect natural resources, and (4) improve health, education, and economic and community development. Association staff members, in five offices around the U.S., respond to observed problems and requests for assistance through a variety of means, including:

Direct advocacy	Public education	Policy development
Grants	Legislation drafting	Technical support
Legal assistance	Research	Congressional testimony
amicus curiae briefs	Advice to agencies	Scholarship programs

For additional information, contact:

Association on American Indian Affairs
245 Fifth Avenue
New York, New York 10016
(212) 689-8720

International Indian Treaty Council

The International Indian Treaty Council (IITC) was established in 1974 as an advocacy and educational organization concerned with issues affecting indigenous people from all areas of the world (Scheurkogel 1992). Besides having a mission of countering the negative effects of 500 years of Euro-American influence, the Council is involved in a variety of specific issues important to Native people, including the environment, religious freedom, protection of sacred sites, and other socio-political issues. IITC is a non-governmental organization, in consultative status (category II), with the United Nations Economic and Social Council. Representatives annually present testimony and documentation on Native issues before the U.N. Commission on Human Rights (International Indian Treaty Council 1992). In the San Francisco Bay area, the Council is also active in hosting noted speakers, sponsoring a regular radio broadcast on news in Indian country, distributing timely information on Native issues to the media, and holding fund-raising events (Stanley 1992).

For additional information, contact:

International Indian Treaty Council
710 Clayton St., Apt. 1
San Francisco, California 94117
(415) 566-0251

Leonard Peltier Defense Committee

The Leonard Peltier Defense Committee (LPDC) is a national and international support group organized for the purpose of gaining the release of Leonard Peltier, a Dakota-Ojibwa, from federal prison. Mr. Peltier is serving two consecutive life sentences in Leavenworth Federal Penitentiary for the deaths of two FBI agents in 1975 (Leonard Peltier Defense Committee 1991).

On June 26, 1975, two FBI agents drove onto private Indian land on the Pine Ridge Reservation in South Dakota, where Peltier and other AIM members were staying at the invitation of the owners. Confusion remains as to why the agents were there and what happened to precipitate the shootout. The LPDC asserts the incident was the culmination of an FBI conspiracy against AIM and its members. The agents' abrupt appearance and behavior, LPDC suggests, directly caused the shootout, and Peltier and others were acting in self-defense. The FBI, however, claims the agents were ambushed by distant gunfire from AIM members and were subsequently executed at close range. Initially, four Indian men were charged equally with aiding and abetting in the deaths of the agents. Two were acquitted and the government dropped the charges on the third. Concentrating its efforts on Peltier, the government obtained a conviction in April 1977 in U.S. District Court in North Dakota (Matthiessen 1991).

U.S. Circuit Court Judge Gerald W. Heaney (1991), who served as a member of the appellate court in two of the Peltier appeals (in 1984 and 1986), has concluded that "the United States government must share the responsibility with the Native Americans for the June 26 [1975] firefight....The government's role in escalating the conflict into a firefight...can properly be considered as a mitigating circumstance. ...The FBI used improper tactics in securing Peltier's extradition from Canada and in otherwise investigating and trying the Peltier case."

Although his name is not widely known in the United States, Leonard Peltier is known to millions of Europeans as a "political prisoner" who was targeted by the FBI, in its efforts in the 1970s, to disintegrate AIM and other activist groups of the era (Savilla 1991). Currently, LPDC is campaigning to obtain Peltier's freedom through Executive Clemency by the President. This campaign has many who oppose it, including some members of the Indian community, but it also has the support of Judge Heaney, several important members of

Congress, and numerous U.S. and foreign citizens who believe
Leonard Peltier was the victim of an abuse of the justice system. The
recently released motion picture, *Incident at Oglala*, is a docu-drama on
Leonard Peltier's story and the broader issues surrounding it.

For additional information, contact:

Leonard Peltier Defense Committee
P.O. Box 583
Lawrence, Kansas 66044
(913) 842-5774

National Congress of American Indians

The National Congress of American Indians (NCAI) was founded in
1944. The dual purposes of this non-profit organization are to (1) provide unity and cooperation among American Indian governments for
the protection of individual and tribal rights and (2) promote the
common welfare of American Indians. NCAI began with fewer than
100 members, from a small number of tribes. It now has 136 member
tribes with a constituency of approximately 600,000 Native people.
Organized as a confederation of member tribal governments, NCAI is
now the largest, second oldest, and perhaps most representative
national American Indian and Alaska Native organization in the
country (National Congress of American Indians 1991 and 1992).

The five operating principles of the NCAI are:

1. Protect Indian and Native traditional cultural and religious rights.
2. Seek appropriate, equitable, and beneficial services and programs
   for Indian and Native governments and people.
3. Secure and preserve Indian and Native rights under treaties and
   agreements with the United States, as well as under federal
   statutes, case law, and administrative decisions and rulings.
4. Promote the common welfare and enhance the quality of life of
   Indian and Native people.
5. Promote a better understanding among the general public concerning Indian and Native governments, Native sovereignty, and
   Native people and their rights.

For additional information, contact:

National Congress of American Indians
900 Pennsylvania Avenue, S.E.
Washington, D.C. 20003
(202) 546-9404

National Indian Education Association

The National Indian Education Association (NIEA) is a non-profit organization that was chartered in 1970. With a nationwide membership of between 1,500 and 2,000 individuals actively concerned with Indian education, it is considered by many to be the foremost voice for Indian education in the U.S. The Association is dedicated to promoting high quality education for American Indian and Alaska Native people, while protecting traditional cultures and values. The NIEA's chartered goals are:

(1) Communication–to conduct an annual National Conference on American Indian education and hold specific workshops in conjunction with the conference; to disseminate specific issue alerts; to issue a bimonthly newsletter and other presentations; to conduct hearings and surveys; to construct position papers.

(2) Advocacy–to evaluate and improve delivery of state and local educational services; to intercede and establish liaison with state and federal agencies; to issue analysis and reaction strategies; to define issues in anticipation rather than in reaction; to work in the area of legislative analysis; and to work in the area of employment opportunities.

(3) Technical Assistance–to assess and coordinate existing technical assistance sources; to add services where needed, given NIEA resources and capacity.

(4) Long-Range Issues and Goals of NIEA–to perform a clearinghouse function; to coordinate NIEA efforts closely with state, tribal, and local Indian education associations; to maintain a directory of Indian professionals; to conduct education workshops on Indian education for non-Indians; to improve the quality of education in both Bureau of Indian Affairs and Public Schools. [National Indian Education Association 1991, p. 2]

For additional information, contact:

National Indian Education Association
1819 "H" Street, N.W., Suite 800
Washington, D.C. 20006
(202) 835-3001

National Indian Media Association

The National Indian Media Association is a non-profit group that was formed late in 1991. Besides providing help to Indians who work in the professional media, the association serves as a focal point or clearinghouse to direct mainstream media through the complex network of contacts for Native American information. It does this by arranging interviews with tribal leaders and personalities. Through these efforts, the association works to help overcome the many misunderstandings and stereotypes about Native people that continue to be presented by the media. Membership in the organization is open to all media professionals, whether Indian or non-Indian (The Lakota Times 1991).

For additional information, contact:

National Indian Media Association
National Press Building
Suite 2091
Washington, D.C. 20056
(202) 822-7226

National Indian Youth Council

The National Indian Youth Council (NIYC) is one of the country's oldest national Indian organizations. It was founded in 1961 to help protect traditional tribal rights and values through education and litigation. Since then it has grown to a national membership of more than 15,000 (National Indian Youth Council 1991a).

In the 1960s, the Council was primarily a civil rights organization, pressing such issues as treaty rights for northwestern tribes and coordinating Indian aspects of the "Poor Peoples' Campaign" in Washington, D.C. In the 1970s, the NIYC was chiefly an environmental organization, aiding tribes beset by problems associated with environmental issues such as coal strip mining and uranium mining. As times have changed, the Council has expanded its activities to encompass other concerns, including freedom of religion, increased Indian political participation, voting rights protection, Indian education, job training and placement, education of the general public about Indian issues, and international Indian issues (National Indian Youth Council 1991b). Regarding the latter topic, the NIYC now has Non-Governmental Organization status with the Economic and Social Council of the United Nations. The Youth Council now works with the U.N. to promote Indian interests and causes throughout the hemisphere. Its representatives attend relevant international meetings, disseminate information to U.S. tribes about indigenous people in other countries, and promote cultural exchanges among Indians of different countries (National Indian Youth Council 1991c).

For additional information, contact:

> National Indian Youth Council
> 318 Elm Street
> Albuquerque, New Mexico 87102
> (505) 247-2251

Native American Rights Fund

The Native American Rights Fund, affectionately referred to as "NARF," is a non-profit organization that was incorporated in 1971. NARF specializes in protection of the rights of Indians and Alaska Natives. Its principal activities involve (a) preservation of tribal existence, (b) protection of tribal natural resources, (c) promotion of human rights, (d) accountability of governments to Native Americans, and (e) development of Indian law.

NARF is known primarily for its legal research and advocacy roles. In its more than 20 years of operation, the organization and its sophisticated legal staff have successfully represented Indian tribes and individuals in nearly every state in the country. Through its involvement in hundreds of cases, it has touched on every area and issue in the complex field of Indian law. NARF has also developed an Indian law library of significant national stature.

For additional information, contact:

> Native American Rights Fund
> 1506 Broadway
> Boulder, Colorado 80302
> (303) 447-8760

SECTION M: ALASKA

> *The name "Alaska" is said to have its origin in the Aleut word*
> *"Alaxaxaq." Its meaning is "the mainland" or, more literally,*
> *"the object toward which the action of the sea is directed."*
>
> Arnold 1976

M-1. *How did Euro-American control and influence over Alaska*
and its Native people begin and evolve?

The vast majority of the history of contact between Alaska Natives
and Euro-American nations involves only two countries—Russia and
the United States. The general experience of Alaska Natives with the
Russians and the Americans contrasts greatly, in several respects,
from that of other Native groups in the lower 48 states. For example,
there was little armed conflict between whites and Alaska Natives.
No treaties were made by the U.S. or Russian governments with
Native groups. Except for Russian enslavement of Aleuts in the
1700s, neither government assumed the type of control over Native
lives that developed in other parts of the U.S. And, a reservation system was never permanently instituted (Spicer 1982). Because specifics
of Alaska history are unfamiliar to many people, the two eras of
Russian and American possession of Alaska merit some review.

The Russian Era

Spanish and Portuguese explorers may have ventured into Alaskan
waters in the late-1500s. However, it wasn't until the mid-1700s, 250
years after Columbus landed in the Bahamas, that Alaska was officially "discovered" in the name of Russia.

Vitus Bering, a Danish navigator sailing on behalf of Russia in
1728, traveled through the strait that now bears his name. He landed
on and named the Diomede Islands, but heavy fog prevented him
from discovering the Alaska mainland which lay just 30 miles to the
east. On his second voyage, in 1741, however, Bering and his expedition sighted Mt. St. Elias, in the southeast region of Alaska, and
briefly explored the coastal area. One of the first of several Russian
reconnaissance parties was lost near present-day Sitka in a hostile
encounter with Native people, probably Tlingit warriors. Bering died

216

from poor health and depression during the latter portion of this second voyage. Nonetheless, his voyages established Russia's claim to Alaska. The second expedition had returned to Russia with an impressive collection of valuable sea otter furs, thus launching what proved to be a remarkably rich fur trade (Rogers 1990).

By 1763, independent Russian trading companies and adventurers had moved across the Aleutian Island chain and penetrated as far east as Kodiak Island. It was there, at Three Saints Bay, that the first permanent Russian settlement was established in 1784 (Lynch 1990). During their tenure, the Russians went on to occupy most of the economically strategic areas of coastal Alaska, except for the northern part of the territory.

Apart from one or two locations, like Kodiak and Sitka, permanent Russian settlements were very small, often having only a dozen inhabitants. Most locations were simple trading posts that were manned by one or two Russians who dealt primarily with Aleuts, Koniags, Chugachmuit, some of the southwestern Eskimos, and perhaps a few Tanainas. The Athapaskans and Russians had almost no contact. (The principal Native cultural areas are shown in Figure 10.)

The first 50 years of Russian activity in Alaska were marked by murder and enslavement of the peaceful Aleuts and, probably, some of the Pacific Eskimo people. It was also a period when the formerly vast populations of fur-bearing animals were plundered. The brutal fur traders had simple reasons for the way they treated the Aleuts. Because the Aleuts were excellent hunters of the valuable sea otter, the traders wanted their service. When the Aleuts resisted enslavement, the Russians frequently killed whole groups of them to induce the remaining people to submit (Arnold 1976).

To establish some kind of constructive control, the Czarist government chartered the Russian American Company in 1799 as the sole trading enterprise, with absolute domination over all aspects of Russian America. For more than two decades, relative peace, order, systematic exploration, and expansion of the fur trade occurred. At any one time, probably fewer than 800 Russians were found in all of Alaska (Lynch 1991). They and their hundreds of Aleut "employees" accomplished the work for the Russian American Company. Many Aleuts even joined the Russian Orthodox Church, learned Russian, and made a career out of working for the Company. (Even today, a

Figure 10. This map shows the principal Native cultural areas in Alaska at the beginning of Russian occupancy in the mid-18th century. (After Prucha 1990a.)

number of middle-aged and older Aleuts speak English, Russian, and Aleut.) Most of the other Alaska Natives were largely left to themselves, though many along the coastal regions did engage in regular activity with non-Indian trading interests.

In the 18th and 19th centuries, English, French, Spanish, and American explorers and whalers charted Alaskan waters, explored much of the coastline, and traded with some of the Native groups along the coast. The Russians, in the meantime, tried repeatedly to expand their operations eastward, to control southeast Alaska. They never quite succeeded, however. For example, all the residents of one early settlement near Yakutat were killed by Tlingits. The first Russian settlement at Sitka in 1802 had the same fate. The Russians resorted to a combined naval-ground operation to drive the Tlingits out of Sitka in 1804. After that, the Tlingits merely tolerated the Russian presence in the immediate Sitka area and remained a serious threat to the intruders through the 1850s.

Continued intrusions by British and American fur traders forced the Russians to grant equal trading rights to these interests in an 1824 agreement. That resulted in an increase in multi-national contact for most coastal and near-interior Native people. By 1839, the Hudson's Bay Company had encroached on southeastern Alaska territory to such an extent that Russians were forced to lease the entire region to this competitor (Rogers 1990).

Over the next three decades, Russian profits from Alaska declined steadily while costs of administration kept rising. The adverse economic situation, disastrous effects of the Crimean War (1853-1856), and the lingering threat of further armed conflict in Europe caused Russia to try to interest the United States in purchasing Alaska in 1859. Preoccupied with domestic problems, the U.S. declined the offer until after the Civil War. A treaty of purchase was signed on March 30, 1867, ratified by the Senate on April 9, and signed by President Andrew Johnson on May 28. A formal transfer of the territory was made during a ceremony at Sitka on October 18, 1867. The purchase price was an incredibly low $7.2 million, or roughly two cents an acre (Lynch 1990)

The American Era

Even prior to the payment of the money for Alaska, Americans began moving in to take control of the assets of the Russian American Company. These included forts, schools, foundries, coal mines, farms, livestock operations, and, of course, the Native trade infrastructure (Lynch 1990).

As was similar with other Euro-American land transfers, the Native people of Alaska were not consulted in any way regarding the change in "ownership" of their land and resources–or their overnight change in nationality. The 1867 land cession treaty with Russia, hastily negotiated and drawn, did not clearly define the legal status, basic rights, and matters of land ownership relevant to Alaska Natives (Arnold 1976). Article III of the treaty did mention them however.

> The uncivilized tribes will be subject to such laws and regulations as the United States may, from time to time, adopt in regard to aboriginal tribes of that country.

In the beginning years of U.S. control of Alaska, the area was commonly viewed as being useless and was referred to as "Seward's

Folly" or "Seward's Icebox." This was because Secretary of State William Seward had championed the land purchase. Although some limited economic development took place in the early period of U.S. possession, the region was generally neglected by the government. For 17 years, Alaska was successively under the nominal administration of the War Department, Treasury Department, and the Navy. The government largely stayed out of the everyday lives of Natives and non-Natives, with the exception of several forced intrusions by the Army and Navy into Tlingit affairs (Arnold 1976; Lynch 1990).

In 1884, Congress passed an Alaska "Organic Act" establishing a civilian government for the area, which was declared to be a "civil and judicial district." The "general laws of the State of Oregon" and the mining laws of the U.S. were to be applied. A gold discovery near Juneau prompted this legislative action. Its main purpose was the legal control of mining activity and adjudication of disputes over land. Significantly, the general land laws of the U.S. were not applied to Alaska, and the issue of Native land claims was deferred.

> [T]he Indians or other persons in said district shall not be disturbed in the possession of any lands actually in their use or occupation or now claimed by them, but the terms under which said persons may acquire title to such lands is reserved for future legislation by Congress.... [Organic Act, p. 26]

From 1880 to 1910, establishment of fish canneries, discoveries of gold, the large influx of non-Natives, the increased importation of outside influences, and the spread of diseases like influenza and tuberculosis greatly disrupted the Native population. Many of the best of the traditional fishing and hunting sites were taken by non-Natives, food became scarce as the fish and game populations decreased, and living conditions deteriorated. Many Native people simply did not survive the transition.

When the Russians arrived in Alaska in the mid-1700s, it is estimated that the Native population consisted of 74,000 Indians, Eskimos, and Aleuts (Arnold 1976). When the U.S. took possession in 1867, the Native population, including 1,400 mixed-bloods, had fallen to an official count of 28,254 (Case 1984). In 1880, at the beginning of three decades of feverish economic development, there were 32,996 Natives and only 430 non-Natives in Alaska. By the end of the gold rush era, in 1910, the Native population had fallen 23 percent from the 1880 level, to 25,331. The non-Native population, however, had increased 9,000 percent, to 39,035. The non-Native population had done well enough during that time period to enable them to push Congress to move Alaska's status one step up from a "judicial district" to a United States territory in 1912.

Where was the BIA all this time? The primary legal status of Alaska Natives–following the 1867 purchase and the 1884 Organic Act, and up until Congressional action in 1905–was presumed by most people to equate with non-Native legal status. That is, Natives were not considered to have separate "Indian" status such as that held by Native people in the lower 48 states. The BIA, therefore, did not get involved. Significantly, there had been no distinction between Native and non-Native residents of Alaska with regard to federal educational services. There was no Indian agency in Alaska, and the Bureau of Education–not the Bureau of Indian Affairs–provided educational services "without regard to race" (Case 1984).

In 1905, Congress passed an education bill, called the Nelson Act, in which it recognized Alaska Natives as a separate group of Alaska residents and specifically allowed for appropriations for the "education and support of the Eskimos, Indians and other Natives of Alaska." This was one of the first of a number of legislative, judicial, and

PHOTO COURTESY OF THE SMITHSONIAN INSTITUTION

This photo from the Smithsonian archives shows Eskimos and store houses at Togiak, Alaska, about the beginning of the twentieth century.

administrative developments which finally led to assumption of responsibility for Alaska Native affairs by the Bureau of Indian Affairs
in 1931. Seven years earlier, Alaska Natives had also gained U.S. citizenship under the Indian Citizenship Act of 1924.

As described in Part III of this book, the Indian Reorganization
Act of 1934 provided American Indians with increased opportunities
for land retention, self-government, and economic development.
Originally, the act did not fully apply to Alaska. A 1936 amendment,
however, applied the bill to the unique circumstances of Alaska.
Numerous Native village governments were organized under the act,
a few reservations were established (later to be dissolved), and some
Native businesses were chartered or financed.

World War II brought great change to Alaska and its Native people. The Japanese invaded the Aleutian Islands in 1942, even taking a
small group of Aleuts back to Japan as prisoners of war. Military personnel numbering 200,000 were sent by the U.S. to the territory. The
Alcan Highway was completed. Many Native people were displaced
for security reasons or voluntarily left their homes to work in
defense-related jobs. Military construction boomed, bringing in more
civilians; and many military personnel remained in Alaska after their
tours of duty or else later retired to the territory. As the population
increased, so did the desire for statehood. On January 3, 1959, Alaska
became the 49th state.

Alaska Native government, BIA administration, and efforts at
defining and protecting Native rights limped along through the
1940s, the 1950s, and the early-1960s. One very positive development
was the beginning of widespread provision of health care services to
Native people, initiated in the 1950s. A growing "background noise,"
however, was the long-ignored question of Native land claims. In the
1960s, it rose to a thunder and resulted in passage of the revolutionary and far-reaching Alaska Native Claims Settlement Act (ANCSA)
of 1971. (A discussion of ANCSA is provided in the answer to question M-4 in this section of the book.)

M-2. *What is the legal definition of an Alaska Native?*

The Alaska Native Claims Settlement Act (1971) contains the definition shown below. It combines a blood quantum and document standard, and it includes the more socially realistic community standard for "Indians" put forth by Cohen (1982). (That standard is mentioned in the answer to question A-1 of this book.)

> (b) "Native" means a citizen of the United States who is a person of one-fourth degree or more of Alaska Indian...Eskimo, or Aleut blood, or combination thereof. The term includes any Native as so defined either or both of whose adoptive parents are not Natives. It also includes, in the absence of proof of a minimum blood quantum, any citizen of the United States who is regarded as an Alaska Native by the Native village or Native group of which he claims to be a member and whose father or mother is (or, if deceased, was) regarded as Native by any village or group. [43 USC 1602]

Technical definitions are also given in the act for "village" and "group." The act further states that, in any questions regarding eligibility for enrollment (i.e., whether or not someone is a Native), the decisions of the Secretary of the Interior are final.

M-3. *What is the Alaska Federation of Natives, and what are its history, mission, and current concerns?*

The Alaska Federation of Natives, or AFN, is the major advocacy and lobbying organization for the Native people of Alaska. It is a corporation formed largely to represent the concerns of Alaska Natives before Congress, the Alaska State Legislature, and federal and state government agencies. AFN's board of directors includes representatives of Native non-profit regional associations, Native regional corporations, and the Alaska Native village corporations formed under the Alaska Native Claims Settlement Act, or ANCSA (1971).

In 1966, more than 400 Alaska Natives, representing 17 Native organizations, gathered in Anchorage for a conference. Their purpose was to address aboriginal land rights and other common problems and to begin the process of organizing AFN. From 1966 to 1971, AFN worked primarily to achieve a fair land claims settlement, which resulted in the signing into law of ANCSA on December 8, 1971.

After passage of ANCSA, the AFN provided technical assistance to Native groups to help implement the terms of the act, including the establishment of corporations mandated by ANCSA. Subsequently, the AFN managed several statewide human service programs, which were later transferred to regional associations, as the latter grew in strength and independence.

In the late-1970s and the 1980s, AFN was a key figure in passage of the Alaska National Interest Lands Conservation Act (1980) and the very important 1987 amendments to ANCSA, known as the "1991 legislation." Today the Federation continues to work at the federal, state, and local levels on pressing social, tribal, and economic issues.

The overall mission of the AFN is to enhance and promote the cultural, economic, and political voice of the entire community of Alaska Natives. The Federation's declared goals for the 1990s reveal the problems currently faced by Native people and the Federation's resolve to address those problems affirmatively. These goals are presented in the box on the following page.

All information for this answer was provided courtesy of the Alaska Federation of Natives, Inc. (1991a and 1991c). For further information, contact the AFN, 1577 "C" Street, Suite 100, Anchorage, Alaska 99501; phone (907) 274-3611.

M-4. *What is the history of the Native land claims issue, and what is the Alaska Native Claims Settlement Act?*

Background

When Alaska was purchased by the U.S. in 1867, and again when the first civil government was organized by Congress in 1884, the issue of Native land claims was put on hold. As stated earlier, no treaty was ever entered into with Alaska Natives. The coming decades of economic and military development led to increasing encroachment on what had always been Native land. Little of real substance was done to address the land and resource rights of Alaska Natives until the

GOALS OF THE ALASKA FEDERATION OF NATIVES

With respect for our elders and ancestors, and in dedication to our children and future generations, we are hereby committed to:

- Protect the use, occupancy and ownership of Native lands
- Promote the highest possible quality of life for Alaska Native people
- Promote control by Alaska Natives over their lives and communities and the institutions that affect them
- Promote pride in heritage and development of self-esteem among Alaska Natives
- Preserve and strengthen Alaska Native cultures
- Foster an understanding of Alaska Native cultures within the larger society
- Secure equitable participation in the educational, health, social, political and economic systems that affect Alaska Natives
- Promote and protect the unique, special relationship and entitlements that exist between Alaska Natives (and Native institutions) and the federal government
- Promote the recognition and development of Alaska Native organizations and institutions
- Strengthen and promote the family unit
- Eliminate alcohol and drug abuse among Alaska Natives
- Protect all benefits and rights of ANCSA and its amendments
- Secure economic employment opportunities and benefits enjoyed by the larger society
- Ensure the spiritual well-being and the physical, mental and emotional health and safety of Alaska Natives
- Protect rights and opportunities to pursue Native subsistence activities and lifestyles
- Eliminate family violence, child neglect and abuse among Alaska Natives
- Promote educational goals and academic achievement levels that provide real opportunities for each person to excel in today's society and that meet the special needs of Alaska Natives
- Urge Alaska Native leaders to actively participate in youth activities as role models and mentors
- Foster statewide unity and trust in representing the common interest of Native people and in celebrating Native cultures

1960s. A series of significant events then brought the land claims issue to a head.

In 1957, major oil fields were discovered in the Kenai Peninsula and Cook Inlet regions. The associated population increase helped lead to Alaskan statehood in 1959. The statehood act granted the State of Alaska the right to select 103 million acres of federal public domain land for itself. In 1961, state land selections were threatening lands which Native peoples considered to be their own. Native protests and complaints to the government began in earnest. At the same time, proposals for federal land withdrawals also threatened lands claimed by Natives.

A statewide conference of Native groups in 1966 resulted in formation of the Alaska Federation of Natives (AFN) which helped spearhead the land rights battle. Also in 1966, Secretary of the Interior Stewart Udall stopped the transfer, to the State of Alaska, of lands claimed by Natives until Congress could act upon the claims. By then, the amount of land claimed had grown to 380 million acres. The first bills designed to settle land claims were introduced in Congress in 1967.

In 1968, huge oil and gas reserves were discovered along Alaska's North Slope. That same year a state-supported Land Claims Task Force recommended a 40 million-acre settlement, and a newly published government study supported the validity of Native land claims. Sales of oil leases in the North Slope area brought the State $900 million in 1969. Also in 1969, oil companies and other business interests placed their full support behind efforts to reach a land settlement quickly so the Alaska pipeline project could get in motion.

A land claims bill passed the Senate in 1970, but the legislation provided only the relatively small amount of 10 million acres of land. Native interests protested successfully in the House. In 1971, Congress passed the Alaska Native Claims Settlement Act (ANCSA) and it was signed into law by President Nixon on December 18. (For additional background on ANCSA, see Arnold 1976, Lynch 1990 and 1991, Rogers 1990, and Tundra Times 1991.)

Basic Provisions of ANCSA

Arnold (1976) summarized the provisions of the Alaska Native Claims Settlement Act. Alaska Natives were to receive full title to 44 million acres of the 380 million acres they had claimed. Native claims based on aboriginal title were said to be "extinguished." The several existing reservations, except for the Annette Island Reserve in far southeast Alaska, were revoked. In addition, monetary compensation for the extinguished land claims was set at $962.5 million. Congress authorized $462.5 million of the monetary award to be appropriated from the federal treasury and to be paid into the Alaska Native Fund over an 11-year period. The remaining $500 million was to be paid into the fund from a percentage of oil and gas revenues as these minerals were developed on federal and state lands. Payments from the Alaska Native Fund were to be made only to regional Native corporations. They, in turn, were to retain part of the funds and pay out part to village corporations and individual Natives. The amount of money each regional corporation received was to be based on the proportion which its enrolled Natives represented to the total number enrolled for all regional corporations.

All U.S. citizens of one-fourth or more Alaska Native blood, and who were alive on December 18, 1971, were qualified to participate in the settlement—unless they were members of the Annette Island Reserve community (which had no relevant claims to be settled).

Unique to federal Indian law, benefits under the settlement were to accrue to eligible Natives through modern Native corporations, and *not* through the traditional entities of tribes, clans, families, or similar communities. All eligible Natives were to become stockholders of their appropriate corporations. Those Natives born after December 18, 1971, were barred from corporate membership and from obtaining stock, except through inheritance.

The initial step for Natives to become stockholders was for them to be enrolled as corporate members. This involved the registering of names, communities, and regions of permanent residence, and the required proving of Indian, Inuit, or Aleut heritage. Based upon the region of one's permanent residence, he or she would be enrolled in one of 12 regional corporations created under the act. ANCSA was later amended to allow the formation of a 13th "regional" corporation for those Alaska Natives living outside the state.

Regarding land distribution, 22 million acres of the total were to be for Native village selection. Just as with the monetary distribution, the number of acres to which a village was entitled was to be determined by its enrollment. Village corporations would own only the surface rights to their land selections. The subsurface of the village corporation land, and most of the remaining land of the 44 million acres, went to the 12 regional corporations. The comparatively small amount of remaining acreage was allocated for a few special corporations that were organized in largely non-Native communities. These lands were intended for Natives or groups of Natives residing away from villages, for pending Native allotments, and for cemeteries and historic sites.

Afterthoughts

When ANCSA was passed, it was heralded as a monumental piece of legislation and the most generous land claims settlement ever made with Native Americans. Alaska Natives were granted title to more land than was held in trust for all tribes, combined, in the rest of the United States. In addition, compensation for lands surrendered by the Native people was about four times greater than the amount which all the tribes in the lower 48 states had won from the Indian Claims Commission over its 25-year history (Worl 1988).

Delegates in Anchorage, Alaska, at the 1991 convention of the Alaska Federation of Natives. The banner marks the 20th anniversary of enactment of the Alaska Native Claims Settlement Act. Photo by Jeff Silverman, Alaska Federation of Natives.

Alaska Natives were, at first, elated with the settlement. Only five years later, however, it was seen as a flawed victory. Some analysts questioned if ANCSA was actually a new form of termination–the disastrous 1950s policy of "terminating" the legal existence of tribes and their reservations. At the base of Native apprehension was the novel corporate approach employed in settling the land claims. The potential long-term effects of the corporate approach had somehow gone unchallenged until after passage of the act (Getches 1985).

The settlement was a distinct departure from previous Indian settlements. ANCSA land would be held by the Native corporations under fee simple title rather than as tribal reservation land held in trust by the federal government. Thus, the Alaska lands would not be protected under trust status. Congress clearly intended that ANCSA assets would provide a means for economic development and Native assimilation into the larger society (Worl 1988).

Traditional cultures and Native subsistence hunting and fishing were now seen as being threatened by potential development at the hands of Native corporations. These "for profit" corporations were designed to make money for shareholders. It soon became evident that the removal of restrictions on the alienation of corporate stock to non-Natives could result in the loss of Native ownership and control of their own corporations. Ironically, some Native leaders are now looking for legislative, judicial, and administrative means of estab lishing reservation status, tribal governments, sovereignty, and feder- al trusteeship over lands and resources to help protect their land set tlement legacy and traditional cultures (Alaska Federation of Natives 1992; Getches 1985; Worl 1988).

ANCSA hasn't been a failure, but it has been a disappointment in some ways. A number of flaws have been addressed in amendments and related legislation, including the Alaska National Interest Lands Conservation Act (ANILCA) of 1980, the ANCSA Amendments of 1987, the 1990 act authorizing a Joint Federal-State Commission on Policies and Programs Affecting Alaska Natives, and a more recent bill (Title III of Public Law 102-201) that extended certain protections against alienation of stock and hostile corporate takeovers until July 1993. The Joint Commission's activities and investigations, just under way, are intended to lead to additional corrective actions relating to ANCSA as well as to other actions relating to non-ANCSA issues.

Delegates of the Alaska Federation of Natives meet in caucus to discuss the issue of hostile corporate takeovers at their 1991 convention. Photo by Jeff Silverman, Alaska Federation of Natives.

M-5. *How much land is held by the Native people of Alaska?*

To be able to put the Native landholdings of Alaska into perspective, one should first understand just how large Alaska is. The total area of the state, including land and interior water, covers 591,000 square miles. That is 378,240,000 acres–more than twice the size of Texas and a dozen times the size of New York state. Border-to-border distances are also immense. Measuring the north-to-south and east-to-west extremities, Alaska stretches roughly 1,400 and 2,400 miles, respectively, including the Aleutian Island chain.

The Native landholding situation in Alaska is quite different from that in the lower 48 states. Whereas the great majority of Indian land in the 48 states is reservation-related trust land, 98 percent of the Native land in Alaska is privately owned, non-reservation land that is *not* held in trust by the United States. There are three categories of Native land in Alaska and they are discussed separately below.

Tribal trust land

Annette Island Indian Reservation, also known as Metlakatla, is the only remaining Indian reservation in the state. It contains all of the tribal trust land in Alaska–86,741 acres (Bureau of Indian Affairs 1985a). Again, title to this category of land is held in trust by the U.S. The reservation is located in the far southeastern tip of Alaska, where it is home to the Tsimshian Indians. They migrated to Annette Island from nearby British Columbia, Canada, in 1887, under the leadership of the Anglican missionary, William Duncan. In 1891, Congress enacted legislation making the Island a reservation (Case 1984).

Individually owned trust land

Some 884,100 acres of numerous, individually owned, allotments of trust land are located in several areas of Alaska (Bureau of Indian Affairs 1985). This acreage is the legacy of federal land policies predating the Alaska Native Claims Settlement Act (ANCSA) of 1971.

Native corporation land

The provisions of ANCSA led to the formation of 12 Native regional corporations, a 13th "regional" corporation for non-resident Alaska Natives (without a defined area), and just over 200 village corporations distributed throughout the 12 regional corporations. (See Figure 11.) These are all for-profit entities. Full private ownership of 40 million acres was promised to the Native corporations as partial compensation for the extinguishing of aboriginal title to the state. In addition, seven village corporations, on five revoked reservations, voted to accept full title to their former reservations and forego other benefits of the settlement act. This brought the total ANCSA land to 43.7 million acres of widely distributed parcels for the Native corporations, or 11.6% of the state. About 80 percent of the land selections and title transfers had been completed as of December 1991 (Silverman 1991b). Much of the allocation of ANCSA land to the Native corporations is based on corporate enrollment numbers which relate to eligibility requirements at the time the act was passed (Arnold 1976).

The U.S. Bureau of Land Management (BLM) is the agency responsible for the ANCSA land distribution process. Data originating from the Anchorage office of the BLM are presented in the table on the next page. This shows how the 43.7 million acres will have been allotted when the process is completed.

ALASKA NATIVE LAND ALLOCATIONS

Region	Regional Corporation Lands	Village Corporation Lands	Former Reservation Village Lands	Totals
	(to the nearest acre)			
Ahtna	1,038,256	691,200		1,729,456
Aleut	142,533	1,221,120		1,363,653
Arctic Slope	4,177,586	852,480		5,030,066
Bering Straits	293,420	1,820,160	1,433,932	3,547,512
Bristol Bay	234,303	2,718,720		2,953,024
Calista	570,132	5,644,800		6,214,932
Chugach	427,976	460,800		888,776
Cook Inlet	1,590,667	668,160		2,258,827
Doyon	8,748,591	3,248,640	2,543,087	14,540,317
Koniag	116,756	923,520		1,040,276
NANA	954,523	1,198,080		2,152,603
Totals	18,294,743	19,447,680	3,977,019	*41,719,442

*Total excludes a 2,000,000-acre land fund from which land is conveyed to Natives (not corporations) pursuant to ANCSA for special purposes, i.e., for cemetery sites and historical places; for Natives living in Sitka, Kenai, Juneau, and Kodiak; for primary places of residence of Natives; and for individual allotments. The excess between the 2,000,000 acres and the total special purpose conveyances will be distributed pro-rata to the regional corporations based on their Native populations. Sealaska Corporation was not entitled to any land under ANCSA because of a pre-ANCSA government settlement with the Tlingit and Haida people. The Thirteenth Regional Corporation received only cash in the ANCSA settlement. [Table information is from Getches 1985.]

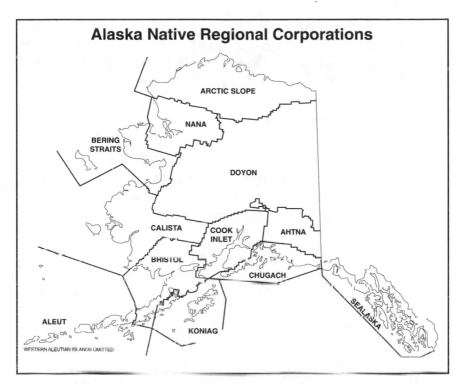

Alaska Native Regional Corporations

Figure 11. Geographic limits of the 12 Native regional corporations established under provisions of the Alaska Native Claims Settlement Act are shown here.

M-6. What is the conflict known as the subsistence issue?

> In the eyes of Native people, "subsistence" is not primarily a question of animals, or their habitats, or the efficiency of their management by public agencies, or even the constitutionality of their allocation among competing user groups. For us, subsistence is a critical part of a much broader historical question about the status, rights, aspirations and future development of the people who are from Alaska. Subsistence law is social policy on a grand scale. It poses the fundamental question of cultural tolerance in modern society: whether all citizens must be made identical in order to be made equal.
>
> Alaska Federation of Natives 1991b, p. 6

In the early 1990s, the subsistence issue is the dominant political concern for the statewide Native community (Alaska Federation of Natives 1991c). From an all-Alaska perspective, including the views of non-Natives, *the* issue is actually several very emotion-packed issues. In one way or another, all are related to hunting and fishing rights and activities (Burch 1984).

One issue involves the question of whether Alaska lands should be developed–and thus cause interference with fish and wildlife populations–or left in a natural or nearly natural state. Concerns about development of oil and gas in the Alaska National Wildlife Refuge have been the most public of recent development conflicts.

A second issue, being hotly contested in the political arena and in the courts, concerns who should legally control hunting and fishing. Should it be the federal government, the state government, organized regional user groups, or a combination thereof? The Alaska Federation of Natives (AFN) favors management of all fish and game by the state government.

Another heated issue focuses on the question of who is to be permitted to hunt and fish in a state where (1) the population has grown too large for everyone to hunt and fish at a substantial harvest level and (2) important fish and game populations have declined or been

Village elder testifies on the subsistence issue at a public meeting. The earphone is for translation into Yupik Eskimo language. Photo by Jeff Silverman, Alaska Federation of Natives.

Fish drying at Kotzebue Sound, Alaska, in the spring of 1986. Photo by Jimmy Evak, Maniilaq Association.

threatened with decline in recent decades. AFN has urged the legislature and the people of Alaska to adopt a constitutional amendment allowing a statutory subsistence preference for rural residents.

Some of the more prominent interest groups involved in the various aspects of the subsistence issue include sport hunting and fishing organizations, commercial hunting and fishing interests (Native and non-Native), conservation groups, development interests, Native organizations, rural communities, state and federal agencies, and the statewide Native community. Natives believe it is important that others understand they do not view subsistence as an "issue" but, rather, as a cultural and economic fact of life (Silverman 1991a).

M-7. *What are the most pressing socio-economic problems of Alaska Natives, and how are they going to be addressed?*

In 1989, the Alaska Federation of Natives (AFN) produced a startling document titled "The AFN Report on the Status of Alaska Natives: A

Call for Action." The report declared that "the fundamental issue confronting Alaska Natives is the struggle of previously self-sufficient individuals and family units to adjust to rapid social change largely imposed from the outside." It also publicized several significant findings. Among them:

1. A plague of alcohol abuse, violence, and self-destruction is afflicting Alaska Natives.
2. Alaska Natives are more vulnerable to serious injury, infectious disease, and death than non-Natives.
3. Alaska Natives have a growing "at risk" population. (Young adult Natives are adrift between cultures and are often excluded from meaningful and gainful employment.)
4. The village economy cannot meet the needs of the growing Native population.
5. Villages are precariously dependent upon public sector spending, and the cost of living in villages is exorbitant.
6. Native children enter and exit village schools with serious educational handicaps, and their education is worse than mediocre.

ALEUT MONTHS

January—Month of the black cormorant

February—Month when last stored food is eaten

March—Month of hunger, gnawing thongs and straps

April—Month of near hunger

May—Month of flowers

June—Month seals are born

July—Month when young amphibians flourish

August—Month when the grass begins to wither and animals grow thin

September—Month when animals shed fur

October—Month of Autumn

November—Month devoted to hunting

December—Long month

Oliver 1988

Existing efforts directed toward issue definition, analysis, and resolution–by Native groups and state and federal agencies–were found to be inadequate for the severity of the problems and the rapid social change at their core. AFN approached the U.S. Senate Select Committee on Indian Affairs for advice on what should be done and asked the committee to make some recommendations. The result was an important piece of legislation that was added as a rider to the Indian Law Enforcement Reform Act of 1990.

Section 12 of this act (1) acknowledged the existence of "a growing social and economic crisis" among Alaska Natives, (2) declared it was timely and essential to conduct a comprehensive review of federal and state policies affecting these Native people, and (3) authorized establishment of the "Joint Federal-State Commission on Policies and Programs Affecting Alaska Natives." The Commission has 14 voting members, seven appointed by the President and seven by the Governor. All appointments have now been made to the commission and it is now undertaking its responsibilities. As charged by Congress:

(c) The Commission shall —

 (1) conduct a comprehensive study of—

  (A) the social and economic status of Alaska Natives, and

  (B) the effectiveness of those policies and programs of the United States, and the State of Alaska, that affect Alaska Natives,

 (2) conduct public hearings on the subject of such study,

 (3) recommend specific actions to the Congress and to the State of Alaska that —

  (A) help to assure that Alaska Natives have life opportunities comparable to other Americans, while respecting their unique traditions, cultures, and special status as Alaska Natives,

  (B) address, among other things, the needs of Alaska Natives for self-determination, economic self-sufficiency, improved levels of educational achievement, improved health status, and reduced incidence of social problems,

 (4) in developing those recommendations, respect the important cultural differences which characterize Alaska Native groups,

 (5) submit, by no later than the date that is eighteen months after the date of the first meeting of the Commission, a report on the study, together with the recommendations developed under

paragraph (3), to the President, the Congress, the Governor of the State of Alaska, and the legislature of the State of Alaska, and

(6) make such a report available to Alaska Native villages and organizations and to the public.

Expectations are running high in Alaska and Washington, D.C., and much may come from the Joint Commission's endeavors. Time will tell.

SECTION N: THE FUTURE

What is the greatest single issue facing Native Americans in the future?

The same one facing us all–the end of Nature. Without denying the seriousness of the many native issues that require ongoing attention, it is absolutely clear that, unless the planet's immense environmental problems are solved, all other concerns, save nuclear conflagration, won't matter.

> *Respect the Earth or all is a waste.*
>
> Lakota Times
> June 3, 1992

A little over two decades ago, at the time of the first Earth Day, many of us naively thought the overall environmental problem had hit bottom and that the only direction we could reasonably choose to travel from there was up. Instead, following the "me generation" of the 1970s and the selfish decade of the 1980s, things have deteriorated much more than anyone in 1970 would have wanted to imagine. We are now regularly updated by the media with stories that essentially go like this: "Remember how very bad we said it was a little while back? Well, we were wrong. It's much worse."

In early October 1991, Oren Lyons, an Onondaga elder, appeared in an interview on a segment of the CBS television magazine "Sunday Morning." Describing his concerns about environmental degradation, he first made the point that there is plenty of blame to be shared by "all of us." He went on to make a very graphic statement summarizing the effect of environmental damage on the future. He simply said, "We have taken our grandchildren by the hair, tilted their heads back, and slit their throats."

This statement startles and even offends some people. But, unless the reality that caused its expression startles and offends them–and the rest of us–even more, we will continue to go precipitously down the road to virtual destruction of the world's biosphere.

Potentially, the *one* issue over which Indian and non-Indian Americans can most strongly come together–and through which we

can positively contribute to each others' futures—is environmental
cleanup and protection.

The days of tea-and-crumpets conservation are over. We are
talking about deadly issues here, issues that necessitate a most
courageous, sweeping, and accelerated solution in order for the
world's environment to be fit for habitation....

The causes of the environmental crisis are well-known, as
are the solutions....[K]ey social institutions, primarily national
governments, lack the direction and high level of motivation necessary to implement solutions. It is therefore imperative, and
exceedingly appropriate...that "We the People" of the world's
nations [including the Indian nations] begin to resolutely provide our leaders with the strong motivation and direction so des-
perately needed.

Utter, Valen, and Cantu 1989

PART III

A SUMMARY HISTORY

OF

UNITED STATES INDIAN POLICY

One of the enduring issues facing the government and the people of the United States through two centuries of existence is the place of American Indians in American society.

Francis Paul Prucha 1985
In *The Indians in American Society*

History is the essential foundation for an understanding of American Indian law and policy.

American Indian Lawyer Training Program 1988

COLONIAL BEGINNINGS

At its earliest stages, United States Indian policy was most directly influenced by two things: (1) former policies of the British Empire and (2) Indian-U.S. conflicts of the Revolutionary War (Prucha 1985).

British policies toward Indians in what is now U.S. territory evolved over more than a century and a half, from the time of the empire's first permanent settlement in North America in 1607 to the American takeover. Unlike the Spanish, who relied heavily on Native labor and economic activity in their colonization of the Western Hemisphere, the British did not consider indigenous people as particularly necessary to colonial life (United States Commission on Civil Rights 1981). During most of their tenure, the British viewed the Indians under their influence, as trading partners and as potential allies against the ambitions of other European powers. When international intrigue grew during the early- and mid-1700s, however, the Indian tribes were seen to represent a strong balance of power among Spain, France, and England (Bureau of Indian Affairs 1975). Accordingly, the tribes were treated as sovereign nations with whom binding agreements could be made for the benefit of the signatory tribes and European powers.

Until 1755, each of the English colonies had its own policy on Indian affairs. In that year, however, control over Indian affairs was placed directly under the British government. This was in response to competing policies of the French, who were attracting the loyalties of frontier tribes. The British government established a policy intended to (1) protect the tribes from unscrupulous traders and speculators, (2) negotiate boundaries by treaties, (3) enlist tribes on the side of the British in the French and Indian War, and (4) exercise as much control over the fur trade as possible (Bureau of Indian Affairs 1975).

Shortly after the conclusion of the French and Indian War, King George III issued the Proclamation of 1763. It established a boundary along the crest of the Appalachian Mountains, separating "Indian country" to the west from the white settlement territory to the east. (See Figure 12.) The proclamation represented, for the first time in the history of European colonization of the hemisphere, the concrete formalization of the concept of Indian land titles. It prohibited issuance of colonial patents to any lands claimed by a tribe unless the Indian

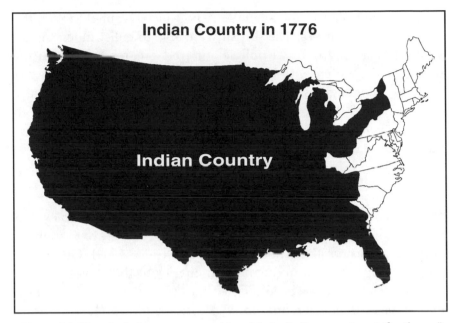

Figure 12. The shaded area was considered to be Indian country at the time of the American Revolution. An earlier boundary line, proclaimed in 1763 by King George III of England, ran along the Appalachian crest. It lay somewhat to the east of the boundary shown here. None of these were sanctioned by law.

or "aboriginal" title had first been extinguished by treaty or purchase. This policy remained in effect through the end of British rule and set the tone for some of the subsequent U.S. approach.

> And whereas it is just and reasonable, and essential to our interest, and the security of our colonists, that the several nations or tribes of Indians, with whom we are connected, and who live under our protection, should not be molested or disturbed in the possession of such parts of our dominions and territories as, not having been ceded to, or purchased by us, are reserved to them or any of them, as their hunting grounds; we do therefore... declare it to be our royal will and pleasure, that no governor...do presume, upon any pretense whatever, to grant warrants of survey, or pass any patents for lands beyond the bounds of their respective governments,...or upon any lands whatever, which not having been ceded to, or purchased by us, as aforesaid, are reserved to the said Indians, or any of them.
>
> Proclamation of 1763
> (Quoted from O'Brien 1989, p. 48)

In the first years of the Revolution, both sides wanted to keep the friendship of the tribes. The British were able to enlist much Indian support because the royal policies offered greater protection for Indian lands. Siding with the British was, therefore, seen by many tribes as siding against the land-grabbing frontiersmen. The enmity that developed during the fighting of the Revolution continued to influence some of the bureaucrats and politicians who later shaped Indian policy in the early years after the war (Horsman 1988).

THE U. S. LEGACY

Numerous works have been published to describe the complex and often fickle history of federal Indian policy. Some are extremely detailed and serve the scholar well (e.g., Prucha 1984). Others are more appropriate as introductory summaries to the subject matter. One such summary has been selected for use as the core of this third part of the book and is reproduced here in its entirety. The material is taken directly from the second chapter of a report by the United States Commission on Civil Rights (1981), titled *Indian Tribes: A Continuing Quest for Survival*. It includes the sections which begin with "Early United States–Indian Relations: 1776-1830" and run through "The Termination Period: 1945-1960." The final section, "Self-Determination: Post-1960," represents the author's effort to update this brief summary of U.S. Indian policy to the 1990s.

Early United States-Indian Relations: 1776-1830

Conflict regarding relations with Indian tribes was not resolved by the outcome of the Revolutionary War. The United States replaced the Crown, and the States replaced the colonies, but the issue of local versus national interest and control was not settled. The newly formed Continental Congress reserved to itself the power of "managing all affairs with the Indians not members of any of the States," but also provided that the "legislative right of any State, within its own limits, be not infringed" (Articles of Confederation 1781). This essentially codified a dichotomy between national and local views on Indian affairs.

Both the emerging central government and the States agreed that the Indians were needed as allies in the Revolutionary War. As a military imperative they sought to maintain friendly relations with as

many tribes as possible. By 1778 the American government had negotiated its first treaty, with the Delawares.

The role of the central government with respect to the tribes and
the policy it would follow toward them was a much debated issue in
revolutionary times. George Washington played an important role in
formulating policy and made clear in his writings that the Federal
Government would need to intercede on behalf of the tribes:

> To suffer a wide extended Country to be over run with Land
> Jobbers, Speculators, and Monopolisers or even with scattered
> settlers, is, in my opinion, inconsistent with that wisdom and
> policy which our true interest dictates, or that an enlightened
> People ought to adopt and, besides, is pregnant of disputes both
> with the Savages, and among ourselves, the evils of which are
> easier, to be conceived than described; and for what? but to
> aggrandize a few avaricious Men to the prejudice of many, and
> the embarrassment of Government.
>
> Washington 1783

The policy that General Washington would ultimately recommend was pragmatic:

> I am clear in my opinion, that policy and economy point very
> strongly to the expediency of being upon good terms with the
> Indians, and the propriety of purchasing their Lands in prefer-
> ence to attempting to drive them by force of arms out of their
> Country.... In a word there is nothing to be obtained by an Indian
> War but the Soil they live on and this can be had by purchase at
> less expence [sic], and without that bloodshed....
>
> Washington 1783

Washington's advice, accepted by a Nation that was exhausted
and weak, was codified as a proclamation of the Continental Congress
on September 22, 1783. The Ordinance for the Regulation of Indian
Affairs followed in 1786, and in 1787, the Northwest Ordinance. This
often quoted and much violated document expresses the following:

> The utmost good faith shall always be observed towards the
> Indians; their lands and property shall never be taken from them
> without their consent; and, in their property, rights, and liberty,
> they shall never be invaded or disturbed, unless in just and law-
> ful wars authorized by Congress; but laws founded in justice and
> humanity shall from time to time be made for preventing wrongs

being done to them, and for preserving peace and friendship with them.

When the Revolutionary War ended in 1783, the United States embarked on a round of treaties with its former allies as well as with the tribes that had aligned themselves with the British. The United States Constitution, ratified in 1789, confirmed the federal role in Indian policy by assigning Congress the authority to involve itself in Indian affairs. Through the treaty process the United States would acquire both lands and legal responsibilities; the tribes would cede lands and obtain Federal commitments in return. It was believed to be in the clear interest of both the United States Government and the Indian nations, under the military circumstances of the era, to live without war and by contract. Between the end of the French and Indian War (1763) and the end of the War of 1812, the Indian nations were secure in the use and occupancy of their lands. They "in effect parlayed their claims to land into claims for services from the new American government" (Kickingbird and Ducheneaux 1973). The treaty process would continue for almost a hundred years and would acquire millions of acres of land for the U.S. Government to provide to non-Indian settlers. The treaties also built a reservoir of material and political promises to the tribes.

The quest for land for the use of non-Indian settlers took on new impetus at the turn of the 19th century. The Louisiana Purchase in 1803 and the acquisition of Florida in 1812-1819 doubled the United States in size. With this expansion, coupled with the consolidation of military and political strength by the new government and the development of the philosophy of "manifest destiny," Indian tribes faced a dramatic and damaging change in Federal Indian policy.

The Removal Era

The eastern tribes, particularly those in Georgia, faced continuing pressures from State and local authorities to give up their lands and political status. Major court battles were fought. (See *Cherokee Nation v. Georgia* 1831 and *Worcester v. Georgia* 1832.) Influential leaders of the day proposed moving the eastern tribes to the western territories. Thomas Jefferson proposed a constitutional amendment to exchange the Indian land east of the Mississippi for land west of that boundary. This amendment failed, but subsequently congressional authorization was obtained on the same question (in 1804). The western area to which Indians were to be moved was then considered uninhabitable by white people.

The political-military realities between the tribes and the United States had shifted by this period, and the tribes were unable to resist removal. The euphemistic "exchange of lands" began in 1817 and continued until mid-century. Thousands of Indian people, including nearly the entire Indian population that had existed in the southeastern United States, were moved west. (See Figure 13.) The first removal treaty, following soon after the Indian Removal Act of 1830, was the Treaty of Dancing Rabbit Creek with the Choctaw Nation (1830). Although removal was theoretically based on the consent of those removed, it is clear that the eastern tribes were coerced. The ideal of "progress" was invoked to rationalize the forced migrations as inevitable and to obscure the material greed of American expansionism. This period has been described as one of the blackest chapters in American history:

> Tens of thousands of helpless Indians, many of whom had white blood, were wholly or partly civilized, and owned homes, livestock, and farms, suffered incredible hardships.... All their efforts to halt or reverse the government's policy failed, and in the end almost all the members of each of the tribes were removed to different areas in the present State of Oklahoma. Some of them went reluctantly but without defiance; others went in chains. Most of them streamed westward under the watchful eyes of troops who made sure that they kept moving.
>
> Josephy 1968, p. 323

Some tribes did remain in the East. The Nation for the most part, however, acted from this time on as if no Indians existed east of the Mississippi.

The assimilationist movement grew in tandem with the policy of removal. Thomas Jefferson was one of the major supporters of the view that with adequate resources and coaxing Indians could be "civilized" and live in harmony with their white neighbors. The responsibility of civilizing Indians fell to the various benevolent societies and missionary organizations. Until the end of the War of 1812 the missionary effort had been hampered by a lack of funding and a clear sense of direction. The change in national mood accompanying

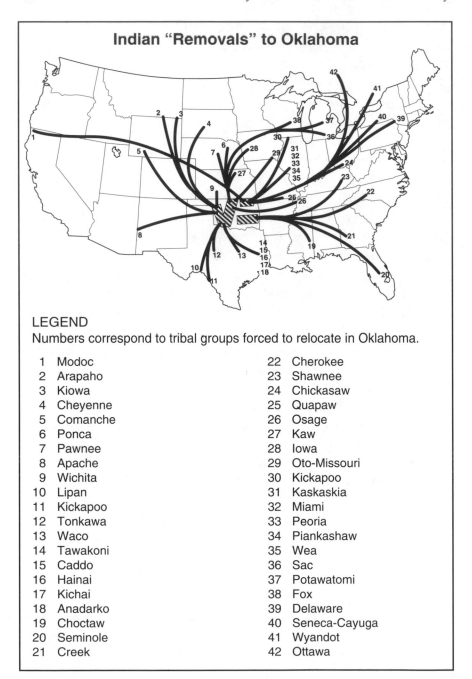

Indian "Removals" to Oklahoma

LEGEND

Numbers correspond to tribal groups forced to relocate in Oklahoma.

1	Modoc	22	Cherokee
2	Arapaho	23	Shawnee
3	Kiowa	24	Chickasaw
4	Cheyenne	25	Quapaw
5	Comanche	26	Osage
6	Ponca	27	Kaw
7	Pawnee	28	Iowa
8	Apache	29	Oto-Missouri
9	Wichita	30	Kickapoo
10	Lipan	31	Kaskaskia
11	Kickapoo	32	Miami
12	Tonkawa	33	Peoria
13	Waco	34	Piankashaw
14	Tawakoni	35	Wea
15	Caddo	36	Sac
16	Hainai	37	Potawatomi
17	Kichai	38	Fox
18	Anadarko	39	Delaware
19	Choctaw	40	Seneca-Cayuga
20	Seminole	41	Wyandot
21	Creek	42	Ottawa

Figure 13. Major "removals" or relocations of Indians to Oklahoma ("Indian Territory") from all across the United States are indicated on this map. Tribal groups were forced to relocate in Oklahoma, beginning in 1817 and continuing into the 1880s.

removal led to the establishment in 1819 of a Civilization Fund, which provided an annual appropriation from Congress to these organizations and gave impetus to the assimilationist movement. The removal period saw the massive movement of missionary stations to west of the Mississippi. From this vantage the missionaries "directed their attention to Indians indigenous to the Indian territory as well as to regaining the confidence of their former eastern charges" (Berkhofer 1967, p. 2).

Indians were seen as being historically anterior and morally inferior to Protestant Christian settlers, and with expectations of their demise as a people, there was pressure to civilize and Christianize them before it was too late. Large and small missions were strung out across America. They were to provide the Indians with European concepts of work, time, savings, and Christian orthodoxy to the end that "as tribes and nations the Indians must perish and live only as men!" (Berkhofer 1967, p. 7).

Mid-Century – Reservations and Wars: 1860-1880

Although land reservations had existed since colonial times, they did not become a primary ingredient in Federal Indian policy until the mid-19th century. Reservations were defined as areas of land, usually within former Indian land holdings, that were set aside for the exclusive use and occupancy of individual tribes or groupings of tribes. Government policy had been to move the tribes westward from areas of white settlement into unsettled territories denoted as Indian country. Areas without white occupation and trade were to become scarce after the mid-19th century. Expansion brought newcomers to all parts of the continent. Wagon trains trekked to Oregon and California as early as 1841. Texas joined the Union in 1846, and the Treaty of Guadalupe Hidalgo in 1848 extended the United States' dominion to the Pacific.

The western tribes and the relocated eastern tribes were challenged for land and resources, such as Black Hills gold, by the new white settlers. The United States embarked on an aggressive policy of establishing Indian reservations by treaty. The treaties would secure land for the settlers, set aside preserves for the tribes, and once again promise material and political assistance to the tribes. Between 1853 and 1856, 52 treaties were negotiated, sometimes peacefully, sometimes not. The desperate saga of the Indian tribes of the Great Plains, the Northwest, and the Southwest has been told in detail elsewhere (Brown 1970). It is clear that in the taking of Indian lands any device that was deemed effective was used, including theft, fraud, deceit, and military force. Even those tribes that had been friendly toward the United States were unable to protect their lands.

Throughout the first half of the 19th century Indian tribes, individuals, and their allies had used the political and legal system of the United States to redress grievances. Sometimes this path proved effective. But even in the face of setbacks, the tribes continued to pursue constitutional mechanisms for grievances.

Congress established in 1855 a Court of Claims that allowed private parties to sue the United States for violations of contracts. A number of Indian tribes and individuals subsequently filed suits for treaty violations involving the taking of land. As the suits progressed, Congress perceived the danger of potential Indian claims and amended the Court of Claims statute to exclude those deriving from treaties. Another century would pass before any systematic process would be available for hearing claims of illegal land taking.

Nothing ultimately prevented the taking of Indian lands. Their holdings were reduced, and the tribes were placed firmly in the reservation system. Indians refusing to stay within reservation boundaries were dealt with by military measures. Reservation occupants were placed under total control of a Federal agent-in-charge whose duty was to acculturate and foster the assimilation of the Natives. Christian churches also played a major role on reservations. President Ulysses Grant delegated to the churches the right to nominate Indian agents and direct educational activities on reservations. The direct result manifested itself in later years:

> [M]any reservations had come under the authority of what had amounted to stern missionary dictatorships whose fanatic zealousness had crushed Indian culture and institutions, suppressed religious and other liberties, and punished Indians for the least show of independence.
>
> Josephy 1968, p. 340

Assimilation and Allotment: 1880-1930

The drive to assimilate Indians into the mainstream of American life by changing their customs, dress, occupations, language, religion, and philosophy has always been an element in Federal-Indian relations. In the latter part of the 19th century and the early part of the 20th century, this assimilationist policy became dominant.

A major thrust of assimilation efforts was to educate Indians in American ways. In 1879 the Carlisle Indian Training School was established by a former military officer. Its philosophy of separating Indian children totally from their Indian environment and forcing them to adopt white ways became the basis for a widescale boarding school movement that eventually removed thousands of Indian children from their cultural settings and families. In addition, traditional tribal governing systems, particularly justice systems, came under strong attack during this period. The Bureau of Indian Affairs established tribal police forces and courts under the administrative control of its agents, the reservation superintendents. These and other efforts were designed to erode the power and influence of Indian leaders and traditions. Everything "Indian" came under attack. Indian feasts, languages, certain marriage practices, dances, and any practices by medicine or religious persons were all banned by the Bureau of Indian Affairs.

The Great Sioux Nation was a focus of much of the assimilation activity, and Black Hills gold provided much impetus for reducing the size of the Sioux Reservation as non-Indians flocked by the thousands into South Dakota. The defeat of Custer and his troops at Little Big Horn in 1876 was a direct outgrowth of the discovery of gold in the Black Hills and tribal resistance to the miners who came seeking it. The Sioux were ultimately forced to cede the Black Hills in 1876. Pressure on the Sioux to give up more land continued up to the time of the allotment legislation, and even then it did not end. In 1889 the Great Sioux Nation was divided into six smaller, generally noncontiguous reservations.

Concurrently, the Bureau of Indian Affairs banned Ghost Dancing. The new Ghost Dance religion had gained prominence by promising an Indian messiah. The 1890 Wounded Knee massacre is now clearly understood as a tragic overreaction on the part of the United States in its efforts to suppress Indian religious practices. Those participating in the massacre, however, were awarded medals at the time.

The latter part of the 19th century was also a period when the traditional Indian means of economic support were no longer viable.

Subsistence hunting and gathering, which had supported many nomadic tribes, were precluded by the advent of reservations and the
mass destruction of wildlife, particularly buffalo, that had accompanied white westward expansion. Many tribes were forced into economic dependency and a dole system of goods and supplies operated
by the Bureau of Indian Affairs. This period of economic hardship
was accompanied by widespread and severe health problems.

Even those tribes whose economies were strong were unable to
escape efforts to subjugate them. The Five Civilized Tribes, removed
from Georgia in the 1830s, had organized themselves economically
and politically in a manner similar to the American States and territories. By the latter part of the 19th century, these tribes were at least as
self-sufficient as the States and territories, but they were nevertheless
stripped of most of their governmental powers in 1898. (See the
Curtis Act of 1898.)

All of these factors played critical roles in undermining tribal self-
sufficiency, but the single most devastating development was the
allotment system. Allotment was advocated as a means of further
civilizing Indians by converting them from a communal land system
to a system of individual ownership. It was argued that ownership
would make farmers out of the "savages." In 1887 Congress passed
the General Allotment Act, also known as the Dawes Act. Although
many other acts of Congress would follow, the general formula of the
Dawes Act set the pattern for allotting Indian reservations. Each family head was to received 160 acres, and a single person was to receive
80 acres. Title to the land was to be held in trust for at least 25 years.
Civilized Indians could end the trust period and receive United
States citizenship and fee simple title to their land. Citizenship would
be unilaterally granted all Indians in 1924 by the Indian Citizenship
Act. Surplus lands within the reservation boundaries, lands not allotted or otherwise set aside, were to be sold to the United States and
then opened for homesteading. The proceeds from the sales were also
to be placed in trust and used by the United States as an account for
supplies provided to the Indians.

Allotment and other assimilationist practices received strong
support from "friends" of the Indians. Many believed that these policies represented the only alternative to Indian extinction. Not everyone defended the policies of the government, however. Dissenters in

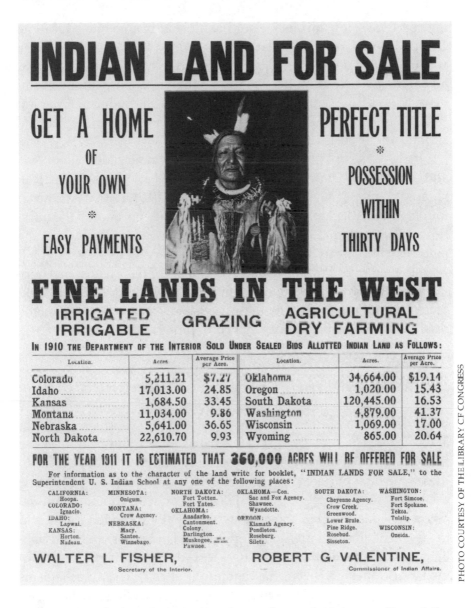

Congress and elsewhere pointed out the underlying reality of the period: whites were securing vast quantities of Indian land.

Toward the end of the allotment period, the Federal Government commissioned a major study of conditions on Indian reservations. The study, known as the Meriam Report (1928), enumerated the disastrous conditions afflicting Indians at that time: high infant death rates, high mortality rates for the entire population, appalling housing conditions, low incomes, poor health, and inadequate education. The policy of forced assimilation was judged a failure. The failure was that it had not worked: "It has resulted in much loss of land and an enormous increase in the details of administration without a compensating advance in the economic ability of the Indians" (Meriam Report 1928, p. 41). But such criticism did not challenge ultimate assimilationist goals.

In the wake of the damaging results of the reservation allotments and assimilation efforts, some Indians moved to use the American legal system on behalf of their people. By 1910 a small group of Indian lawyers had emerged to do battle in the courts over the questions of Indian lands, citizenship, allotment procedures, and the enforcement of treaty rights. Even though reservations were originally conceived of as a means to deprive Indians of their lands, they represented the last remnants of Indian land and, as such, were held sacred by the tribes. Despite the prison-like aspects of life on many reservations, Indian advocates moved to protect this land base.

The Indian Reorganization Act: 1930-1945

The Meriam Report and several other investigations produced major changes in Federal Indian practices. Federal policy would ultimately favor restoration of some measure of tribal self-government and tribal resources. The strategy was to use tribal culture and institutions as transitional devices for the complete assimilation of Indian life into the dominant white society. The major instrument for this policy was the Indian Reorganization Act of 1934, which, with companion legislation affecting the Oklahoma tribes, essentially provided for an end to allotment, for measures to restore Indian land bases, and for establishment of a revolving credit fund to promote economic development. Also included were the regulation of resources, mechanisms for chartering and reorganizing tribal governments, and the establishment of an employment preference policy for Indians within the Federal Government.

The Indian Reorganization Act, however, did not go as far as its advocates would have liked, and several key features were not in the legislation as it finally was passed. The elements lost included an appellate Indian court system, mechanisms to assure tribal independence from bureaucratic control, and a national policy to promote and support the study and understanding of Indian cultures.

Another major development during this period was the passage by Congress of the Johnson O'Malley Act (1934) as a means to promote Federal and State cooperation in the provision of services to Indians, particularly in education. This development involved States more aggressively in Indian affairs and was a natural outgrowth of the Meriam Report's view that the Federal Government had performed poorly as a service provider and that the States had a better record.

Finally, during the Great Depression, the Department of the Interior assisted hundreds of tribes in drafting new constitutions, codes, and governmental structures. These efforts produced essentially standardized approaches promoted by Department of the Interior lawyers. Some land was purchased and returned to tribal control during this time, but the Indian land base remained essentially unaltered. This period for reviving tribal governments was a relatively short one.

The Termination Period: 1945-1960

Probing examination of the living conditions of Indians has periodically served as a stimulus to promote change in the manner in which the Federal Government deals with tribes. The United States Senate in 1943 conducted a survey of Indian conditions and found serious and troubling problems. The Bureau of Indian Affairs and Federal bureaucracy were held culpable for these conditions. The administrative and financial costs of achieving slow progress toward assimilation were viewed as excessive.

Criteria were developed by the Commissioner of Indian Affairs to identify Indian tribal groups that could be removed from Federal aegis. The theory was that some tribes were sufficiently acculturated and that the Federal protective role was no longer necessary. But another development of the same period suggests a less benign interpretation of events—some 133 separate bills were introduced in Congress to permit the transfer of trust land from Indian ownership to non-Indian ownership. There was also pressure to terminate particular tribes, such as the Klamaths, who possessed valuable timber resources, and the Agua Caliente, who owned much of the area near Palm Springs, California. In 1949, the Hoover Commission (although not established to deal with Indian issues) recommended the full and complete integration of Indians into American society.

During the 1950s, Federal Indian policy was a three-pronged program: (1) termination of tribes over which Federal responsibility was thought unnecessary, (2) transfer of Federal responsibility and jurisdiction to State governments (e.g., under Public Law 280), and (3) physical relocation of Indian people from reservations to urban areas. The cornerstone of the termination era was House Concurrent Resolution 108, which declared, "Indian tribes and individual members thereof...should be freed from Federal supervision and control and from all disabilities and limitations specially applicable to Indians."

The three-pronged policy was aggressively carried out by Dillon Myer, former director of detention camps for Japanese Americans, who became the Commissioner of Indian Affairs in 1950. The Bureau of Indian Affairs, which had been a target of congressional criticism in 1943, grew in budget and staff as it administered terminationist policies. Between 1954 and 1962, statutes were passed authorizing the termination of more than 100 tribes, bands, or Indian rancherias. Most of those affected were small bands on the West Coast, but two sizable tribes, the Klamaths and Menominees, were also terminated. In all, approximately 12,000 individual Indians lost tribal affiliations that included political relationships with the United States. Approximately 2.5 million acres of Indian land were removed from protected status.

Self-Determination: Post-1960

The self-determination era can be traced back to the presidential election campaign of 1960 (Sanders 1985). Candidates John Kennedy and Richard Nixon both pledged there would be no change in treaty or contractual relationships without tribal consent. They also declared there would be protection of the Indian land base, credit assistance, and encouragement of tribal planning for economic development.

The newly-elected President Kennedy further promised the inclusion of Indians in legislative programs for segments of the nation's population that were depressed and impoverished. He also appointed Stewart Udall as Secretary of the Interior, and Udall promptly commissioned a task force on Indian affairs. The task force recommended a shift away from termination of the federal trust relationship and toward the development of human and natural resources in Indian country (Cohen 1982).

Kennedy's promise of Indian inclusion in social programs only began to take shape in a substantial way during President Johnson's administration. Johnson's "Great Society" programs made Indians an integral part of the expanding human concern of the times (Deloria and Lytle 1983). In 1968, President Johnson proposed

> ...a new goal for our Indian programs: A goal that ends the old debate about "termination" of Indian programs and stresses self-determination; a goal that erases old attitudes of paternalism and promotes partnership self-help. (p. 336)

Also in 1968, the Indian Civil Rights Act was passed–the first major piece of legislation enacted during the post-termination era that dealt specifically with Indian matters. A relevant and significant part of the act prohibited states from assuming jurisdiction over Indian country, under Public Law 280, without first obtaining tribal consent (Deloria and Lytle 1983).

President Johnson came close to being the first federal official to formally repudiate the termination policy. It didn't happen under his administration, however. It was President Nixon, in a speech on July 8, 1970, who said:

> This policy of forced termination is wrong.... The special relationship between Indians and the Federal government is the result...of solemn obligations which have been entered into by the United States Government.... To terminate this relationship would be no more appropriate than to terminate the citizenship rights of any other American.... Self-determination among the Indian people can and must be encouraged.... This, then, must be the goal of any new national policy toward the Indian people...(p. 564-567)

President Nixon reinforced his message by declaring that it was necessary to strengthen Indian autonomy without any threat of ending federal concern and federal support. He asked Congress to repeal House Concurrent Resolution 108, passed in 1953, which embodied the termination mentality. Ironically, it took Congress 18 more years to *officially* repeal the resolution. This was accomplished through the addition of the following short paragraph to section 5203 of the Tribally Controlled Schools Act of 1988.

> (f) TERMINATION. —The Congress hereby repudiates and rejects House Concurrent Resolution 108 of the 83rd Congress

and any policy of unilateral termination of Federal relations with
any Indian Nation.

Nixon also made a number of specific legislative recommendations. Following upon his urgings, along with those of growing numbers of Indian activists, traditional tribal leaders, and an American
public that was reawakening to Native needs, a flurry of Indian legislation was passed into law in the 1970s.

Several pieces of legislation among the many passed during this
period are notable because they are indicative of the change in federal policy from the days of termination. The Indian Education Act of
1972 set a statutory foundation for more comprehensive funding of
Indian education and greater focus on Indian education at the local
level (Sanders 1985). The act provided for special training programs
for teachers of Indian students, for fellowships for students in certain
fields of study, and for basic research in Indian education (Deloria
and Lytle 1983). Not a panacea for the many problems in Indian education, it was a start in the right direction.

A second and very significant statute is the Indian Self-Determination and Education Assistance Act of 1975. It is often referred to
in Indian country as "638" legislation, because it was passed as
Public Law 93-638. Through grants and contracts, the act, as amended, encourages tribes to assume responsibilities for federally funded
Indian programs formerly administered by employees in the Departments of Education, Interior, and Health and Human Services. Tribes
decide if they wish to participate in a particular program. If they do,
then funds and management decisions are subject to tribal control.
This is similar to the ways other local governments participate in federal revenue sharing programs. It means that participating tribal governments can now control their own housing, education, law enforcement, social service, health, and community development programs
(American Indian Lawyer Training Program 1988; Cohen 1982; Kelly
1988; O'Brien 1989).

In 1978, Congress enacted two additional laws of major significance. The Indian Child Welfare Act addressed the long-standing
problem in which as many as a third of Indian children were taken
from their natural parents and adopted out to non-Indian parents pursuant to state adoption and guardianship laws. This act provided that
many adoption and guardianship cases were to take place in tribal

court, and it established a preference for Indian guardians over non-Indian guardians when Indian guardianship cases were heard in state courts. The second law, the American Indian Religious Freedom Act (AIRFA), while much less successful in its implementation, nonetheless recognized the government's obligation to maintain tribal cultural existence. Its language specifically recognized the importance of traditional Indian religious practices. Furthermore, it directed that all federal agencies were to make sure that their policies do not interfere with the free exercise of Native religions (American Indian Lawyer Training Program 1988; O'Brien 1989).

The self-determination movement was accelerated through a series of decisions by the Supreme Court in the 1970s and early 1980s. The Court emphasized "Indian sovereignty" and the inherent power of tribes to assert their economic, political, and cultural authority in appropriate areas (Kelly 1988). (See, for example, *McClanahan v. Arizona State Tax Commission* 1973, *Santa Clara Pueblo v. Martinez* 1978, and *Merrion v. Jicarilla Apache Tribe* 1982.) Other sovereignty-related cases, however, limited tribal powers in various areas, such as law enforcement, regulation of hunting and fishing by non-Indians on non-Indian land within reservation boundaries (if no significant tribal interest is at stake), and litigation of reserved water rights barred by prior court decrees (American Indian Lawyer Training Program 1988). (See, for example, *Oliphant v. Suquamish Tribe* 1978, *Montana v. United States* 1982, and *Nevada v. United States* 1983.)

Overall, the 1980s represented an era of mixed results for Indian self-determination, with much on the positive side. The Reagan administration gave strong vocal support for programs developed for Indian self-betterment and tribal development, but the number of these programs actually soon declined because of the administration's cutbacks (Waldman 1985). Still, the federal policies of the 1980s affirmed many of the sovereign powers of tribes and continued to enunciate the concept of a government-to-government relationship among the federal government, the states, and the tribes (Kelly 1988). During the decade, it became apparent that another dramatic shift to some "new" unilateral and damaging policy–akin to the old one of forced assimilation–was left behind in the pages of history books. The tribes, however, know better than to "never say never." Even so, it may be helpful to consider an example of the changes that have occurred. The publicly stated, positive attitude of Congress and the administration toward the issue of self-determination and the trust relationship at the end of the 1980s is demonstrated by House Concurrent Resolution 331. (See Appendix 9.) The resolution was passed by the House of Representatives on October 4, 1988.

Although the Indian Gaming Regulatory Act became law in 1988, it is the 1990s in which the act, its provisions, and its regulatory implementation are being so hotly debated. Indian gaming business activities and related policies will be among the most public of issues on Indian policy in the 1990s. As the controversy rages, clashes will continue among the various governmental units–federal, state, and tribal–and private gaming entities. Each party with a vested interest will continue its attempts to acquire (or to maintain) a piece of the lucrative "economic pie" associated with gaming.

Some of the more "common" issues from past years will require serious reevaluation, and attention will need to be directed toward resolution of problems. Major issues include the following: housing, health services, environmental concerns, AIDS awareness and prevention programs for the highly vulnerable communities in Indian country, economic development, education, natural resource protection and management, corruption in tribal government, basic issues of sovereignty and self-government, land rights, water rights, hunting and fishing rights, preference for Indians in contracting, alcohol and drug abuse programs, Indian youth at risk, federal recognition of unrecognized tribes, racism, Native suicide, mismanagement of trust accounts, crime and law enforcement, cultural and religious freedom, child welfare, tribal autonomy, sufficiency of government appropriations, general relations among federal, state, and tribal governmental units–including unresponsiveness of government at all levels.

The newly-appointed Joint Federal-State Commission on Policies and Programs Affecting Alaska Natives is scheduled to present its findings and recommendations to Congress, the President, and the State of Alaska before mid-decade. The Commission's actions and recommendations, if they live up to Congressional, state, and Native expectations, should result in some policy changes on a grand scale which address the serious socio-economic challenges faced by Alaska Natives.

Native Hawaiian rights and land claims are likely to receive more congressional debate during the 1990s. At the same time, conflict will probably arise as to whether to (1) leave Native Hawaiian affairs under state control, (2) include their rights, land claims, and social services under federal Indian programs, or (3) develop a separate federal program or independent classification for their unique needs for status, culture, socio-political concerns, and a viable land base.

In 1989, after two years of investigation and hearings, the Special Committee on Investigations (a subcommittee of the Senate Select Committee on Indian Affairs) published its final, bipartisan report. The report is a general indictment of the handling of Indian affairs at all levels. Consider the following excerpts from the report:

> We indeed found fraud, corruption and mismanagement pervading the institutions that are supposed to serve American Indians. (p. 4)

> Paternalistic federal control over American Indians has created a federal bureaucracy ensnarled in red tape and riddled with fraud, mismanagement and waste. Worse, the Committee found that federal officials in every agency knew of the abuses but did little or nothing to stop them. (p. 5)

> In every area it touches, the BIA is plagued with mismanagement. (p. 8)

> Free from tough criminal laws and energetic prosecution, some tribal officials have engaged in corrupt practices. (p. 6)

> Like so many of the federal agencies responsible for Indian affairs, mismanagement is pervasive at the Indian Health Service.... (p. 153)

> Like other federal agencies involved in Indian preference contracting, HUD (U.S. Department of Housing and Urban Development) has been vulnerable to fraud and abuse, making it a haven for phony Indian companies that successfully bid contracts away from legitimate Indian firms. (p. 171)

> Since Congress has ultimate responsibility for federal Indian policy, we in the Senate and House must accept the blame for failing to adequately oversee and reform Indian affairs. Rather than becoming actively engaged in Indian issues, Congress has demonstrated an attitude of benign neglect. (p. 7)

Needless to say, the report of the Special Committee on Investigations shook things up in Washington and in Indian country. Besides reporting its findings, the committee also called for some sweeping legislative changes in several areas and "A New Federalism for American Indians." The proposed foundation of the "New Federalism" is (1) the establishment of an Office of Federal-Tribal Relations (OFTR) within the Executive Office of the President and (2) negotiation by the OFTR, on behalf of the United States, of new formal agreements with federally recognized tribes to promote greater tribal self-government.

As frequently happens in big government, reactions to the report settled down, in many cases, after the initial jolt of publication. Even so, some agencies are taking major steps to address the shortfalls and accusations outlined in the report. Reform attempts going on within the BIA itself are among the most active.

In 1990, Secretary of the Interior Manuel Lujan formed an Advisory Task Force on reorganization of the BIA. The task force is composed of 36 tribal leaders, two Interior Department officials, and five BIA officials. This group has been holding meetings in different parts of Indian country since its formation. Among other things, it is attempting to come up with an administrative design for an "ideal" Indian agency, possibly to replace some of the agency offices in the BIA's 12 geographically-defined administrative areas (Bureau of Indian Affairs 1991c). The task force, in its preliminary report, has proposed a revolutionary budget system, transferring more than 86 percent of BIA funds to tribal control (Anquoe 1992c). The tribes now control about 27 percent of the budget. Other suggested measures include staff cuts in the BIA and shifting of some BIA staff members to tribal employment, maximizing the distribution of funding, delegating more authority from Washington to field offices, increasing administrative flexibility at the tribe or agency level, and establishing an independent "National Indian Advisory Board." Congress, of course, will have to approve implementation of the task force recommendations, which it is considering at this writing.

Time will tell how well the BIA, other federal agencies with Indian responsibilities, and the Congress respond to the indictment of the Senate Committee's 1989 report and to the policy challenges of the future.

APPENDIX 1

BACKGROUND ON NATIVE HAWAIIAN ISSUES

[The opinion of the United States is] *that the Government of the [Hawaiian] Islands ought to be respected, that no power ought either to take possession of the islands as a conquest, or for the purpose of colonization, and that no power ought to seek for any undue control over the existing Government, or any exclusive privileges or preferences in matters of commerce.*

U.S. Secretary of State Webster, 1842
(Cohen 1982, p. 799)

Native Hawaiians are descended from the Polynesians who arrived in the Islands between 1,000 and 1,500 years ago. By the time Captain James Cook first landed in 1778, perhaps 300,000 Hawaiians resided there. He found these people to be living under a well established political system and a feudal land tenure system controlled by various chiefs. The clear existence of these cultural/governmental institutions, the islanders' demonstrated ability to defend themselves, and their relative remoteness all worked together to negate application of the discovery doctrine to Hawaii. The Islands were soon recognized as an independent nation by the world community.

Most of the credit for this early recognition of Hawaiian sovereignty goes to King Kamehameha I. Starting in 1782, through conquest and coercion, he progressively consolidated all of the islands under a single monarchy ruled by him. By 1810, he had complete control of Hawaii. Even after Kamehameha's death, in 1819, the monarchy grew in sophistication, and a written constitution was developed in 1840. But the toll from disease, cultural disintegration, and meddling by foreign nations and their resident merchants mounted steadily.

By 1890, the total island population of 90,000 had only 34,000 full-blood Hawaiians and 6,000 mixed-bloods. Foreigners, mostly American merchants, now owned 25 percent of the kingdom's 4,100,000 acres of land. These foreigners also controlled another 25 percent of the country through leasehold interests. But, they wanted more.

In 1893, a coup d'état, sponsored primarily by American businessmen, overthrew the constitutional government of Queen Liliuokalani. The coup was successful only because the U.S. Minister to Hawaii, without authorization from the President, ordered U.S. Marines ashore from nearby war ships and strategically located them to prevent the Queen and her loyalists from putting down the coup.

The coup's conspirators, known as "The Annexation Club," negotiated an annexation agreement with U.S. officials, but President Grover Cleveland refused to submit the agreement to the U.S. Senate for ratification. He adamantly opposed the annexation attempt, declaring Queen Liliuokalani's overthrow to be a stain on U.S. honor; and he called for restoration of the rightful monarchy.

The insurrectionists had to put annexation on hold for awhile and decided to try establishing a republic. They did, and they included Native Hawaiians as citizens. Five years later, with the blessings of the new president, William McKinley, Congress annexed Hawaii to the United States. The Islands were incorporated as a U.S. territory in June 1900.

In the early 1900s, Congress took notice of the terrible social and economic conditions among Native Hawaiians. It was widely acknowledged that loss of the land base which had sustained them in the past was at the heart of the problem. Congress reacted by passing the Hawaii Homes Commission Act of 1921. This act was intended to allow the leasing of certain public lands for Native homesteads—supposedly to "rehabilitate" people of at least one-half Hawaiian ancestry—while ownership of the lands remained in trust status. About 200,000 acres of federal lands were designated as being available for the homestead leasing program. However, Territorial administration of the act failed badly in providing agricultural lands and residential lots for the betterment of Native Hawaiians.

When Hawaii became a state in 1959, the Hawaii Homes Commission lands, and administrative responsibility for them, were transferred to the state by the federal government. Administration improved notably under state control, and increasing numbers of Hawaiian families were provided leased homesteads for some agricultural and residential purposes. However, 60 years after its inception, the program had accommodated only 15 percent of Native Hawaiians and only about 25 percent of the designated lands had been utilized for homesteads.

The statehood act of 1959 included a provision which allowed, at state discretion, use of income from state lands "for the betterment of conditions of Native Hawaiians...." The state generally opted, however, to make other uses of state land proceeds. This changed in 1978 when a provision was added to the Hawaiian Constitution calling for at least partial contribution of state land income toward improvement of conditions among Native Hawaiians.

Today, despite the constitutional change, large numbers of Native Hawaiians continue to be acutely disadvantaged. Statistics on health, education, crime, unemployment, and underemployment graphically bear this out. Many Hawaiians are convinced that these adverse conditions would not exist if they had not been deprived of their land base and other pre-1893 elements of their heritage.

Concerned for their people's well being, more Hawaiians are becoming politically active. They are pursuing a variety of issues including redress of past American conduct, land rights, subsistence hunting and fishing rights, inclusion within federal service programs for other Native Americans, access to beaches and other traditional sites, and federally recognized tribal status with some level of self-government or "sovereignty." Several initial successes have been achieved in Congress, such as inclusion of Native Hawaiians in the Native American Programs Act of 1975, the American Indian Religious Freedom Act of 1978, the Elementary and Secondary Education Act Amendments of 1988, and the Native American Graves Protection and Repatriation Act of 1990. In addition, Congress has passed specific legislation pertaining to Native Hawaiians, namely the Native Hawaiians Study Commission Act of 1980 and the Native Hawaiian Health Care Act of 1988.

The 1990 Census Report shows that 138,742 individuals with Native Hawaiian ancestry account for 12.5 percent of the total Hawaii state population of 1,111,800. (The Native ancestry number includes an estimated 9,400 full-blood Hawaiians, which is down from an estimated 11,000 for 1980.) These people clearly constitute a significant minority and they will no longer allow themselves to be largely left out of the state or national political scenes. Many will continue to press further to reclaim some of the numerous rights of which they and their ancestors were deprived following Euro American contact. Unless they falter in their resolve, additional gains are sure to be achieved for Native Hawaiians in the future.

NOTE: Primary sources for this appendix are: American Indian Lawyer Training Program 1988; Cohen 1982; State of Hawaii 1991; Sutton 1985; and Wilkinson 1988. Also, see the case of *Hou Hawaiians v. State of Hawaii* (1985) where an organized group of Native Hawaiians unsuccessfully attempted to gain federal recognition under laws and regulations pertaining to Indian tribes. With respect to population figures, it is instructive to note that the total "Pacific Islander" population of Hawaii (more than 200,000) is sometimes confused with the Native Hawaiian population (State of Hawaii 1991). Beyond Hawaii, legitimate concerns being expressed by Natives of current and former Pacific island territories of the United States (American Samoa, Guam, Bikini Atoll, etc.) merit full consideration by the U.S. government.

APPENDIX 2

INDIAN TRIBAL ENTITIES WITHIN THE CONTIGUOUS 48 STATES RECOGNIZED AND ELIGIBLE TO RECEIVE SERVICES FROM THE UNITED STATES BUREAU OF INDIAN AFFAIRS

Absentee-Shawnee Tribe of Indians of Oklahoma

Agua Caliente Band of Cahuilla Indians of the Agua Caliente Indian Reservation, California

Ak Chin Indian Community of Papago Indians of the Maricopa, Ak Chin Reservation, Arizona

Alabama and Coushatta Tribes of Texas

Alabama-Quassarte Tribal Town of the Creek Nation of Oklahoma

Alturas Rancheria of Pit River Indians of California

Apache Tribe of Oklahoma

Arapahoe Tribe of the Wind River Reservation, Wyoming

Aroostook Band of Micmac Indians of Maine

Assiniboine and Sioux Tribes of the Fort Peck Indian Reservation, Montana

Augustine Bank of Cahuilla Mission Indians of the Augustine Reservation, California

Bad River Band of the Lake Superior Tribe of Chippewa Indians of the Bad River Reservation, Wisconsin

Bay Mills Indian Community of the Sault Ste. Marie Band of Chippewa Indians, Bay Mills Reservation, Michigan

Berry Creek Rancheria of Maidu Indians of California

Big Lagoon Rancheria of Smith River Indians of California

Big Pine Band of Owens Valley Paiute Shoshone Indians of the Big Pine Reservation, California

Big Sandy Rancheria of Mono Indians of California

Big Valley Rancheria of Pomo & Pit River Indians of California

Blackfeet Tribe of the Blackfeet Indian Reservation of Montana

Blue Lake Rancheria of California

Bridgeport Paiute Indian Colony of California

Buena Vista Rancheria of Me-Wuk Indians of California

Burns Paiute Indian Colony, Oregon

Cabazon Band of Cahuilla Mission Indians of the Cabazon Reservation, California

Cachil DeHe Band of Wintun Indians of the Colusa Indian Community of the Colusa Rancheria, California

Caddo Indian Tribe of Oklahoma

Cahuilla Band of Mission Indians of the Cahuilla Reservation, California

Cahto Indian Tribe of the Laytonville Rancheria, California

Campo Band of Diegueno Mission Indians of the Campo Indian Reservation, California

Capitan Grande Band of Diegueno Mission Indians of California:
Barona Group of the Barona Reservation, California
Viejas Group of the Viejas Reservation, California

Cayuga Nation of New York

Cedarville Rancheria of Northern Paiute Indians of California

Chemehuevi Indian Tribe of the Chemehuevi Reservation, California

NOTE: Includes Indian tribes, bands, villages, communities, and pueblos, as of January 1993.

Cher-Ae Heights Indian Community of the Trinidad Rancheria, California

Cherokee Nation of Oklahoma

Cheyenne-Arapaho Tribes of Oklahoma

Cheyenne River Sioux Tribe of the Cheyenne River Reservation, South Dakota

Chickasaw Nation of Oklahoma

Chicken Ranch Rancheria of Me-Wuk Indians of California

Chippewa-Cree Indians of the Rocky Boy's Reservation, Montana

Chitimacha Tribe of Louisiana

Choctaw Nation of Oklahoma

Citizen Band Potawatomi Indian Tribe of Oklahoma

Cloverdale Rancheria of Pomo Indians of California

Coast Indian Community of Yurok Indians of the Resighini Rancheria, California

Cocopah Tribe of Arizona

Coeur D'Alene Tribe of the Coeur D'Alene Reservation, Idaho

Cold Springs Rancheria of Mono Indians of California

Colorado River Indian Tribes of the Colorado River Indian Reservation, Arizona and California

Comanche Indian Tribe of Oklahoma

Confederated Salish & Kootenai Tribes of the Flathead Reservation, Montana

Confederated Tribes of the Chehalis Reservation, Washington

Confederated Tribes of the Colville Reservation, Washington

Confederated Tribes of the Coos, Lower Umpqua and Siuslaw Indians of Oregon

Confederated Tribes of the Goshute Reservation, Nevada and Utah

Confederated Tribes of the Grand Ronde Community of Oregon

Confederated Tribes of the Siletz Reservation, Oregon

Confederated Tribes of the Umatilla Reservation, Oregon

Confederated Tribes of the Warm Springs Reservation of Oregon

Confederated Tribes of the Bands of the Yakima Indian Nation of the Yakima Reservation, Washington

Coquille Tribe of Oregon

Cortina Indian Rancheria of Wintun Indians of California

Coushatta Tribe of Louisiana

Covelo Indian Community of the Round Valley Reservation, California

Cow Creek Band of Umpqua Indians of Oregon

Coyote Valley Band of Pomo Indians of California

Creek Nation of Oklahoma

Crow Tribe of Montana

Crow Creek Sioux Tribe of the Crow Creek Reservation, South Dakota

Cuyapaipe Community of Diegueno Mission Indians of the Cuyapaipe Reservation, California

Death Valley Timbi-Sha Shoshone Band of California

Delaware Tribe of Western Oklahoma

Devils Lake Sioux Tribe of the Devils Lake Sioux Reservation, North Dakota

Dry Creek Rancheria of Pomo Indians of California

Duckwater Shoshone Tribe of the Duckwater Reservation, Nevada

Eastern Band of Cherokee Indians of North Carolina

Eastern Shawnee Tribe of Oklahoma

Elem Indian Colony of Pomo Indians of the Sulphur Bank Rancheria, California

Elk Valley Rancheria of Smith River Tolowa Indians of California

Ely Indian Colony of Nevada

Enterprise Rancheria of Maidu Indians of California

Flandreau Santee Tribe of South Dakota

Forest County Potawatomi Community of Wisconsin Potawatomie Indians, Wisconsin

Fort Belknap Indian Community of the
Fort Belknap Reservation of Montana

Fort Bidwell Indian Community of
Paiute Indians of the Fort Bidwell
Reservation, California

Fort Independence Indian Community
of Paiute Indians of the Fort
Independence Reservation, California

Fort McDermitt Paiute and Shoshone
Tribes of the Fort McDermitt Indian
Reservation, Nevada

Fort McDowell Mohave-Apache Indian
Community of the Fort McDowell
Indian Reservation, Arizona

Fort Mojave Indian Tribe of Arizona

Fort Sill Apache Tribe of Oklahoma

Gay Head Wampanoag Indians of
Massachusetts

Gila River Pima-Maricopa Indian
Community of the Gila River Indian
Reservation of Arizona

Grand Traverse Band of Ottawa and
Chippewa Indians of Michigan

Greenville Rancheria of Maidu Indians
of California

Grindstone Indian Rancheria of Wintun-
Wailaki Indians of California

Guidiville Rancheria of California

Hannahville Indian Community of
Wisconsin Potawatomie Indians of
Michigan

Havasupai Tribe of the Havasupai
Reservation, Arizona

Hoh Indian Tribe of the Hoh Indian
Reservation, Washington

Hoopa Valley Tribe of the Hoopa Valley
Reservation, California

Hopi Tribe of Arizona

Hopland Band of Pomo Indians of the
Hopland Rancheria, California

Houlton Band of Maliseet Indians of
Maine

Hualapai Tribe of the Hualapai Indian
Reservation, California [Arizona]

Inaja Band of Diegueno Mission Indians
of the Inaja and Cosmit Reservation,
California

Iowa Tribe of Kansas and Nebraska

Iowa Tribe of Oklahoma

Jackson Rancheria of Me-Wuk Indians of
California

Jamestown Klallam Tribe of Washington

Jamul Indian Village of California

Jicarilla Apache Tribe of the Jicarilla
Apache Indian Reservation, New
Mexico

Kaibab Band of Paiute Indians of the
Kaibab Indian Reservation, Arizona

Kalispel Indian Community of the
Kalispel Reservation, Washington

Karuk Tribe of California

Kashia Band of Pomo Indians of the
Stewarts Point Rancheria, California

Kaw Indian Tribe of Oklahoma

Keweenaw Bay Indian Community of
L'Anse and Ontonagon Bands of
Chippewa Indians of the L'Anse
Reservation, Michigan

Kialegee Tribal Town of the Creek
Indian Nation of Oklahoma

Kickapoo Traditional Tribe of Texas

Kickapoo Tribe of Indians of the
Kickapoo Reservation in Kansas

Kickapoo Tribe of Oklahoma (includes
Texas Band of Kickapoo Indians)

Kiowa Indian Tribe of Oklahoma

Klamath Indian Tribe of Oregon

Kootenai Tribe of Idaho

La Jolla Band of Luiseno Mission Indians
of the La Jolla Reservation, California

La Posta Band of Diegueno Mission
Indians of the La Posta Indian
Reservation, California

Lac Courte Oreilles Band of Lake
Superior Chippewa Indians of the Lac
Courte Oreilles Reservation of
Wisconsin

Lac du Flambeau Band of Lake Superior
Chippewa Indians of the Lac du
Flambeau Reservation of Wisconsin

Lac Vieux Desert Band of Lake Superior
Chippewa Indians of Michigan

Las Vegas Tribe of Paiute Indians of the Las Vegas Indian Colony, Nevada

Los Coyotes Band of Cahuilla Mission Indians of the Los Coyotes Reservation, California

Lovelock Paiute Tribe of the Lovelock Indian Colony, Nevada

Lower Brule Sioux Tribe of the Lower Brule Reservation, South Dakota

Lower Elwha Tribal Community of the Lower Elwha Reservation, Washington

Lower Sioux Indian Community of Minnesota Mdewakanton Sioux Indians of the Lower Sioux Reservation in Minnesota

Lummi Tribe of the Lummi Reservation, Washington

Lytton Rancheria of California

Makah Indian Tribe of the Makah Indian Reservation, Washington

Manchester Band of Pomo Indians of the Manchester-Point Arena Rancheria, California

Manzanita Band of Diegueno Mission Indians of the Manzanita Reservation, California

Mashantucket Pequot Tribe of Connecticut

Mechoopda Indian Tribe of Chico Rancheria, California

Menominee Indian Tribe of Wisconsin

Mesa Grande Band of Diegueno Mission Indians of the Mesa Grande Reservation, California

Mescalero Apache Tribe of the Mescalero Reservation, New Mexico

Miami Tribe of Oklahoma

Miccosukee Tribe of Indians of Florida

Middletown Rancheria of Pomo Indians of California

Minnesota Chippewa Tribe, Minnesota (Six component Reservations: Bois Forte Band [Nett Lake], Fond du Lac Band, Grand Portage Band, Leech Lake Band, Mille Lac Band, White Earth Band)

Mississippi Band of Choctaw Indians, Mississippi

Moapa Band of Paiute Indians of the Moapa River Indian Reservation, Nevada

Modoc Tribe of Oklahoma

Mooretown Rancheria of Maidu Indians of California

Moronogo Band of Cahuilla Mission Indians of the Morongo Reservation, California

Muckleshoot Indian Tribe of the Muckleshoot Reservation, Washington

Narragansett Indian Tribe of Rhode Island

Navajo Tribe of Arizona, New Mexico and Utah

Nez Perce Tribe of Idaho

Nisqually Indian Community of the Nisqually Reservation, Washington

Nooksack Indian Tribe of Washington

Northern Cheyenne Tribe of the Northern Cheyenne Indian Reservation, Montana

Northfork Rancheria of Mono Indians of California

Northwestern Band of Shoshoni Indians of Utah (Washakie)

Oglala Sioux Tribe of the Pine Ridge Reservation, South Dakota

Omaha Tribe of Nebraska

Oneida Nation of New York

Oneida Tribe of Wisconsin

Onondaga Nation of New York

Osage Tribe of Oklahoma

Ottawa Tribe of Oklahoma

Otoe-Missouria Tribe of Oklahoma

Paiute Indian Tribe of Utah

Paiute-Shoshone Indians of the Bishop Community of the Bishop Colony, California

Paiute-Shoshone Tribe of the Fallon Reservation and Colony, Nevada

Paiute-Shoshone Indians of the Lone Pine Community of the Lone Pine Reservation, California

Pala Band of Luiseno Mission Indians of the Pala Reservation, California

Pascua Yaqui Tribe of Arizona

Passamaquoddy Tribe of Maine

Pauma Band of Luiseno Mission Indians of the Pauma & Yuima Reservation, California

Pawnee Indian Tribe of Oklahoma

Pechanga Band of Luiseno Mission Indians of the Pechanga Reservation, California

Penobscot Tribe of Maine

Peoria Tribe of Oklahoma

Picayune Rancheria of Chukchansi Indians of California

Pinoleville Rancheria of Pomo Indians of California

Pit River Tribe of California (includes Big Bend, Lookout, Montgomery Creek & Roaring Creek Rancherias & XL Ranch)

Poarch Band of Creek Indians of Alabama

Ponca Tribe of Indians of Oklahoma

Ponca Tribe of Nebraska

Port Gamble Indian Community of the Port Gamble Reservation, Washington

Potter Valley Rancheria of Pomo Indians of California

Prairie Band of Potawatomi Indians of Kansas

Prairie Island Indian Community of Minnesota Mdewakanton Sioux Indians of the Prairie Island Reservation, Minnesota

Pueblo of Acoma, New Mexico

Pueblo of Cochiti, New Mexico

Pueblo of Isleta, New Mexico

Pueblo of Jemez, New Mexico

Pueblo of Laguna, New Mexico

Pueblo of Nambe, New Mexico

Pueblo of Picuris, New Mexico

Pueblo of Pojoaque, New Mexico

Pueblo of San Felipe, New Mexico

Pueblo of San Juan, New Mexico

Pueblo of San Lldefonso, New Mexico

Pueblo of Sandia, New Mexico

Pueblo of Santa Ana, New Mexico

Pueblo of Santa Clara, New Mexico

Pueblo of Santo Domingo, New Mexico

Pueblo of Taos, New Mexico

Pueblo of Tesuque, New Mexico

Pueblo of Zia, New Mexico

Puyallup Tribe of the Puyallup Reservation, Washington

Pyramid Lake Paiute Tribe of the Pyramid Lake Reservation, Nevada

Quapaw Tribe of Oklahoma

Quartz Valley Rancheria of Karok, Shasta & Upper Klamath Indians of California

Quechan Tribe of the Fort Yuma Indian Reservation, California

Quileute Tribe of the Quileute Reservation, Washington

Quinault Tribe of the Quinault Reservation, Washington

Ramena Band or Village of Cahuilla Mission Indians of California

Red Cliff Band of Lake Superior Chippewa Indians of Wisconsin

Red Lake Band of Chippewa Indians of the Red Lake Reservation, Minnesota

Redding Rancheria of Pomo Indians of California

Redwood Valley Rancheria of Pomo Indians of California

Reno-Sparks Indian Colony, Nevada

Rincon Band of Luiseno Mission Indians of the Rincon Reservation, California

Robinson Rancheria of Pomo Indians of California

Rohnerville Rancheria of Bear River or Mattole Indians of California

Rosebud Sioux Tribe of the Rosebud Indian Reservation, South Dakota

Rumsey Indian Rancheria of Wintun Indians of California

Sac & Fox Tribe of the Mississippi in Iowa

Sac & Fox Tribe of Missouri in Kansas and Nebraska

Sac & Fox Tribe of Oklahoma

Saginaw Chippewa Indian Tribe of Michigan, Isabella Reservation

Salt River Pima-Maricopa Indian Community of the Salt River Reservation, Arizona

San Carlos Apache Tribe of the San Carlos Reservation, Arizona

San Juan Paiute Tribe of Arizona

San Manual Band of Serrano Mission Indians of the San Manual Reservation, California

San Pasqual Band of Diegueno Mission Indians of California

Santa Rosa Indian Community of the Santa Rosa Rancheria, California

Santa Rosa Band of Cahuilla Mission Indians of the Santa Rose Reservation, California

Santa Ynez Band of Chumash Mission Indians of the Santa Ysabel Reservation, California

Santa Ysabel Band of Diegueno Mission Indians of the Santa Ysabel Reservation, California

Santee Sioux Tribe of the Santee Reservation of Nebraska

Sauk-Suiattle Indian Tribe of Washington

Sault Ste. Marie Tribe of Chippewa Indians of Michigan

Scotts Valley Band of Pomo Indians, California

Seminole Nation of Oklahoma

Seminole Tribe of Florida, Dania, Big Cypress & Brighton Reservations

Seneca Nation of New York

Seneca-Cayuga Tribe of Oklahoma

Shakopee Mdewakanton Sioux Community of Minnesota (Prior Lake)

Sheep Ranch Rancheria of Me-Wuk Indians of California

Sherwood Valley Rancheria of Pomo Indians of California

Shingle Springs Band of Me-Wuk Indians, Shingle Springs Rancheria (Verona Tract), California

Shoalwater Bay Tribe of the Shoalwater Bay Indian Reservation, Washington

Shoshone Tribe of the Wind River Reservation, Wyoming

Shoshone-Bannock Tribes of the Fort Hall Reservation of Idaho

Shoshone-Paiute Tribes of the Duck Valley Reservation, Nevada

Sisseton-Wahpeton Sioux Tribe of the Lake Traverse Reservation, South Dakota

Skokomish Indian Tribe of the Skokomish Reservation, Washington

Skull Valley Band of Goshute Indians of Utah

Smith River Rancheria of California

Soboba Band of Luiseno Mission Indians of the Soboba Reservation, California

Sokoagon Chippewa Community of the Mole Lake Band of Chippewa Indians, Wisconsin

Southern Ute Indian Tribe of the Southern Ute Reservation, Colorado

Spokane Tribe of the Spokane Reservation, Washington

Squaxin Island Tribe of the Squaxin Island Reservation, Washington

St. Croix Chippewa Indians of Wisconsin, St. Croix Reservation

St. Regis Band of Mohawk Indians of New York

Standing Rock Sioux Tribe of North & South Dakota

Stockbridge-Munsee Community of Mohican Indians of Wisconsin

Stillaguamish Tribe of Washington

Summit Lake Paiute Tribe of Nevada

Suquamish Indian Tribe of the Port Madison Reservation, Washington

Susanville Indian Rancheria of Paiute, Maidu, Pit River & Washoe Indians of California

Swinomish Indians of the Swinomish Reservation, Washington

Sycuan Band of Diegueno Mission Indians of California

Table Bluff Rancheria of Wiyot Indians of California

Table Mountain Rancheria of California

Te-Moak Tribe of Western Shoshone Indians of Nevada

Thlopthlocco Tribal Town of the Creek Nation of Oklahoma

Three Affiliated Tribes of the Fort Berthold Reservation, North Dakota

Tohono O'odham Nation of Arizona (formerly known as the Papago Tribe of the Sells, Gila Bend & San Xavier Reservation, Arizona)

Tonawanda Band of Seneca Indians of New York

Tonkawa Tribe of Indians of Oklahoma

Tonto Apache Tribe of Arizona

Torres-Martinez Band of Cahuilla Mission Indians of California

Tule River Indian Tribe of the Tule River Reservation, California

Tulalip Tribes of the Tulalip Reservation, Washington

Tunica-Biloxi Indian Tribe of Louisiana

Tuolumne Band of Me-Wuk Indians of the Tuolumne Rancheria of California

Turtle Mountain Band of Chippewa Indians of North Dakota

Tuscarora Nation of New York

Twenty-Nine Palms Band of Luiseno Mission Indians of California

United Keetoowah Band of Cherokee Indians, Oklahoma

Upper Lake Band of Pomo Indians of Upper Lake Rancheria of California

Upper Sioux Indian Community of the Upper Sioux Reservation, Minnesota

Upper Skagit Indian Tribe of Washington

Ute Indian Tribe of the Uintah & Ouray Reservation, Utah

Ute Mountain Tribe of the Ute Mountain Reservation, Colorado, New Mexico & Utah

Utu Utu Gwaitu Paiute Tribe of the Benton Paiute Reservation, California

Walker River Paiute Tribe of the Walker River Reservation, California

Washoe Tribe of Nevada & California (Carson Colony, Dresslerville & Washoe Ranches)

White Mountain Apache Tribe of the Fort Apache Reservation, Arizona

Wichita Indian Tribe of Oklahoma

Winnebago Tribe of Nebraska

Winnemucca Indian Colony of Nevada

Wisconsin Winnebago Indian Tribe of Wisconsin

Wyandotte Tribe of Oklahoma

Yankton Sioux Tribe of South Dakota

Yavapai-Apache Indian Community of the Camp Verde Reservation, Arizona

Yavapai-Prescott Tribe of the Yavapai Reservation, Arizona

Yerington Paiute Tribe of the Yerington Colony & Campbell Ranch, Nevada

Yomba Shoshone Tribe of the Yomba Reservation, Nevada

Ysleta Del Sur Pueblo of Texas

Yurok Tribe of the Hoopa Valley Reservation, California

Zuni Tribe of the Zuni Reservation, New Mexico

APPENDIX 3

NATIVE ENTITIES WITHIN THE STATE OF ALASKA RECOGNIZED AND ELIGIBLE TO RECEIVE SERVICES FROM THE UNITED STATES BUREAU OF INDIAN AFFAIRS

Afognak

Ahkiok-Kaguyak Native Corp.

AHTNA, Inc. (Cantwell, Chistochina, Copper Center, Gakona, Gulkana, Mentasta & Tazlina)

AHTNA, Incorporated

Akhiok

Akiachak

Akiachak, Akiachak Native Community

Akiachak, Ltd.

Akiak

Akiak Native Community

Akutan

Akutan Corp.

Alakanuk

Alakanuk Native Corp.

Alaska Peninsula Corp. (Kokhanok, Newhalen, Port Heiden, South Naknek & Ugashek)

Alatna

Aleknagik (aka Alegnagik)

Aleknagik Natives, Ltd.

Aleut Corporation

Alexander Creek

Alexander Creek, Inc.

Allakaket

Ambler

Anaktuvuk Pass

Andreafsey

Angoon

Angoon Community Association

Aniak

Anton Larsen, Inc.

Anvik

Arctic Slope Regional Corporation

Arctic Village

ARVIQ, Inc. (Platinum)

Askinuk Corp. (Scammon Bay)

Atka

Atka, Native Village of Atka

Atkasook

Atkasook Corp.

Atmauthluak, Ltd.

Atmautluak

Atxam Corp. (Atka)

Ayakulik

Ayakulik, Inc.

Azachorok, Inc. (Mountain Village)

Baan-o-yeel kon Corp. (Rampart)

Barrow

Bay View, Inc. (Ivanof Bay)

Bean Ridge Corp. (Manley Hot Springs)

Beaver

Beaver Kwit'chin Corp.

Becharof Corp. (Egegik)

Belkofski Corp.

Belkofsky (aka Belkofski)

Bells Flats

Bells Flats Natives, Inc.

Bering Straits Native Corporation

Bethel (aka Orutsararmuit)

Bethel Native Corp.

NOTE: This list includes all of the Alaska entities meeting any of the following criteria which are used in one or more Federal statutes for the benefit of Alaska Natives: (1) "Tribes" as defined or established under the Indian Reorganization Act as supplemented by the Alaska Native Act; (2) Alaska Native Villages defined in or established pursuant to the Alaska Native Claims Settlement Act (ANCSA); (3) Village corporations defined in or established pursuant to ANCSA; (4) Regional corporations defined in or established pursuant to ANCSA; (5) Urban corporations defined in or established pursuant to ANCSA; (6) Alaska Native groups defined in or established pursuant to ANCSA; (7) Alaska Native group corporations defined in or established pursuant to ANCSA; (8) Alaska Native entities that receive assistance from the Bureau [of Indian Affairs] in matters relating to the settlement of claims against the United States government...; and (9) Tribes which have petitioned to be acknowledged and have been determined to exist as tribes pursuant to 25 CFR Part 83.

Bill Moore's (aka Bill Moore's Slough)

Birch Creek

Brevig Mission

Brevig Mission Native Corp.

Bristol Bay Native Corp.

Buckland

Buckland, Native Village of Buckland

Calista Corporation

Candle

Cantwell

Canyon Village

Cape Fox Corporation (Saxman)

Caswell

Caswell Native Assn.

Central Council of Tlingit and Haida Indian Tribes of Alaska

Chalkyitsik

Chalkyitsik Native Corp.

Chaloonawick

Chaluka Corp. (Nikolski)

Chanega, Native Village of Chanega

Chanilut

Chefarnmute, Inc. (Chefornak)

Chenaga Corporation

Cherfornak

Chevak

Chevak Company Corp.

Chickaloon

Chickaloon Moose Creek Native Association, Inc.

Chignik

Chignik Lagoon

Chignik Lagoon Native Corporation

Chignik Lake

Chignik River, Ltd. (Chignik Lake)

Chilkat Indian Village of Klukwan

Chilkoot Indian Assn. of Haines

Chistochina

Chitina

Chitina Native Corp.

Choggiung, Ltd. (Dillingham, Ekuk, Portage Creek)

Chuathbaluk

Chugach Alaska Corp.

Chuloonawick Corp.

Circle

Clark's Point

Cook Inlet Region, Inc.

Copper Center

Council

Council Native Corp.

Craig

Craig Community Assn.

Crooked Creek

Cully Corp. (Point Lay)

Danzhit Hanlaii Corp. (Circle)

Deering

Deering, Native Village of Deering

Deloycheet, Inc. (Holy Cross)

Dillingham

Dineega Corp. (Ruby)

Dinyee Corp. (Stevens)

Diomede Native Corp.

Diomede, Native Village of Diomede (aka Inalik)

Dot Lake

Dot Lake Native Corp.

Douglas Indian Assn.

Doyon, Limited

Eagle

Eek

Egegik

Eklutna

Eklutna, Inc.

Ekuk

Ekwok

Ekwok Natives, Ltd.

Elim

Elim Native Corp.

Elim, Native Village of Elim

Emmonak

Emmonak Corporation

English Bay

English Bay Corp.

Evanville

Evanville, Inc.

Eyak

Eyak Corporation

False Pass

Far West, Inc. (Chignik)

Fort Yukon

Fort Yukon, Native Village of Fort Yukon

Gakona

Galena

Gambell

Gambell, Native Village of Gambell

Gana-'Yoo, Limited (Galena, Kaltag, Koyukuk & Nulato)

Georgetown

Gold Creek-Susitna

Gold Creek-Susitna, Inc.

Goldbelt, Inc. (Juneau)

Golovin

Golovin Native Corp.

Goodnews Bay

Grayling

Grayling, Organized Village of Grayling (aka Holikachuk)

Gulkana

Gwitchyaa Zhee Corp.
  (Fort Yukon)
Haida Corporation
  (Hydaburg)
Hamilton
Healy Lake
Hee-Yea-lindge Corp.
  (Grayling)
Holy Cross
Hoonah Indian Assn.
Hooper Bay
Hughes
Huna Totem (Hoonah)
Hungwitchin Corp. (Eagle)
Huslia
Hydaburg
Hydaburg Cooperative
  Association
Igiugig
Igiugig Native Corp.
Iliamna
Iliamna Natives, Ltd.
Inalik (aka Diomede)
Ingalik, Inc. (Anvik)
Inupiat Community of the
  Arctic Slope
Iqfijouaq Company (Eek)
Isanotski Corporation
  (False Pass)
Ivanof Bay
K'oyitl'ots'ina, Ltd.
  (Alatna, Allakaket,
  Hughes & Huslia)
Kaguyak
Kake
Kake, Organized Village
  of Kake
Kake Tribal Corporation
Kaktovik
Kaktovik Inupiat Corp.
Kalskag
Kaltag
Kanatak, Native Village
  of Kanatak

Karluk
Karluk, Native Village of
  Karluk
Kasaan, Organized
  Village of Kasaan
Kasaan
Kasigluk
Kasigluk, Inc.
Kavilco, Inc. (Kasaan)
Kenai Native Assn, Inc.
Kenaitze Indian Tribe
Ketchikan Indian Corp.
Kiana
KianT'ree
  (Canyon Village)
Kijik Corporation
  (Nondalton)
Kikiktagruk Inupiat Corp.
  (Kotzebue)
King Cove
King Cove Corporation
King Island Native
  Community
King Island Native
  Corporation
Kipnuk
Kiutsarak, Inc.
  (Goodnews Bay)
Kivalina
Kivalina, Native Village
  of Kivalina
Klawock
Klawock Cooperative Assn.
Klawock Heenya
Klukwan, Inc.
Knik
Knikatnu, Inc. (Knik)
Kobuk
Kokarmiut Corp. (Akiak)
Kokhanok
Koliganek
Koliganek Natives, Ltd.
Kongiganak

Kongnikilnomiut Yuita
  Corp. (Bill Moore's)
Koniag, Incorporated
Koniag, Inc. (Karluk &
  Larsen Bay)
Kootznoowoo, Inc.
  (Angoon)
Kotlik
Kotlik Yupik Corp.
Kotzebue
Kotzebue, Native
  Village of Kotzebue
Koyuk
Koyuk Native Corp.
Koyuk, Native Village
  of Koyuk
Koyukuk
Kugkaktlik, Ltd.
  (Kipnuk)
Kuskokwim Native Corp.
  (Aniak, Chuathbaluk,
  Crooked Creek,
  Georgetown, Lower
  Kalska, Red Devil,
  Napaimute,
  Sleetmute, Stony
  River, Upper Kalskag)
Kuugpik Corporation
  (Nooiksut)
Kwethluk
Kwethluk, Inc.
Kwethluk, Organized
  Village of Kwethluk
Kwigillingok
Kwigillingok, Native
  Village of Kwigilingok
Kwik, Inc.
  (Kwigillingok)
Kwinhagak, Native
  Village of Kwinhagak
  (aka Quinhagak)
Larsen Bay
Leisnoi, Inc. (Woody
  Island)
Levelock

Levelock Natives, Ltd.
Lime Village
Lime Village Company
Litnik
Litnik, Inc.
Lower Kalskag
Manley Hot Springs
Manokotak
Manokotak Natives, Ltd.
Marshall
Mary's Igloo
Mary's Igloo Native Corp.
Maserculiq, Inc. (Marshall)
McGrath
Mekoryuk
Mekoryuk, Native Village
    of Mekoryuk, Island of
    Nunivak
Mendas Chaag Native
    Corp. (Healy Lake)
Mentasta Lake
Metlakatla Indian Comm.,
    Annette Island Reserve
Minto
Minto, Native Village of
    Minto
Montana Creek
Montana Creek Native
    Association
Mountain Village
MTNT, Ltd. (McGrath,
    Nikolai, Takotna &
    Telida)
Nagamut
Naknek
NANA Regional Corp.
    (Ambler, Buckland,
    Deering, Kiana,
    Kivalina, Kobuk,
    Noatak, Noorvik,
    Selawik & Shungnak)
Napaimute
Napakiak Corporation
Napakiak Native Village
    of Napakiak

Napakiak
Napakiak Corporation
Natives of Afognak, Inc.
    (Afognak & Port Lions)
Natives of Kodiak
Neets' ai Corporation
    (Arctic Village)
Nelson Lagoon
Nelson Lagoon Corp.
Nenana
Nerklikmute Native Corp.
    (Andreafski)
New Stuyahok
Newhalen
Newtok
Newtok Corporation
NGTA, Inc. (Nightmute)
Nightmute
Nikolai
Nikolski
Nikolski, Native Village
    of Nikolski
Nima Corp. (Mekoryuk)
Ninilchik
Ninilchik Native Assn.
Noatak
Noatak, Native Village of
    Noatak
Nome (aka Nome Eskimo)
Nome Eskimo
    Community
Nondalton
Nooiksut (aka Nuiqsut)
Noorvik
Noorvik Native Comm.
Northway
Northway Natives, Inc.
Nulato
Nunakauiak Yupik Corp.
    (Tooksok Bay)
Nunamiut Corporation
    (Anaktuvuk Pass)
Nunapiglluraq Corp.
    (Hamilton)

Nunapitchuk
Nunapitchuk, Ltd.
Nunapitchuk, Native
    Village of Nunapitchuk
Oceanside Corporation
    (Perryville)
OHOG, Inc.
    (Ohogamiut)
Ohogamiut
Old Harbor
Old Harbor Native
    Corporation
Olgoonik Corporation
    (Wainwright)
Olsonville
Oscarville
Oscarville Native Corp.
Ounalashka Corp.
    (Unalaska)
Ouzinkie
Ouzinkie Native Corp.
Paimiut
Paimiut Corporation
Paug-vik, Incorporated,
    Ltd. (Naknek)
Pauloff Harbor
Pedro Bay
Pedro Bay Native Corp.
Perryville
Perryville, Native
    Village of Perryville
Petersburg Indian Assn.
Pilot Point
Pilot Point Native Corp.
Pilot Station
Pilot Station, Inc.
Pitka's Point
Pitka's Point Native
    Corporation
Platinum
Point Hope
Point Hope, Native
    Village of Point Hope
Point Lay

Point Lay, Native Village
of Point Lay

Point Possession

Point Possession, Inc.

Port Alsworth

Port Graham

Port Graham Corp.

Port Heiden (Meshick)

Port Lions

Port Williams (Shuyak)

Portage Creek
(Ohgsenakale)

Pribilof Aleut
Communities of St. Paul
& St. George Islands

Qanırtuuq, Inc.
(Quinhagak aka
Kwinhagak)

Qemirtalek Coast Corp.
(Kongiganak)

Quinhagak (aka
Kwinhagak)

Rampart

Red Devil

Ruby

Russian Mission or
Chauthalue
(Kuskokwim)

Russian Mission (Yukon)

Russian Mission Native
Corporation

Saguyak, Inc. (Clark's
Point)

Salamatof

Salamatof Native Assn., Inc.

Sanak Corporation
(Pauloff Harbor)

Sand Point

Savoonga

Savoonga Native Corp.

Savoonga, Native Village
of Savoonga

Saxman

Saxman, Organized
Village of Saxman

Scammon Bay

Sea Lion Corporation
(Hooper Bay)

Sealaska Corporation

Selawik

Selawik, Native Village of
Selawik

Seldovia

Seldovia Native
Association, Inc.

Seth-de-ya-ah Corp.
(Minto)

Shaan-Seet, Inc. (Craig)

Shageluk

Shageluk Native Village

Shaktoolik

Shaktoolik Native Corp.

Shaktoolik, Native Village
of Shaktoolik

Shee Atika, Inc. (Sitka)

Sheldon's Point

Shishmaref

Shishmaref Native Corp.

Shishmaref, Native
Village of Shishmaref

Shumagin Corporation
(Sand Point)

Shungnak

Shungnak, Native Village
of Shungnak

Shuyak, Inc. (Port
Williams)

Sitka Community Assn.

Sitnasuak Native Corp.
(Nome)

Sleetmute

Solomon

Solomon Native Corp.

South Naknek

St. George

St. George Tanaq Corp.

St. Mary's (aka Algaaciq)

St. Mary's Native Corp.

St. Michael

St. Michael Native
Corporation

St. Michael, Native
Village of St. Michael

St. Paul

Stebbins

Stebbins Community
Association

Stebbins Native Corp.

Stevens, Native Village
of Stevens

Stevens Village

Stony River

Stuyahok, Ltd. (New
Stuyahok)

Swan Lake Corp.
(Sheldon's Point)

Takotna

Tanacross

Tanacross, Inc.

Tanacross, Native
Village of Tanacross

Tanadgusix Corp. (St.
Paul)

Tanalian, Inc. (Port
Alsworth)

Tanana

Tanana, Native Village
of Tanana

Tatitlek

Tatitlek Corporation

Tatitlek, Native Village
of Tatitlek

Tazlina

Telida

Teller

Teller Native Corp.

Tetlin

Tetlin, Native Corp.

Tetlin, Native Village of
Tetlin

Thirteenth Regional
Corp.

Tigara Corporation
(Point Hope)

Tihteet'Aii, Inc. (Birch Creek)

Toghottele Corporation (Nenana)

Togiak

Togiak Natives, Ltd.

Toksook Bay

Tozitna, Ltd. (Tanana)

Tulkisarmute, Inc. (Tuluksak)

Tuluksak

Tuluksak Native Community

Tuntutuliak

Tuntutuliak Land, Ltd.

Tununak

Tununak, Native Village of Tununak

Tununrmiut Rinit Corp. (Tununak)

Twin Hills

Twin Hills Native Corp.

Tyonek

Tyonek, Native Corp.

Tyonek, Native Village of Tyonek

Uganik

Uganik Natives, Inc.

Ugashik

Ukpeagvik Inupiat Corp. (Barrow)

Umkumiut

Umkumiut, Ltd.

Unalakleet

Unalakleet Native Corp.

Unalakleet, Native Village of Unalakleet

Unalaska

Unga

Unga Corporation

Upper Kalskag

Uyak

Uyak Natives, Inc.

Venetie

Venetie, Native Village of Venetie

Wainwright

Wales

Wales Native Corp.

Wales, Native Village of Wales

White Mountain

White Mountain Native Corporation

White Mountain, Native Village of White Mountain

Woody Island

Wrangell Cooperative Association

Yak-tat Kwaan, Inc. (Yakutat)

Yakutat

Zho-Tse, Inc. (Shageluk)

APPENDIX 4

BIA SUMMARY OF 25 CFR, PART 83

PROCEDURES FOR ESTABLISHING THAT AN AMERICAN INDIAN GROUP EXISTS AS AN INDIAN TRIBE

The regulations contain seven specific criteria which must be met for a group to qualify as a "tribe." The petitioner (the group) must be traceable as an identifiable Indian group, containing a membership core which has exerted a governing influence over its members from historic times to the present. Briefly, to gain acknowledgment, the petitioners must:

(1) establish that they have been identified, from historical times to the present, on a substantially continuous basis as "American Indian" or "aboriginal;"

(2) establish that a substantial portion of the group inhabits a specific area or lives in a community viewed as American Indian, distinct from other populations in the area, and that its members are descendants of an Indian tribe which historically inhabited a specific area;

(3) furnish a statement of facts which establishes that the group has maintained tribal political influence, or other authority, over its members as an autonomous entity throughout history until the present;

(4) furnish a copy of the group's present government document or, in the absence of such a written document, a statement describing in full the membership criteria and the procedures through which the group currently governs its affairs and its members;

(5) furnish a list of known current members of the group, and a copy of each available former list of members, based on the group's own defined membership criteria. The membership must consist of individuals who have established (using evidence acceptable to the Secretary of the Interior) descendancy from a tribe which existed historically or from historical tribes which combined and functioned as a single autonomous entity;

(6) establish that the membership of the group is composed principally of persons who are not members of any other North American tribe; and,

NOTE: The information in this appendix pertains to Indian groups not previously recognized as tribes by the federal government (BIA 1985b). CFR refers to the Code of Federal Regulations.

(7) establish that neither the group nor its members are subject to congressional legislation which has expressly terminated or forbidden the Federal relationship.

The Assistant Secretary of the Interior for Indian Affairs evaluates each petition and the accompanying evidence and makes one of two determinations. The petitioning group either meets the criteria or does not. Petitions that are denied can be reconsidered at the special request of the Secretary of the Interior. Only if the petitioners qualify, however, will they be acknowledged as a tribe. Otherwise, their pre-petition status remains the same or they must obtain special legislation from Congress – an unlikely event under their circumstances. Title 25 of the Code of Federal Regulations (CFR), Sec. 83.11, describes what takes place after a petition is successful:

(a) Upon final determination that the petitioner is an Indian tribe, the tribe shall be eligible for services and benefits from the Federal Government available to other federally recognized tribes and entitled to the privileges and immunities available to other federally recognized tribes by virtue of their status as Indian tribes with a government-to-government relationship to the United States as well as having the responsibilities and obligations of such tribes. Acknowledgment shall subject such Indian tribes to the same authority of Congress and the United States to which other federally acknowledged tribes are subject.

(b) While the newly recognized tribe shall be eligible for benefits and services, acknowledgment of tribal existence will not create an immediate entitlement to existing Bureau of Indian Affairs programs. Such programs shall become available upon appropriation of funds by Congress. Requests for appropriations shall follow a determination of the needs of the newly recognized tribe.

APPENDIX 5

MEMBERSHIP IN THE NAVAJO TRIBE

GENERAL PROVISIONS

§ 501. Composition

The membership of the Navajo Tribe shall consist of the following persons:

(1) All persons of Navajo blood whose names appear on the official roll of the Navajo Tribe maintained by the Bureau of Indian Affairs.

(2) Any person who is at least one-fourth degree Navajo blood, but who has not previously been enrolled as a member of the Tribe, is eligible for Tribal membership and enrollment.

(3) Children born to any enrolled member of the Navajo Tribe shall automatically become members of the Navajo Tribe and shall be enrolled, provided they are at least one-fourth degree Navajo blood.

§ 502. Adoption as not possible

(a) No Tribal law or custom has ever existed or exists now, by which anyone can ever become a Navajo, either by adoption, or otherwise, except by birth.

(b) All those individuals who claim to be a member of the Tribe by adoption are declared to be in no possible way an adopted or honorary member of the Navajo people.

§ 503. Member of another tribe

No person, otherwise eligible for membership in the Navajo Tribe, may enroll as a member of said Tribe, who, at the same time, is on the roll of any other tribe of Indians.

§ 504. Authority of Advisory Committee

The Advisory Committee of the Navajo Tribal Council is authorized and directed:

(1) to make and promulgate all necessary rules and regulations for establishing eligibility for membership and enrollment in the Navajo Tribe;

(2) to establish basic standards and requirements of proof required to determine eligibility for membership and enrollment;

(3) to prescribe forms of application for enrollment, and establish dates or designated periods for enrollment.

NOTE: This information is from the Navajo Tribal Code (N.T.C.), courtesy of the Navajo Nation.

§ 505. Renunciation of membership

Any enrolled member of the Navajo Tribe may renounce his membership by written petition to the Chairman of the Navajo Tribe requesting that his name be stricken from the Tribal roll. Such person may be reinstated in the Navajo Tribe only by the vote of a majority of the Navajo Tribal Council.

ENROLLMENT PROCEDURE

§ 551. Application for enrollment

Anyone wishing to apply for enrollment in the Navajo Tribe may submit an application in the form set out in 1 N.T.C. § 556. Such application must be verified before a notary public.

§ 552. Enrollment Screening Committee; action by Advisory Committee

An Enrollment Screening Committee consisting of the Chairman, the Vice-Chairman, and the Director of Land Investigations, the Agency Census Clerk, and the Tribal Legal Advisor is established. The Enrollment Screening Committee shall consider all applications for enrollment in the first instance.

In all cases where the records of the Navajo Agency do not show that the applicant is of at least one-fourth degree Navajo blood or the applicant does not establish such fact by documentary evidence independent of his own statement, consisting of the affidavits of disinterested persons, certified copies of public or church records, or the like, the Screening Committee shall reject the application. In all cases where the applicant appears to be enrolled in another Indian tribe, the Screening Committee shall reject the application. In all cases the Screening Committee or any successor committee lawfully established shall inform the applicant of his rights of appeal under this section. The Committee or its successor shall establish a record of any hearing or proceeding on any application, and this record shall contain the evidence used by the Committee in making its decision, a statement of its decision, and its reasons therefore, and the date. The Committee or its successor shall transmit this record to an appropriate Trial Court of the Navajo Tribe, and a copy to the Office of the Prosecutor.

§ 553. Standards for Screening Committee recommendations

The Screening Committee shall be guided by the following standards in making its recommendations:

(1) If the applicant appears to be a Navajo Indian of full blood it shall recommend approval.

(2) If the applicant appears to have Navajo blood of one-fourth degree or higher, but not full blood, it shall base its recommendations on his degree of Navajo blood, how long he has lived among the Navajo people, whether he is presently living among them, whether he can be identified a member

of a Navajo clan, whether he can speak the Navajo language, and whether he is married to an enrolled Navajo. The Screening Committee is authorized to make investigations to determine such facts, but the burden of proof in all cases shall rest on the applicant.

§ 554. Appeals from Screening Committee – Trial Courts

The Trial Courts of the Navajo Tribe shall have original jurisdiction to hear and decide appeals from decisions of the Enrollment Screening Committee or any successor committee lawfully established by the Advisory Committee of the Navajo Tribal Council pursuant to 1 N.T.C. § 504.

§ 560. Form of application

APPLICATION FOR ENROLLMENT IN THE NAVAJO TRIBE
OF INDIANS

STATE OF..)
)
COUNTY OF...) ss.
)

I hereby apply for enrollment in the Navajo Tribe. I am a man/woman. All the names by which I have ever been known are as follows:

....

....

....

My present address is ....

....

I was born .... at ....
               (Date)   (Place)

My mother's name was ....

Her degree of Navajo blood was ....

Census number, if any ....

Her clan was ....

She was born .... at ....
               (Date)   (Place)

If living, her present address is ....

....

My maternal grandmother's name was ....

Her degree of Navajo blood was ....

Census number, if any ....

Her clan was ....

She was born .... at ....
                (Date)   (Place)

If living, her present address is ....
....

My maternal grandfather's name was ....
His degree of Navajo blood was ....
Census number, if any ....
His clan was ....
He was born .... at ....
         (Date)   (Place)

If living, his present address is ....
....

My father's name was ....
His degree of Navajo blood was ....
Census number, if any ....
His clan was..
He was born .... at ....
     (Date)   (Place)

If living, his present address is ....
....

My paternal grandmother's name was ....
Her degree of Navajo blood was ....
Census number, if any ....
Her clan was ....
She was born .... at ....
     (Date)   (Place)

If living, her present address is ....
....

My paternal grandfather's name was ....
His degree of Navajo blood was ....
Census number, if any ....
His clan was ....
He was born .... at ....
     (Date)   (Place)

If living, his present address : ....
....

I have lived among Navajo people during the following periods at the following places:
From .... to .... at..
     (Year)   (Year)

From .... to .... at...
      (Year)   (Year)

From .... to .... at...
      (Year)   (Year)

From .... to .... at...
      (Year)   (Year)

I can/cannot speak the Navajo language.

My wife's/husband's name is ....

She/he is/is not an enrolled member of the Navajo Tribe. If such a member, her/his census number is ....

I am not at the present time enrolled in any other Indian Tribe.

I have/have not been previously enrolled in the Navajo Tribe. If previously enrolled, my census number was ....

If previously enrolled, I was dropped from the official roll of the Navajo Tribe on .... for the following reason

....

....

....

      (A person who has voluntarily renounced membership
      in the Navajo Tribe may be reinstated only by a vote of
      majority of the Navajo Tribal Council.)

Remarks: ....

....

....

....

....

                    Signature: ....

                            (Use name in current use)

Subscribed and sworn to before me, a notary public, this ....

day of ...., 19................, by ....

                                    (Name of applicant)

My commission expires ....

                ....

                      Notary Public

(SEAL)

NOTE: In all cases where the records of the Navajo Agency do not show that the applicant is of at least one-fourth degree Navajo blood, such fact must be established by documentary evidence independent of the applicant's own statement. Such evidence may consist of the affidavits of disinterested persons, certified copies of public or church records or the like.

APPENDIX 6

TREATY WITH THE DELAWARES, 1778

Articles of agreement and confederation, made and entered into by Andrew and Thomas Lewis, Esquires, Commissioners for, and in Behalf of the United States of North-America of the one Part, and Capt. White Eyes, Capt. John Kill Buck, Junior, and Capt. Pipe, Deputies and Chief Men of the Delaware Nation of the other Part.

ARTICLE I.

That all offences or acts of hostilities by one, or either of the contracting parties against the other, be mutually forgiven, and buried in the depth of oblivion, never more to be had in remembrance.

ARTICLE II.

That a perpetual peace and friendship shall from henceforth take place, and subsist between the contracting parties aforesaid, through all succeeding generations: and if either of the parties are engaged in a just and necessary war with any other nation or nations, that then each shall assist the other in due proportion to their abilities, till their enemies are brought to reasonable terms of accommodation: and that if either of them shall discover any hostile designs forming against the other, they shall give the earliest notice thereof, that timeous measures may be taken to prevent their ill effect.

ARTICLE III.

And whereas the United States are engaged in a just and necessary war, in defence and support of life, liberty and independence, against the King of England and his adherents, and as said King is yet possessed of several posts and forts on the lakes and other places, the reduction of which is of great importance to the peace and security of the contracting parties, and as the most practicable way for the troops of the United States to some of the posts and forts is by passing through the country of the Delaware nation, the aforesaid deputies, on behalf of themselves and their nation, do hereby stipulate and agree to give a free passage through their country to the troops aforesaid, and the same to conduct by the nearest and best ways to the posts, forts or towns of the enemies of the United States, affording to said troops such supplies of corn, meat, horses, or whatever may be in their power for the accommodation of such troops, on the commanding officer's, &c paying, or engageing to pay, the full value of whatever they can supply them with. And the said deputies, on the behalf of their nation, engage to join the troops of the United States aforesaid, with such a number of their best and most expert warriors as they can spare, consistent with their own safety, and act in concert with them; and for the better security of the old men, women and children of the aforesaid nation, whilst their warriors are engaged against the common enemy, it is agreed on the part of the United States, that a fort of sufficient strength and capacity be built at the expense of the said States, with such assistance as it may be in the power of the said Delaware Nation to give, in the most convenient place, and advantageous situation, as shall be agreed on by the commanding officer of the troops aforesaid, with the advice and concurrence of the deputies of the aforesaid Delaware Nation, which fort shall be garrisoned by such a number of the troops of the United States, as the commanding officer can spare for the present, and hereafter by such numbers, as the wise men of the United States in council, shall think most conducive to the common good.

ARTICLE IV.

For the better security of the peace and friendship now entered into by the contracting parties, against all infractions of the same by the citizens of either party, to the prejudice of the other, neither party shall proceed to the infliction of punishments on the citizens of the other, otherwise then by securing the offender or offenders by imprisonment, or any other competent means, till a fair and impartial trial can be had by judges or juries of both parties, as near as can be to the laws, customs and usages of the contracting parties and natural justice: The mode of such trials to be hereafter fixed by the wise men of the United States in Congress assembled, with the assistance of such deputies of the Delaware nation, as may be appointed to act in concert with them in adjusting this matter to their mutual liking. And it is further agreed between the parties aforesaid, that neither shall entertain or give countenance to the enemies of the other, or protect in their respective states, criminal fugitives, servants or slaves, but the same to apprehend, and secure and deliver to the State or States, to which such enemies, criminals, servants or slaves respectively belong.

ARTICLE V.

Whereas the confederation entered into by the Delaware nation and the United States, renders the first dependent on the latter for all the articles of clothing, utensils and implements of war, and it is judged not only reasonable, but indispensably necessary, that the aforesaid Nation be supplied with such articles from time to time, as far as the United States may have it in their power, by a well-regulated trade, under the conduct of an intelligent, candid agent, with an adequate salary, one more influenced by the love of his country, and a constant attention to the duties of his department by promoting the common interest, than the sinister purposes of converting and binding all the duties of his office to his private emolument: Convinced of the necessity of such measures, the Commissioners of the United States, at the earnest solicitation of the deputies aforesaid, have engaged in behalf of the United States, that such a trade shall be afforded said nation, conducted on such principles of mutual interest as the wisdom of the United States in Congress assembled shall think most conducive to adopt for their mutual convenience.

ARTICLE VI.

Whereas the enemies of the United States have endeavored, by every artifice in their power, to possess the Indians in general with an opinion, that it is the design of the States aforesaid, to extirpate the Indians and take possession of their country: to obviate such false suggestion, the United States do engage to guarantee to the aforesaid nation of Delawares, and their heirs, all their territorial rights in the fullest and most ample manner, as it hath been bounded by former treaties, as long as they the said Delaware nation shall abide by, and hold fast the chain of friendship now entered into. And it is further agreed on between the contracting parties should it for the future be found conducive for the mutual interest of both parties to invite any other tribes who have been friends to the interest of the United States, to join the present confederation, and to form a state whereof the Delaware nation shall be the head, and have a representation in Congress: Provided, nothing contained in this article to be considered as conclusive until it meets with the approbation of Congress. And it is also the intent and meaning of this article, that no protection or countenance shall be afforded to any who are at present our enemies, by which they might escape the punishment they deserve.

In witness whereof, the parties have hereunto interchangeably set their hands and seals, at Fort Pitt, September seventeenth, anno Domini one thousand seven hundred and seventy-eight.

> Andrew Lewis,
> [L. S.]
> Thomas Lewis,
> [L. S.]
> White Eyes, his x mark,
> [L. S.]
>
> The Pipe, his x mark,
> [L. S.]
>
> John Kill Buck, his x mark,
> [L. S.]

In presence of—
  Lach'n McIntosh, brigadier-general, commander the Western Department.
  Daniel Brodhead, colonel Eighth Pennsylvania Regiment,
  W. Crawford, colonel,
  John Campbell,
  John Stephenson,
  John Gibson, colonel Thirteenth Virginia Regiment,
  A. Graham, brigade major,
  Lach. McIntosh, jr., major brigade,
  Benjamin Mills,
  Joseph L. Finley, captain Eighth Pennsylvania Regiment,
  John Finley, captain Eighth Pennsylvania Regiment.

APPENDIX 7

A PUBLIC DECLARATION

TO THE TRIBAL COUNCILS AND TRADITIONAL SPIRITUAL LEADERS OF THE INDIAN AND ESKIMO PEOPLES OF THE PACIFIC NORTHWEST

November 21, 1987

Dear Brothers and Sisters,

This is a formal apology on behalf of our churches for their long-standing participation in the destruction of traditional Native American spiritual practices. We call upon our people for recognition of and respect for your traditional ways of life and for protection of your sacred places and ceremonial objects. We have frequently been unconscious and insensitive and have not come to your aid when you have been victimized by unjust Federal policies and practices. In many other circumstances we reflected the rampant racism and prejudice of the dominant culture with which we too willingly identified. During the 200th Anniversary year of the United States Constitution we, as leaders of our churches in the Pacific Northwest, extend our apology. We ask for your forgiveness and blessing.

As the Creator continues to renew the earth, the plants, the animals and all living things, we call upon the people of our denominations and fellowship to a commitment of mutual support in your efforts to reclaim and protect the legacy of your own traditional spiritual teachings. To that end we pledge our support and assistance in upholding the American Religious Freedom Act (P. L. 95-134, 1978) and within that legal precedent affirm the following:

1) The rights of the Native Peoples to practice and participate in traditional ceremonies and rituals with the same protection offered all religions under the Constitution.

2) Access to and protection of sacred sites and public lands for ceremonial purposes.

3) The use of religious symbols (feathers, tobacco, sweet grass, bones, etc.) for use in traditional ceremonies and rituals.

The spiritual power of the land and the ancient wisdom of your indigenous religions can be, we believe, great gifts to the Christian churches. We offer our commitment to support you in the righting of previous wrongs: To protect your peoples' efforts to enhance Native spiritual teachings; to encourage the members of our churches to stand in solidarity with you on these important religious issues; to provide advocacy and mediation, when appropriate, for ongoing negotiations with State agencies and Federal officials regarding these matters.

May the promises of this day go on public record with all the congregations of our communions and be communicated to the Native American Peoples of the Pacific Northwest. May the God of Abraham and Sarah, and the Spirit who lives in both the cedar and Salmon People be honored and celebrated.

Sincerely,

The Rev. Thomas L. Blevins, Bishop
Pacific Northwest Synod –
  Lutheran Church in America

The Most Rev. Raymond G. Hunthausen
  Archbishop of Seattle
Roman Catholic Archdiocese of Seattle

The Rev. Dr. Robert Bradford,
  Executive Minister
American Baptist Churches of the
  Northwest

The Rev. Elizabeth Knott, Synod Exec.
Presbyterian Church
  Synod Alaska-Northwest

The Rev. Robert Brock
N.W. Regional Christian Church

The Rev. Lowell Knutson, Bishop
North Pacific District
  American Lutheran Church

The Right Rev. Robert H. Cochrane,
  Bishop, Episcopal Diocese of Olympia

The Most Rev. Thomas Murphy
  Coadjutor Archbishop
Roman Catholic Archdiocese of Seattle

The Rev. W. James Halfaker
  Conference Minister
Washington North Idaho Conference
  United Church of Christ

The Rev. Melvin G. Talbert, Bishop
United Methodist Church –
  Pacific Northwest Conference

APPENDIX 8

STATE INDIAN COMMISSIONS

Individual states have developed commissions to address American Indian issues.

ALABAMA
Alabama Indian Affairs Commission
339 Dexter Ave., Suite 113
Montgomery, AL 36130

ALASKA
Assistant for Alaska Native Affairs
Office of the Governor
Pouch A
Juneau, AK 99811

ARIZONA
Arizona Commission on Indian
    Affairs
1645 W. Jefferson, Suite 433
Phoenix, AZ 85007

CALIFORNIA
California Native American
    Heritage Commission
915 Capitol Mall
Sacramento, CA 95814

COLORADO
Colorado Commission of Indian
    Affairs
130 State Capitol
Denver, CO 80203

CONNECTICUT
Connecticut Indian Affairs Council
Department of Environmental
    Protection
165 Capitol Ave.
Hartford, CT 06106

DELAWARE
Office of Human Relations
630 State College Rd.
Dover, DE 19901

FLORIDA
Florida Governor's Council
    on Indian Affairs
521 E. College Ave.
Tallahassee, FL 32301

GEORGIA
Office of Indian Heritage
330 Capitol Ave. S.E.
Atlanta, GA 30334

HAWAII
Hawaii Council of American
    Indian Nations
Box 17627
910 N. Vineyard Blvd.
Honolulu, HI 96817

IDAHO
American Indian Coordinator
State House
Boise, ID 83720

IOWA
Office of the Governor
State Capitol
Des Moines, IA 50319

LOUISIANA
Governor's Commission on
Indian Affairs
Box 44455, Capitol Station
Baton Rouge, LA 70804

MAINE
Maine Indian Affairs Commission
State Health Station #38
Augusta, ME 04333

MARYLAND
Commission on Indian Affairs
45 Calvert St.
Annapolis, MD 21401

MASSACHUSETTS
Massachusetts Commission on
Indian Affairs
One Ashburn Pl., Rm. 1004
Boston, MA 02108

MICHIGAN
Michigan Commission on Indian
Affairs
Dept. of Management and Budget
Box 30026
611 W. Ottawa St.
Lansing, MI 48909

MINNESOTA
Minnesota Council on Indian
Affairs
127 University Ave.
St. Paul, MN 55155

MONTANA
Governor's Office of Indian Affairs
1218 E. Sixth Ave.
Helena, MT 59620

NEBRASKA
Nebraska Indian Commission
Box 94914, State Capitol
Lincoln, NE 68701

NEVADA
Nevada Indian Commission
3100 Mill St., Suite 206
Reno, NV 89502

NEW HAMPSHIRE
New Hampshire Indian Council
913 Elm St., Room 201
Manchester, NH 03101

NEW JERSEY
New Jersey Indian Office
300 Main St., Suite 3F
Orange, NJ 07050

NEW MEXICO
New Mexico Office on Indian
Affairs
La Villa Rivera Building
Santa Fe, NM 87501

NEW YORK
Dept. of Indian Services
Donovan State Office Bldg.
125 Main St., Rm. 471
Buffalo, NY 14203

NORTH CAROLINA
North Carolina Commission on
Indian Affairs
Box 27228
227 E. Edenton St. #229
Raleigh, NC 27611

NORTH DAKOTA
North Dakota Indian Affairs
Commission
State Capitol Bldg.
Bismarck, ND 58505

OHIO
Ohio Indian Affairs Coordinator
Outdoor Recreation Service
Fountain Square Bldg. E
Columbus, OH 43224

OKLAHOMA
Oklahoma Indian Affairs Commission
4010 N. Lincoln
Oklahoma City, OK 73105

OREGON
Commission on Indian Affairs
454 State Capitol Bldg.
Salem, OR 97310

RHODE ISLAND
Rhode Island Commission for
    Indian Affairs
444 Friendship St.
Providence, RI 02907

SOUTH CAROLINA
Assistant to the Governor
Box 11450
Columbia, SC 29211

SOUTH DAKOTA
South Dakota Office of Indian Affairs
Kneip Bldg.
Pierre, SD 57501

TEXAS
Texas Indian Commission
Box 2960
Austin, TX 78768

TENNESSEE
Tennessee Indian Council
1110 12th Ave. S.
Nashville, TN 30273

UTAH
Utah Division of Indian Affairs
6220 State Office Bldg.
Salt Lake City, UT 84114

VIRGINIA
Indian Affairs Coordinator
Secretary of Human Resources
9th Street Office Bldg., Rm. 622
Richmond, VA 23219

WASHINGTON
Washington Commission for
    Indian Affairs
1057 Capitol Way
Olympia, WA 98504

WISCONSIN
Wisconsin Governor's Indian Desk
Box 7863
Madison, WI 53701

WYOMING
Wyoming State Indian Commission
2660 Peck Ave.
Riverton, WY 82501

Source: Giago, Tim, ed. 1991. *The American Indian and the Media*. The National
    Conference on Christians and Jews. Minneapolis, Minn. 84 p.

APPENDIX 9

100th Congress 2d Session
H. Con. Res. 331

CONCURRENT RESOLUTION

To acknowledge the contribution of the Iroquois Confederacy of Nations to the development of the United States Constitution and to reaffirm the continuing government-to-government relationship between Indian tribes and the United States established in the Constitution.

Whereas the original framers of the Constitution, including, most notably, George Washington and Benjamin Franklin, are known to have greatly admired the concepts of the Six Nations of the Iroquois Confederacy;

Whereas the confederation of the original Thirteen Colonies into one republic was influenced by the political system developed by the Iroquois Confederacy as were many of the democratic principles which were incorporated into the Constitution itself; and

Whereas, since the formation of the United States, the Congress has recognized the sovereign status of Indian tribes and has, through the exercise of powers reserved to the Federal Government in the Commerce Clause of the Constitution (art. I, s. 2, cl. 3), dealt with Indian tribes on a government-to-government basis and has, through the treaty clause (art. II, s. 2, cl. 2) entered into three hundred and seventy treaties with Indian tribal Nations;

Whereas, from the first treaty entered into with an Indian Nation, the treaty with the Delaware Indians of September 17, 1778, the Congress has assumed a trust responsibility and obligation to Indian tribes and their members;

Whereas this trust responsibility calls for Congress to "exercise the utmost good faith in dealings with Indians" as provided for in the Northwest Ordinance of 1787, (1 Stat. 50);

Whereas the judicial system of the United States has consistently recognized and reaffirmed this special relationship: Now, therefore, be it

Resolved by the House of Representatives (the Senate concurring), That—

 (1) the Congress, on the occasion of the two hundredth anniversary of the signing of the United States Constitution, acknowledges the contribution made by the Iroquois Confederacy and other Indian Nations to the formation and development of the United States;

(2) the Congress also hereby reaffirms the constitutionally recognized government-to-government relationship with Indian tribes which has been the cornerstone of this Nation's official Indian policy;

(3) the Congress specifically acknowledges and reaffirms the trust responsibility and obligation of the United States Government to Indian tribes, including Alaska Natives, for their preservation, protection, and enhancement, including the provision of health, education, social, and economic assistance programs as necessary, and including the duty to assist tribes in their performance of governmental responsibility to provide for the social and economic well-being of their members and to preserve tribal cultural identity and heritage; and

(4) the Congress also acknowledges the need to exercise the utmost good faith in upholding its treaties with the various tribes, as the tribes understood them to be, and the duty of a great Nation to uphold its legal and moral obligations for the benefit of all of its citizens so that they and their posterity may also continue to enjoy the rights they have enshrined in the United States Constitution for time immemorial.

Passed the House of Representatives October 4, 1988.

Attest: DONNALD K. ANDERSON,
                                                                Clerk.

BIBLIOGRAPHY

Administration for Native Americans. 1991a. Availability of financial assistance. 56 *Federal Register* No. 151, p. 37396.

———. 1991b. Fact sheet. Washington, D.C. 6 p.

Alaska Federation of Natives. 1989. *The AFN report on the status of Alaska Natives: A call for action.* Anchorage. 78 p.

———. 1991a. No title. Information pamphlet on history, mission, and organizational structure. Anchorage. 3-leaf fold-out.

———. 1991b. *AFN Newsletter.* Vol IX, No. 4 (Dec.). 16 p.

———. 1991c. *ANCSA twenty years later.* Annual Report. Anchorage. 24 p.

———. 1992. *AFN Newsletter.* Vol. X, No. 2 (Mar.). 8 p.

Alaska Native Claims Settlement Act. 1971. P.L. 92-203, 85 Stat. 688, 43 USC 1601 et seq.

Alaska Native Claims Settlement Act Amendments of 1987. 1988. P.L. 100 241, 101 Stat. 1788.

Alaska National Interest Lands Conservation Act. 1980. P.L. 96-487, 94 Stat 2371, 16 USC 3111 et seq.

American Indian Anti-Defamation Council. 1991. Mission statement. Denver, Colo. 1 p.

American Indian Lawyer Training Program. 1988. *Indian tribes as sovereign governments: A sourcebook on federal-tribal history, law, and policy.* AIRI Press, Oakland, Calif. 156 p.

American Indian Movement. 1991. Fact sheet. Leonard Peltier Defense Committee, Lawrence, Kans. 6 p.

American Indian Policy Review Commission. 1977. Final report. U.S. Govt. Printing Office, Washington, D.C. Vol. I, 624 p., Vol. II, 923 p.

American Indian Religious Freedom Act (Joint Resolution). 1978. P.L. 95-341, 92 Stat. 469, 42 USC 1996.

Anderson, George E., W.H. Ellison, and Robert F. Heizer. 1978. *Treaty making and treaty rejection by the federal government in California, 1850–1852.* Ballena Press, Socorro, N.Mex. 124 p.

Andrews, Patsy J. 1991. Personal communication. Advisory Services Specialist, Indian Arts and Crafts Board, Washington, D.C., Oct. 28.

Anquoe, Bunty. 1991b. Oklahoma tribes ink treaty. In *Lakota Times*, Oct. 16.

———. 1991a. Canadian Eskimos win fifth of Canada. In *Lakota Times*, Dec. 24.

———. 1992a. BIA mismanagement blasted. In *Lakota Times*, Apr. 8.

———. 1992b. Brown defends budget. In *Lakota Times*, Apr. 8.

———. 1992c. Task force reworks budgetary process. In *Lakota Times*, Feb. 4.

Antoine v. Washington 1975. 420 U.S. 194.

Arizona v. California. 1963. 373 U.S. 546.

Arizona Commission on Indian Affairs. 1991. Legislative statement of Executive Director. Sept. 23. 6 p.

Arnold, Robert D. 1976. *Alaska Native land claims*. Alaska Native Foundation, Anchorage. 348 p.

Articles of Confederation. 1781. Art. IX. 1 Stat. 4, 7 (1845).

Associated Press. 1991a. Alaska churches apologize to Indians. In *Lakota Times*, Nov. 6.

———. 1991b. BIA blames sloppy bookkeeping for $23.8 million in lost equipment. In *Arizona Daily Star*, Nov. 3.

———. 1991c. Environmental racism claim to be studied at meeting. In *Arizona Daily Star*, Aug. 25.

———. 1991d. Eskimos to gain control of a fifth of Canada. Reprinted in *Arizona Daily Star*, Dec. 17.

———. 1991e. Indian gaming funds cited as aid to culture. In *Arizona Daily Star*, Aug. 25.

———. 1991f. Probe blames government for deficient Indian schools. In *Tucson Citizen*, Aug. 5.

———. 1991g. Thanksgiving no holiday for U.S. Indians. In *Arizona Daily Star*, Nov. 28.

———. 1991h. Tribal leaders may debate legalization of alcohol sales on Navajo Reservation. In *Arizona Daily Star*, Nov. 29.

———. 1992. Indian task force report to Congress urges BIA overhaul, tribal control of funds. In *Arizona Daily Star*, Feb. 2.

Association on American Indian Affairs. 1991. Annual report. New York. 20 p.

———. 1992. *Indian Affairs*, No. 125, Winter/Spring. 8 p.

Axtell, James. 1988. *After Columbus: Essays in ethnohistory of colonial North America*. Oxford Univ. Press, New York. 300 p.

Axtell, James, and William C. Sturtevant. 1986. The unkindest cut, who invented scalping. *In* Nichols. 1986. p. 47-60.

Basso, Keith H., and Morris E. Opler, eds. 1971. *Apachean culture, history, and ethnology.* Anthropological Papers of the University of Arizona, Tucson. No. 21. 167 p.

Begay, David H., and Martha B. Becktell. 1990. These are ancient traditions and they don't grow old. Paper presented at Conference on Native American Voices: Culture and Learning. Prescott College, Prescott, Ariz. Aug. 4 p.

Benally, Herbert John. 1990. Navajo philosophy of learning. Paper presented at Conference on Native American Voices: Culture and Learning. Prescott College, Prescott, Ariz. Aug. 15 p.

Berkhofer, Robert F., Jr. 1967. *Salvation and the savage: An analysis of Protestant missions and American Indian response, 1787–1862.* Univ. of Kentucky Press, Louisville. 186 p.

————. 1979. *The white man's Indian: Images of the American Indian from Columbus to the present.* Vintage Books, New York. 261 p.

Black's Law Dictionary. 1990. West Publishing Co., St. Paul, Minn. 1657 p.

Bradford, Emle. 1973. *Christopher Columbus.* Viking Press, New York. 288 p.

Brand, Stewart. 1988. Indians and the counterculture, 1960s–1970s. *In* Washburn. 1988. p. 570–572.

Brodeur, Paul. 1985. *Restitution: The land claims of the Mashpee, Passamoquoddy, and Penobscot Indians of New England.* Northeastern Univ. Press, Boston. 148 p.

Brophy, William A., and Sophie D. Aberle. 1966. *The Indian: America's unfinished business. Report of the commission on the rights, liberties, and responsibilities of the American Indian.* Univ. of Oklahoma Press, Norman. 236 p.

Brown, Dee. 1970. *Bury my heart at Wounded Knee–An Indian history of the American West.* Holt, Rinehart, and Winston, New York. 487 p.

Burch, Ernest S., Jr. 1984. The land claims era in Alaska. *In* Damas. 1984. p. 657–661.

Bureau of Indian Affairs. 1903. *Report of the Commissioner of Indian Affairs. Treaties made with Indian tribes in the United States which have been ratified by the Senate.* Annual Rept., Dept. of the Interior, Washington, D.C. 45 p.

————. 1964. *Answers to your questions about the American Indian.* Supt. of Documents, U.S. Govt. Printing Office, Washington, D.C. 38 p.

————. 1966. *Indians, Eskimos, and Aleuts of Alaska.* Washington, D.C. 18 p.

————. 1968. *Answers to your questions about American Indians.* Supt. of Documents, U.S. Govt. Printing Office, Washington, D.C. 42 p.

————. 1974. *The American Indians: Answers to 101 questions.* Supt. of Documents, U.S. Govt. Printing Office, Washington, D.C. 60 p.

————. 1975. *Federal Indian Policy.* Washington, D.C. 21 p.

————. 1978. *The American Indians: Answers to 101 questions.* Supt. of Documents, U.S. Govt. Printing Office, Washington, D.C. 61 p.

————. 1984. *Tribal enrollment.* Phoenix Area Office, Arizona. 172 p.

————. 1985a. *Annual Report of Indian Lands.* Washington, D.C. 89 p.

————. 1985b. *Information about acknowledgment.* Washington, D.C. 5 p.

————. 1987a. *American Indians today: Answers to your questions.* U.S. Dept. of the Interior, Washington, D.C. 24 p.

————. 1987b. *The Bureau of Indian Affairs.* (Mission Statement.) Washington, D.C. 1 p.

————. 1988. *Report on BIA education.* Washington, D.C. 261 p.

————. 1989a. *Indian Land Areas Map.* Washington, D.C.

————. 1989b. *Indian service population and labor force estimates.* U.S. Dept. of the Interior, Washington, D.C. 24 p.

————. 1990. *American Indian and Alaska Native education.* Washington, D.C. 2 p.

————. 1991a. *American Indians today.* Washington, D.C. 36 p.

————. 1991b. *Education fact sheet.* Washington, D.C. 6 p.

————. 1991c. Reorganization task force to meet in Anchorage; "Ideal agencies" to be discussed. *Indian News* 15(13):1–2.

————. 1992a. *Indian forestry career opportunities.* Washington, D.C. 5 p.

————. 1992b. *Tribal horizons.* In *Departmental Highlights*, p. 19–24. Washington, D.C. p. 19-24.

Bush, George. 1991. *President's policy statement on American Indians.* Bureau of Indian Affairs, Washington, D.C. June 14.

Camp, Carter. 1992. Sincere doubts: Tourism diminishes Lakota ceremonies. In *Lakota Times*, Aug. 12.

Campbell, Lyle, and Marianne Mithun, eds. 1979. *The languages of Native America: Historical and comparative assessment.* University of Texas Press, Austin. 1034 p.

Canby, William C., Jr. 1981. *American Indian law in a nutshell.* West Publ. Co., St. Paul, Minn. 288 p.

Capps, Benjamin. 1973. *The Indians.* Time-Life Books, Chicago. 240 p.

————. 1975. *The great chiefs.* Time-Life Books, Chicago. 240 p.

Case, David S. 1984. *Alaska Natives and American laws.* Univ. of Alaska Press, Fairbanks. 586 p.

Ceram, C.W. 1971. *The first Americans: A story of North American archaeology.* Harcourt Brace Jovanovich, Inc., New York. 357 p.

Chasing Horse, Joseph. 1991. Personal communication. Sicangu Lakota, Rosebud Reservation, S.Dak. Dec. 28.

Cherokee Nation v. Georgia. 1831. 30 U.S. (5 Pet.) 1.

Churchill, Ward. 1991. *Jimmy Durham: An artist for Native North America.* Spirit of Crazy Horse, L.P.D.C., Lawrence, Kans. Oct.–Nov., p. 6, 12.

Civilization Fund. 1819. 3 Stat. 516 (1846).

Clifton, James A., ed. 1990. *The invented Indian: Cultural fictions and government policies.* Transaction Publishers, New Brunswick, N.J. 388 p.

Code of Federal Regulations. 1990. Title 25–Indians.

Coggins, George Cameron, and Charles F. Wilkinson. 1981. *Federal public land and resources law.* The Foundation Press, Mineola, N.Y. 849 p.

Cohen, Fay G. 1986. *Treaties on trial: The continuing controversy over Northwest fishing rights.* Univ. of Washington Press, Seattle. 229 p.

Cohen, Felix S. 1942a. *Handbook of federal Indian law.* U.S. Govt. Printing Office, Washington, D.C. 662 p.

———. 1942b. The Spanish origin of Indian rights in the United States. *Georgetown Law Journal* 31:1–21.

———. 1947. Original Indian title. *Minnesota Law Review* 32:28–59.

———. 1953. The erosion of Indian rights, 1950–1953. 62 *Yale Law Journal* 348.

———. 1971. *Handbook of federal Indian law.* (Reprint of 1942 edition.) Univ. of New Mexico Press, Albuquerque. 662 p.

———. 1982. *Felix S. Cohen's handbook on federal Indian law.* The Michie Company, Charlottesville, Va. 912 p.

Collier, John. 1934. *Memorandum, hearings on H.R. 7902.* House Committee on Indian Affairs, 73rd Cong., 2nd sess., p. 16–18.

Committee on Interior and Insular Affairs. 1964. *List of Indian treaties.* 88th Cong., 2nd sess. Committee Print No. 33. 45 p.

Curtis Act. 1898. 30 Stat. 495.

Damas, David, ed. 1984. *Handbook of North American Indians–Arctic.* Smithsonian Institution, Washington, D.C. 829 p.

Davis, Tony. 1992. Apaches split over nuclear waste. *High Country News* 24(1): 12–14. (Jan. 27)

Deloria, Vine, Jr. 1969. *Custer died for your sins: An Indian manifesto.* The Macmillan Company, Toronto. 279 p.

———. 1970. *We talk, you listen: New tribes, new turf.* Macmillan and Company, New York. 227 p.

———. 1973. *God is red.* Grosset and Dunlap, New York. 376 p.

———. 1974a. *Behind the trail of broken treaties: An Indian Declaration of Independence.* University of Texas Press, Austin. 296 p.

———. 1974b. *The Indian affair.* Friendship Press, New York. 95 p.

———. 1979. *The metaphysics of modern existence.* Harper & Row, San Francisco. 223 p.

———. 1989. A simple question of humanity–The moral dimensions of the reburial issue. *Native American Rights Fund Legal Review* 14(4):1–12.

Deloria, Vine, Jr., ed. 1971. *Of utmost good faith.* Straight Arrow Books, San Francisco. 262 p.

———. 1985. *American Indian policy in the twentieth century.* Univ. of Oklahoma Press, Norman. 265 p.

Deloria, Vine, Jr., and Clifford M. Lytle. 1983. *American Indians, American justice.* Univ. of Texas Press, Austin. 292 p.

———. 1984. *The nations within: The past and future of American Indian sovereignty.* Pantheon Books, New York. 293 p.

Demallie, Raymond J. 1977. *Comanche treaties with the Republic of Texas.* Institute for the Development of Indian Law, Washington, D.C. p. 1–4.

Denevan, William M. 1976. *The native population of the Americas in 1492.* Univ. of Wisconsin Press, Madison. 353 p.

Dobyns, Henry F. 1976. *Native American historical demography: A critical bibliography.* Indiana Univ. Press, Bloomington. 95 p.

Driver, Harold E. 1969. *Indians of North America.* Univ. of Chicago Press, Chicago. 632 p.

Drucker, Philip. 1954. *Indians of the northwest coast.* The Natural History Press, Garden City, New York. 224 p.

Dvorchak, Robert. 1992. Without wampum or buffalo, Indians rely on blackjack, bingo. Associated Press article in *Prescott Courier*, Dec. 11.

Elementary and Secondary Education Act Amendments. 1988. P.L. 100-297, 102 Stat. 358, 20 USC 4901.

Encyclopaedia Britannica. 1990. *American Indians.* Vol. 1, p. 318–320. Encyclopaedia Britannica, Inc. Chicago.

Erikson, Jane. 1991. La Frontera gets Indian AIDS grant. In *Arizona Daily Star*, Nov. 19.

Evans, G. Edward, and Jeffrey Clark. 1980. *North American Indian language materials, 1890–1965: An annotated bibliography of monographic works*. American Indian Studies Center, U. of California at Los Angeles. 154 p.

Farb, Peter. 1968. *Man's rise to civilization as shown by the Indians of North America from primeval times to the coming of the Industrial State*. Dutton, New York. 332 p.

Federal Register. 1988. *Indian entities [within the lower 48 states and] Native entities within the state of Alaska recognized and eligible to receive services from the United States Bureau of Indian Affairs*. U.S. Govt., Washington, D.C. Vol. 53(250):52829–52835.

Feraca, Stephen E. 1990. Inside BIA: Or, "We're getting rid of all these honkies." *In* Clifton. 1990. p. 271–289.

Flowers, Ronald B. 1983. *Criminal jurisdiction allocation in Indian country*. Associated Faculty Press, Inc., Port Washington, N.Y. 121 p.

Funke, Karl A. 1976. Educational assistance and employment preference: Who is an Indian. *American Indian Law Review* 4:1–47.

Gallatin, Albert. 1836. A synopsis of the Indian tribes within the United States east of the Rocky Mountains, and the British and Russian possessions in America. In *Archaeologia Americana: Transactions and Collections of the American Antiquarian Society* 2. Cambridge, Mass. p. 1–422.

Gamerman, Ellen. 1992. State blocked gaming pact, Indian chairman tells panel. In *Arizona Daily Star*, Jan. 10.

General Allotment Act. 1887. 24 Stat. 388.

Getches, David H. 1985. Alternative approaches to land claims: Alaska and Hawaii. *In* Sutton. 1985. p. 301–333.

Getches, David H., Daniel M. Rosenfelt, and Charles F. Wilkinson. 1979. *Federal Indian law: Cases and materials*. West Publishing Company. St. Paul, Minn. 660 p.

Giago, Tim. 1991a. Mascots, spirituality, and insensitivity. In *Lakota Times*, Oct. 23.

———. 1991b. Notes from Indian country. In *Lakota Times*, Sept. 11.

———. 1991c. What do you call an Indian. In *Lakota Times*, Dec. 14.

Giago, Tim, ed. 1991d. *The American Indian and the media*. National Conference of Christians and Jews. Minneapolis, Minn. 84 p.

Gibbons, Boyd. 1992. Alcohol: The legal drug. *National Geographic* 181(2):3–35.

Gibson, Ronald, ed. 1977. *Jefferson Davis and the Confederacy, and treaties con-cluded by the Confederate States with Indian tribes.* Occana Publications, Inc., Dobbs Ferry, New York. 205 p.

Gillespie, Beryl C. 1981. Territorial groups before 1821: Athapaskans of the Shield and Mackenzie drainage. *In* Helm. 1981. p. 161–168.

Glaser, Lynn. 1973. *Indians or Jews.* Lorrin L. Morrison Press, Los Angeles. 85 p.

Goldberg, Carole E. 1975. Public Law 280: The limits of state jurisdiction over reservation Indians. 22 *U.C.L.A. Law Review* 535–594.

Graham, Colonel W.A. (USA Ret.). 1959. *The story of the Little Bighorn.* Bonanza Books, New York. 178 p.

Grinde, Donald A., Jr. 1977. *The Iroquois and the founding of the American nation.* American Indian Historian Press, San Francisco. 175 p.

Grinnell, George B. 1910. Coup and scalp among the Plains Indians. *American Anthropologist* 12:296–310.

Hafford, William E. 1989. The Navajo code talkers. *Arizona Highways* 65(2): 36–45.

Hagan, William T. 1981. Tribalism rejuvenated: The Native American since the era of termination. *In* Nichols. 1981. p. 295–304.

Hall, Gilbert L. 1981. *The federal–Indian trust relationship.* Inst. Devel. Indian Law, Washington, D.C. 132 p.

Harlow, Victor E. 1935. *Oklahoma: Its origins and development.* Harlow Publ. Corp., Oklahoma City. 450 p.

Harrison et al. v. Laveen. 1948. 196 P.2d 456.

Hausman, Gerald. 1992. *Turtle Island alphabet: A lexicon of Native American symbols and culture.* St. Martin's Press, New York. 204 p.

Hawaii Homes Commission Act. 1921. P.L. 67-42, 42 Stat. 108.

Hazard, Anne. 1991. Indians need more doctors, Senators told. In *Arizona Daily Star*, Nov. 13.

Heaney, Gerald W., Senior Judge on the U.S. Circuit Court of Appeals for the Eighth Circuit. 1991. Letter to Senator Inouye, Chairman, Senate Select Committee on Indian Affairs. Apr. 18.

Heat-Moon, William Least. 1991. *PrairyErth (a deep map).* Houghton Mifflin Company, Boston. 624 p.

Heinl, Robert Debs, Jr. 1962. *Soldiers of the sea.* United States Naval Institute, Annapolis, Maryland. 692 p.

Helm, June, ed. 1981. *Handbook of North American Indians—Subarctic.* Smithsonian Institution, Washington, D.C. 837 p.

Henige, David. 1990. Their numbers become thick: Native American historical demography as expiation. *In* Clifton. 1990. p. 169–191.

Hill, Edward E. 1974. *The Office of Indian Affairs, 1824–1880: Historical sketches.* Clearwater Publishing Co., Inc., New York. 246 p.

Hill, Edward E., comp. 1981. *Guide to records in the National Archives of the United States relating to American Indians.* U.S. Govt. Printing Office, Washington, D.C. 467 p.

Hill, H.W., ed. 1984. *The consolidated treaty series index, Vol. 3, 1852–1885.* Oceana Publications, Dobbs Ferry, N.J. p. 359, 413, 479.

Hodge, Frederick Webb, ed. 1907. *Handbook of American Indians north of Mexico.* Smithsonian Institution, Bureau of Ethnology, Washington, D.C. Bulletin 30, Part 1, 972 p. and Part 2, 1221 p.

——. 1975. *Handbook of American Indians north of Mexico.* Rowan and Littlefield, Totowa, N.J. Part 1, 972 p. and Part 2, 1221 p.

Hoover Commission—Commission on Organization of the Executive Branch of the Government. 1949. *Indian Affairs: A Report to Congress.* U.S. Govt. Printing Office, Washington, D.C. 81 p.

Horsman, Reginald. 1988. United States Indian policies, 1776–1815. *In* Washburn. 1988. p. 29–39.

Hou Hawaiians v. State of Hawaii. 1985. 764 P.2d 623.

Houghton, Richard H., III. 1989. An argument for Indian status for Native Hawaiians—The discovery of a lost tribe. *American Indian Law Review* 14(1):1–55.

House Concurrent Resolution 108. 1953. 83rd Cong., 1st sess. 67 Stat. B132.

Howe, Henry. 1851. *Historical collections of the great West. Vols. I & II.* Henry Howe. Cincinnati, Ohio. 440 p.

Iacopi, Robert L., ed. 1972. *Look to the mountain top.* Gousha Publications. San Jose, Calif. 121 p.

Indian Arts and Crafts Act. 1990. P.L. 101-644, 104 Stat. 4662, 25 USC Sec. 305.

Indian Arts and Crafts Board. 1991a. *Summary and text of Title I, Public Law 101-644.* U.S. Dept. of the Interior, Washington, D.C. 6 p.

——. 1991b. Fact sheet. U.S. Dept. of the Interior, Washington, D.C. 6 p.

Indian Child Welfare Act. 1978. P.L. 95-608, 92 Stat. 3069, 25 USC Sec. 1901 et seq.

Indian Citizenship Act. 1924. P.L. 68-233, 43 Stat. 253.

Indian Civil Rights Act. 1968. P.L. 90-284, 82 Stat. 73, 77-81.

Indian Education Act of 1972. P.L. 92-318, 86 Stat. 235, 334-345. As amended.

Indian Education Act of 1988. P.L. 100-297, 102 Stat. 363. As amended.

Indian Gaming Regulatory Act. 1988. P.L. 100-497, 102 Stat. 2467.

Indian Health Care Improvement Act. 1976. P.L. 94-437, 90 Stat. 1400. As amended. 25 USC Sec. 1601 et seq.

Indian Health Service. 1988. *Indian Health Service accomplishments: Fiscal year 1988.* Rockville, Md. 32 p.

———. 1991a. *Regional differences in Indian health: 1991.* Rockville, Md. 73 p.

———. 1991b. *Service area population estimates and projections 1980–2010.* Rockville, Md. 38 p.

———. 1991c. *Trends in Indian health: 1991.* Rockville, Md. 93 p.

———. 1992a. Fact sheet. Rockville, Md. 2 p.

———. 1992b. Personal communication. Public Information Office. Jan. 23.

Indian Law Enforcement Reform Act. 1990. P.L. 101-379, 104 Stat. 473, 42 USC 2991a.

Indian Removal Act of 1830. 4 Stat. 411.

Indian Reorganization Act. 1934. 48 Stat. 984, 25 USC 461 et seq.

Indian Self-Determination and Education Assistance Act. 1975. P.L. 93-638, 88 Stat. 2203, 25 USC Sec. 450–450n, 455–458e.

Institute for the Development of Indian Law. 1973. *A chronological list of treaties and agreements made by Indian tribes with the United States.* Washington, D.C. 34 p.

International Indian Treaty Council. 1992. Press Release. San Francisco, Calif. (Mar.)

Jackson, Helen Hunt. 1886. *A century of dishonor: A sketch of the United States government's dealings with some of the Indian tribes.* Roberts Brothers, Boston. 514 p.

Johanson, Bruce E. 1982. *Forgotten founders: How the American Indian helped shape democracy.* Harvard Common Press, Boston. 167 p.

Johnson v. McIntosh. 1823. 21 U.S. 543.

Johnson, Lyndon B. 1968. *Special message to the Congress on the problems of the American Indian: "The Forgotten American."* Public Papers of the President of the United States, p. 335-344. (Mar. 6.)

Johnson-O'Malley Act. 1934. 48 Stat. 596, 25 USC Sec. 452-454.

Johnson, Steven L. 1977. *Guide to American Indian documents in the Congressional Serial Set: 1817–1899.* Clearwater Publ. Co., Inc., New York. 503 p.

Jones, Mike. 1991. Personal communication. Real Estate Office, Bureau of Indian Affairs, Washington, D.C. Dec. 6.

Josephy, Alvin M., Jr. 1968. *The Indian heritage of America.* Alfred A. Knopf, New York. 384 p.

———. 1982. *Now that the buffalo's gone: A study of today's American Indians.* Alfred A. Knopf, New York. 300 p.

Kappler, Charles J., ed. 1904. *Indian affairs: Laws and treaties, Vol. 2, Treaties.* U.S. Govt. Printing Office, Washington, D.C. 1099 p.

Kehoe, Alice B. 1990. Primitivists and plastic medicine men. *In* Clifton. 1990. p. 193–209.

Kelly, Lawrence. 1988. United States Indian policies, 1900–1980. *In* Washburn. 1988. p. 66–80.

Kickingbird, Kirke, and Karen Ducheneaux. 1973. *One hundred million acres.* Macmillan Company, New York. 240 p.

Kickingbird, Kirke, Lynn Kickingbird, Alexander Tallchief Skibine, and Charles Chibitty. 1980. *Indian treaties.* Inst. Devel. Indian Law. Washington, D.C. 90 p.

Kickingbird, Lynn, and Kirke Kickingbird. 1977. *Indians and the U.S. government.* Inst. Devel. Indian Law. Washington, D.C. 115 p.

Kickingbird, Kirke, Lynn Kickingbird, Charles Chibitty, and Curtis Berkey. 1977. *Indian sovereignty.* Inst. Devel. Indian Law. Washington, D.C. 49 p.

Klein, Barry T., ed. 1990. *Reference encyclopedia of the American Indian.* Fifth edition. Todd Publications, West Nyack, N.Y. 1078 p.

Kvasnicka, Robert M. 1988. United States Indian treaties. *In* Washburn. 1988. p. 195–201.

Lakota Times. 1991. Indians in media create resource clearinghouse. Dec. 24.

Lamphere, Louise. 1983. Southwestern ceremonialism. *In* Ortiz. 1983. p. 744–763.

Lantis, Margaret. 1984. Aleut. *In* Damas. 1984. p. 161–184.

Larabee, L.W., ed. 1961. *The papers of Benjamin Franklin.* Yale Univ. Press, New Haven, Conn. 4:117–121.

League of Women Voters. 1976. *Indian country.* League of Women Voters Education Fund, Washington, D.C. 120 p.

Leland, Donald. 1990. Liberty, equality, fraternity: Was the Indian really egalitarian? *In* Clifton. 1990. p. 145–167.

Leonard Peltier Defense Committee. 1991. Information Pamphlet. Lawrence, Kans. Winter 1990–1991. 1 p.

Leubben, Thomas E. 1980. *American Indian natural resources: Oil & gas.* Inst. Devel. Indian Law, Washington, D.C. 91 p.

Lick, Derek. 1991. Indians want reforms in U.S. recognition rules. In *Arizona Daily Star,* Oct. 23.

Little Eagle, Avis. 1991. Braves fans assault protesters. In *Lakota Times,* Oct. 30.

———. 1992. Lakota discuss exploitation of religion, preserving culture. In *Indian Country Today,* Nov. 6.

Little Thunder et al. v. State of South Dakota. 1975. 518 F.2d 1253.

Littman, Jonathan. 1991. Reservation industry not business as usual. *San Francisco Chronicle* article reprinted in *Arizona Daily Star,* Sept. 8.

Lone Wolf v. Hitchcock. 1903. 187 U.S. 553.

Lopach, James J., Margery Hunter Brown, and Richard L. Clow. 1990. *Tribal government today: Politics on Montana Indian reservations.* Westview Press, San Francisco. 193 p.

Lowie, Robert H. 1954. *Indians of the Plains.* The Natural History Press, Garden City, N.Y. 258 p.

Lynch, Donald F. 1990. Alaska. In *Academic American Encyclopedia.* Grolier Corporation, Danbury, Conn. Vol. 1, p. 240-247.

———. 1991. Alaska. In *Encyclopedia Americana.* Grolier Corporation, Danbury, Conn. Vol. 1, p. 457-473.

Lyng v. Northwest Indian Cemetery Protective Assn. 1988. 485 U.S. 439.

MacNeish, Richard S. 1971. Early man in the Andes. *Scientific American* 224(4): 36,46.

Mahon, John K. 1988. Indian-United States military situation, 1775-1848. *In* Washburn. 1988. p. 144-162.

Maine Indian Land Claims Settlement Act. 1980. P.L. 96-420, 94 Stat. 1785.

Martin, Phillip. 1984. Foreword. *In* Taylor. 1984. p. ix.

Martinez v. Southern Ute Tribe. 1957. 249 F.2d 915.

Mashpee Tribe v. New Seabury Corp. 1979. 592 F.2d 575.

Matthiessen, Peter. 1991. *In the spirit of Crazy Horse.* Viking Penguin, New York. 645 p.

McClanahan v. Arizona State Tax Commission. 1973. 411 U.S. 164.

McLuhan, T.C. 1971. *Touch the earth: A self-portrait of Indian existence.* Promontory Press, New York. 185 p.

McNeley, James K. 1990. *A Navajo curriculum in the national context.* Paper presented at Conference on Native American Voices: Culture and Learning. Prescott College, Prescott, Ariz. Aug. 12 p.

McNickle, D'Arcy. 1975. *They came here first.* Harper & Row, San Francisco. 325 p.

Meriam Report. 1928. *The problem of Indian administration.* Inst. for Govt. Research, Washington, D.C. 872 p.

Merrion v. Jicarilla Apache Tribe. 1982. 455 U.S. 130.

Meyer, Michael A. 1984. *Special chronological list, special chronologies (A) Colonial and like treaties (B) Postal and telegraphic etc. agreements, Vol. 2.* Oceana Publications, Inc., Dobbs Ferry, New York. 425 p.

Montana v. United States. 1982. 450 U.S. 544.

Montoya v. Bolack. 1962. 372 P.2d 387.

Montoya v. United States. 1901. 180 U.S. 261.

Mooney, James. 1928. *The aboriginal population of America north of Mexico.* Smithsonian Misc. Coll., Vol. 80, No. 7. Smithsonian Institution, Washington, D.C. 40 p.

Morton v. Mancari. 1974. 417 U.S. 535.

Nash, Philleo. 1988. Map. *In* Washburn. 1988. p. 274.

National Archives and Records Administration. n.d. *Ratified Indian treaties, 1722–1869.* National Archives Microfilm M668. Washington, D.C.

National Congress of American Indians. 1976. *Treaties and trust responsibilities.* Major Policy Resolution Number One. Adopted Oct. 21.

———. 1991. *The 1990s: A new federalism on our terms.* Washington, D.C. 3 p.

———. 1992. Personal communication. Public Information Office. Apr. 1.

National Geographic Society. 1991. 1491: America before Columbus. *National Geographic* 180(4):1–99. (Oct. issue)

National Indian Education Association. 1991. *Description and history of the NIEA.* Washington, D.C. 6 p.

National Indian Gaming Commission. 1991. *Commission fees.* 56 Federal Register, No. 158. p. 56282.

———. 1992a. *25 CFR Part 502–Definitions under the Indian Gaming Regulatory Act; Rule.* Vol. 57 Federal Register No. 69, p. 12382. (Apr. 9)

———. 1992b. *25 CFR Parts 515, 519, 522, 523, 524, 556, 558 – Service: approval of Class II and Class III gaming ordinances under the Indian Gaming Regulatory Act procedures; proposed rules and notice.* (July 8)

———. 1992c. *25 CFR Parts 571, et al. – Compliance and enforcement procedures under the Indian Gaming Regulatory Act: Proposed rule.* Vol. 57 Federal Register No. 132, p. 30584. (July 9)

National Indian Policy Center. 1991. Fact sheet. Washington, D.C. 1 p.

———. 1992. *Report to Congress: Recommendations for the establishment of a National Indian Policy Center.* Washington, D.C. 81 p.

National Indian Youth Council. 1991a. *Americans Before Columbus* 19(1):1–8.

———. 1991b. *The choice is yours.* Albuquerque, N.Mex. 1 p.

———. 1991c. Information pamphlet. Albuquerque, N.Mex. 1 p.

National Museum of the American Indian Act. 1989. P.L. 101-185, 103 Stat. 1336.

Native American Graves Protection and Repatriation Act. 1990. P.L. 101-601, 104 Stat. 3048.

Native American Programs Act. 1975. P.L. 93-644, 88 Stat. 2324, 42 USC 2991a.

Native Hawaiian Health Care Act. 1988. P.L. 100-579, 102 Stat. 2916, 42 USC 11701.

Native Hawaiians Study Commission Act. 1980. P.L. 96-565 (Title III), 94 Stat. 3324.

Native Village of Tyonek v. Puckett et al. 1992. U.S. Circuit Court of Appeals for the Ninth Circuit. No. 87-3569. (Jan. 13)

Neihardt, John G. 1959. *Black Elk speaks.* Simon & Schuster, New York. 238 p.

Nelson Act. 1905. 33 Stat. 617.

Nevada v. United States. 1983. 463 U.S. 110.

Nez Perce Treaty. 1868. 15 Stat. 693.

Nichols, Roger L., ed. 1986. *The American Indian: Past and present.* Alfred A. Knopf, New York. 312 p.

Nixon, Richard M. 1970. *Special message to the Congress on Indian affairs.* Public Papers of the President of the United States: Richard Nixon. p. 564–576. (July 8)

O'Brien, Sharon. 1989. *American Indian tribal governments.* Univ. of Oklahoma Press, Norman. 349 p.

Office of Indian Education. 1991. OIE Information pamphlet. U.S. Dept. of Education, Washington, D.C. 4 p.

Office of the Federal Register. 1990. *United States government manual 1990/91.* Supt. of Documents, U.S. Govt. Printing Office, Washington, D.C. 907 p.

Oklahoma Enabling Act. 1906. 34 Stat. 267.

Oklahoma Indian Affairs Commission. 1991. *Proceedings–Sovereignty symposium IV.* June 10–12. 675 p.

Oklahoma Organic Act. 1890. 26 Stat. 81.

Oklahoma Tax Commission v. Citizen Band Potawatomi Indian Tribe of Oklahoma. 1991. 111 S. Ct. 905.

Old Army Press. 1979. *Chronological list of actions, etc. with Indians from January 15, 1837, to January 1891.* Fort Collins, Colo. 79 p.

Oliphant v. Suquamish Tribe. 1978. 435 U.S. 191.

Oliver, Ethel Ross. 1988. *Journal of an Aleutian year.* Univ. of Washington Press, Seattle. 248 p.

Oregon v. Smith. 1990. 494 U.S. 872.

Organic Act–Alaska. 1884. 23 Stat. 24.

Ortiz, Alfonso, ed. 1979. *Handbook of North American Indians–Southwest. Vol. 9.* Smithsonian Institution, Washington, D.C. 701 p.

———. 1983. *Handbook of North American Indians–Southwest. Vol. 10.* Smithsonian Institution, Washington, D.C. 868 p.

Owen, Roger C., James J. F. Deetz, and Anthony D. Fisher. 1967. *The North American Indians: A sourcebook.* The Macmillan Company, New York. 752 p.

Oxford English Dictionary. 2nd ed. 1989. Oxford Univ. Press, New York.

Park, Charles. 1975. Enrollment: Procedures and consequences. *American Indian Law Review* 3:109–111.

Parker, Alan R. 1992. Personal communication. Director, National Indian Policy Center, Washington, D.C. March 24.

Parry, Clive, ed. 1969. *The consolidated treaty series.* Oceana Publications, Inc., Dobbs Ferry, N.Y. 231 Vols.

People v. Woody. 1964. 394 P.2d 813.

Peyote Way Church of God, Inc. v. Thornburgh. 1991. 922 F.2d 1210.

Price, H. Marcus III. 1991. *Disputing the dead: U.S. law on aboriginal remains and grave goods.* Univ. of Missouri Press, Columbia. 136 p.

Price, John A. 1978. *Native studies: American and Canadian Indians.* McGraw-Hill Ryerson Ltd., Toronto. 309 p.

Prince v. Board of Education of Central Consolidated School District No. 22. 1975. 543 P.2d 1176. (N.Mex.)

Prucha, Francis Paul, S.J. 1977. *United States Indian policy: A critical bibliography.* Indiana Univ. Press, Bloomington. 54 p.

———. 1981. *Indian policy in the United States: Historical essays.* Univ. of Nebraska Press, Lincoln. 272 p.

———. 1982. *Indian–white relations in the United States: A bibliography of works published 1975–1980.* Univ. of Nebraska Press, Lincoln. 179 p.

———. 1984. *The great father: The United States government and the American Indians. Vol. II.* Univ. of Nebraska Press, Lincoln. 1302 p.

———. 1985. *The Indians in American society: From the Revolutionary War to the present.* UCLA Press, Los Angeles. 127 p.

———. 1990a. *Atlas of American Indian affairs.* Univ. of Nebraska Press, Lincoln. 191 p.

———. 1990b. *Documents of United States Indian policy.* Univ. of Nebraska Press, Lincoln. 338 p.

Public Law 280. 1953. 67 Stat. 588.

Puyallup Tribe of Indians Settlement Act. 1989. P.L. 101-41, 103 Stat. 83.

Reid, John Phillip. 1970. *A law of blood.* New York Univ. Press, New York. 340 p.

Reynolds, Jerry. 1991. Border run drinking style reinforces old stereotypes. In *Lakota Times*, Oct. 2.

Rhoades, Everett R., John Hammond, Thomas K. Welty, Aaron Handler, and Robert W. Ambler. 1987. The Indian burden of illness and future health interventions. Public Health Reports, *Jour. U.S. Public Health Service* 102(4):361-368.

Rhoades, Everett R., Luana Reyes, and George D. Buzzard. 1987. The organization of health services for Indian people. Public Health Reports, *Jour. U.S. Public Health Service* 102(4):352-356.

Rogers, George W. 1990. Alaska. In *Colliers Encyclopedia.* Macmillan Education Company, New York. Vol. 1, p. 438-452.

Rosenstiel, Annette. 1983. *Red & white: Indian views of the white man, 1492–1982.* Universe Books, New York. 192 p.

Royce, Charles C. 1899. *Indian land cessions in the United States.* Bureau of American Ethnology, Washington, D.C., 18th Annual Report, 1896–1897, Part 2. p. 521–997.

Russell, George L. 1991. *A map of American Indian history.* Thunderbird Enterprises, Phoenix, Ariz.

Sanders, Douglas. 1985. *Aboriginal self-government in the United States*. Queen's University, Kingston, Ontario, Canada. 69 p.

Santa Clara Pueblo v. Martinez. 1978. 436 U.S. 49.

Savilla, Elmer. 1991. Yet another chapter in the saga of Peltier's case. In *Lakota Times*, Oct. 9.

Scheurkogel, Norma. 1992. Personal communication. International Indian Treaty Council, San Francisco. Mar. 27.

Schickel, Richard. 1975. Editorial comments. In *New York Times*, Feb. 9.

Scott, Walter. 1991. *Walter Scott's personality parade*. Box 5573, Beverly Hills, Calif.

Seminole Nation v. United States. 1946. 316 U.S. 286.

Seneca Nation Claims Settlement Act. 1990. P.L. 101-503, 104 Stat. 1292.

Service, Elman R. 1963. *Profiles in ethnology*. Harper and Row, New York. 509 p.

Shorris, Earl. 1971. *The death of the Great Spirit*. Signet, New York. 205 p.

Silverman, Jeff. 1991a. Personal communication. Public Information Office, Alaska Federation of Natives, Anchorage. Dec. 9.

————. 1991b. Personal communication. Public Information Office, Alaska Federation of Natives, Anchorage. Dec. 23.

Simard, Jean-Jacques. 1990. White ghost, red shadows: The reduction of North American Natives. *In* Clifton. 1990. p. 333–369.

Simmons, Janice. 1992. Personal communication. Public Affairs Staff, Bureau of Indian Affairs, Washington, D.C. Jan. 21.

Slotkin, James S. 1967. The peyote way. *In* Owen, Deetz, and Fisher. 1967. p. 648–654.

Smith, James G.E. 1981. Western woods Cree. *In* Helm. 1981. p. 256–270.

Smith, Michael T. 1986. The history of Indian citizenship. *In* Nichols. 1986. p. 232–241.

Snyder Act. 1921. 42 Stat. 208.

Sockbeson, Henry. 1990. Repatriation Act protects Native burial remains and artifacts. Native American Rights Fund, *Legal Review* 16(1):1–4.

Sokolow, Gary. 1990. The future of gambling in Indian country. *American Indian Law Review* 15(1):151–183.

Special Committee on Investigations. 1989. *Final report and legislative recommendations*. Senate Select Committee on Indian Affairs, 101st Cong., 1st sess., Report 101-216. U.S. Govt. Printing Office, Washington, D.C. 238 p.

Spicer, Edward H. 1962. *Cycles of conquest: The impact of Spain, Mexico, and the United States on the Indians of the Southwest.* Univ. of Arizona Press, Tucson. 609 p.

————. 1969. *A short history of the Indians of the United States.* Van Nostrand Reinhold Co. New York. 319 p.

————. 1982. *The American Indian.* Belknap Press, Cambridge, Mass. 210 p.

Stallings, Laurence. 1963. *The doughboys.* Harper & Row, New York. 404 p.

Standing Bear, Luther. 1933. *Land of the spotted eagle.* Houghton Mifflin Co., New York. 259 p.

Stanley, Dyanne. 1992. Personal communication. Public Information staff, International Indian Treaty Council, San Francisco. Mar. 26.

State of Hawaii. 1991. Hawaii State Department of Business and Economic Development and Tourism. Personal communication with Documents Librarian. Sept. 17.

Stedman, Raymond W. 1982. *Shadows of the Indian: Stereotypes in American culture.* Univ. of Oklahoma Press, Norman.

Steinmetz, George. 1992. *The preventable tragedy: Fetal alcohol syndrome. National Geographic* 181(2):36–39. (Feb. issue)

Stewart, Omer. 1987. *Peyote religion: A history.* Univ. of Oklahoma Press, Norman. 454 p.

————. 1991. Peyote and the law. *In* Vecsey. 1991. p. 44–62.

Stillman, Pamela. 1991. State experts meet to warn of fetal alcohol problems. In *Lakota Times,* Nov. 13.

Sutton, Imre. 1985. *Irredeemable America: The Indians' estate and land claims.* Univ. of New Mexico Press, Albuquerque. 421 p.

Szasz, Margaret Connell, and Carmelita Ryan. 1988. American Indian education. *In* Washburn. 1988. p. 284–300.

Tallman, Valerie. 1991. Native philosophy can overcome environmental racism, summit told. In *Lakota Times,* Nov. 13.

Taylor, Theodore W. 1984. *The Bureau of Indian Affairs.* Westview Press, Boulder, Colo. 220 p.

Teters, Charlene. 1991. Using Indian team names is cruel, racist. In *Arizona Daily Star,* Nov. 19.

Texas Band of Kickpoo Act. 1983. P.L. 97-429, 96 Stat. 2269.

Thomas, Cyrus. 1899. Introduction. *In* Royce. 1899. p. 527–647.

Time-Life Books. 1990. *The old West*. Prentice Hall Press, New York. 432 p.

Toledo v. Nobel-Sysco, Inc. 1986. 651 F.Supp. 483.

Trask, Mililani B. 1991. Personal communication. Governor of the Sovereign Nation of Hawaii, 152-B Koula Street, Hilo, Hawaii 96720. Nov. 22.

———. 1992. Personal communication. Governor of the Sovereign Nation of Hawaii. Apr. 29.

Treaty of Dancing Rabbit Creek with the Choctaw Nation. 1830. 7 Stat. 333.

Treaty of Guadalupe Hidalgo. 1848. 9 Stat. 922 (1851).

Treaty with Russia. 1867. 15 Stat. 539.

Treaty with the Cherokees. 1817. 7 Stat. 156.

Treaty with the Senecas, et al. 1867. 15 Stat. 517.

Treaty with the Wyandots. 1855. 10 Stat. 1159.

Tribally Controlled Schools Act. 1988. P.L. 100-297, 102 Stat. 385.

Tundra Times. 1991. *Alaska Native Claims Settlement Act: A scrapbook history*. Anchorage. 63 p.

Tyler, Lyman S. 1973. *A history of Indian policy*. Bureau of Indian Affairs, U.S. Dept. of the Interior. Washington, D.C. 328 p.

Underhill, Ruth. 1957. Religion among American Indians. *Annals of American Academy of Political and Social Sciences* 311:127–136.

———. 1965. *Red man's religion: Beliefs and practices of the Indians north of Mexico*. Univ. of Chicago Press, Chicago. 301 p.

———. 1974. Religion among American Indians. *In* Worton. 1974. p. 116–119.

United Effort Trust. 1979. *Federal/Indian trust relationship*. Washington, D.C. 2 p.

U.S. v. Wheeler. 1978. 435 U.S. 313.

U.S. v. Winans. 1905. 198 U.S. 371.

U.S. Bureau of the Census. 1991. *American Indian and Alaska Native areas: 1990*. Racial Stat. Branch, Population Div. Washington, D.C. 52 p. (June)

———. 1991. *1990 Census counts of American Indians, Eskimos, or Aleuts and American Indian and Alaska Native areas*. Racial Stat. Branch, Population Div. Washington, D.C. 16 p. (July)

———. 1991. Release CB91-229. 4 p. (July 5)

———. 1991. Release CB91-232. 6 p. (July 11)

U.S. Department of Commerce. 1974. *Federal and State Indian reservations and Indian trust areas*. U.S. Govt. Printing Office, Washington, D.C. 604 p.

U.S. Department of the Interior. 1894. *Indians taxed and not taxed.* U.S. Govt. Printing Office, Washington, D.C. 683 p.

———. 1931. Secretarial Order No. 494. Mar. 14.

U.S. Indian Claims Commission. 1978. Final report. U.S. Govt. Printing Office, Washington, D.C. 141 p.

U.S. Public Health Service. 1987. Public Health Reports 102(4):350–376.

———. 1991. 43 CFR 36.10 et seq.

United States Commission on Civil Rights. 1981. *Indian tribes: A continuing quest for survival.* Supt. of Documents, U.S. Govt. Printing Office, Washington, D.C. 192 p.

United States Congress. 1964. *List of Indian treaties.* House Committee on Interior and Insular Affairs, 82nd Cong., 2nd sess., Comm. Print No. 30. Sept. 8.

United States Government Manual. 1990. *Census 1990.* U.S. Govt. Printing Office, Washington, D.C. 907 p.

Utley, Robert M. 1963. *The last days of the Sioux Nation.* Yale Univ. Press, New Haven. 314 p.

———. 1988. Indian-United States military situation, 1848–1891. *In* Washburn. 1988. p. 163–184.

Utter, Jack. 1991. *Wounded Knee & the ghost dance tragedy.* National Woodlands Publishing Co., Lake Ann, Mich. 29 p.

Utter, Jack, Bob Valen, and Rita Cantu. 1989. Response to environmental despair, or–Invitation to a revolution. *Jour. Interpretation* 13(5):12–14.

Vaughn, Alden T. 1982. From white man to redskin: Changing Anglo-American perceptions of the American Indian. *American Historical Review* 87:917–953.

Vecsey, Christopher, ed. 1991. *Handbook of American Indian religious freedom.* Crossroad Publishing Co., New York. 180 p.

Verrill, A. Hyatt. 1927. *The American Indian. North, South, and Central America.* The New Home Library, New York. 485 p.

Waldman, Carl. 1985. *Atlas of the North American Indian.* Facts on File, New York. 276 p.

Waldron v. United States. 1905. 143 Fed. Repts. 413.

Walke, Roger. 1991. *Federal programs of assistance to Native Americans.* Senate Report 102-62. Senate Select Committee on Indian Affairs. U.S. Govt. Printing Office, Washington, D.C. 331 p.

Walker, Hans, Jr. 1989. *Federal Indian tax rules: A compilation of Internal Revenue Service rules relating to Indians.* 238 p.

Wall, Steve, and Harvey Arden. 1990. *Wisdom-keepers: Meetings with Native American spiritual Elders*. Beyond Words Publ., Hillsboro, Oreg. 128 p.

Wardwell, Lelia. 1991. *The Native American experience*. Facts on File, New York. 268 p.

Washburn, Wilcomb. 1973. *The American Indian and the United States: A documentary history*. Random House, New York. Vols. I–IV. 3119 p.

Washburn, Wilcomb E., ed. 1988. *Handbook of North American Indians—History of Indian-white relations*. Smithsonian Institution, Washington, D.C. 838 p.

Washington, George. 1783. Letter to James Duane. Sept. 7. Excerpted in Prucha. 1990. p. 1.

Weatherford, Jack. 1988. *Indian givers*. Fawcett Columbine, New York. 272 p.

Weatherhead, L.R. 1980. What is an "Indian tribe?"–The question of tribal existence. *American Indian Law Review* 8:1–47.

Webb, George W. 1966. *Chronological list of engagements between the Regular Army of the United States and various tribes of hostile Indians which occurred during the years 1790–1898*. Argonaut Press, New York. 141 p.

White, Richard, and William Cronon. 1988. Ecological change and the Indian white relation. *In* Washburn. 1988. p. 417–429.

White, Robert H. 1990. *Tribal assets: The rebirth of Native America*. Henry Holt and Company, New York. 291 p.

Wilkinson, Charles F. 1988. The idea of sovereignty: Native peoples, their lands, their dreams. *Legal Review of the American Rights Fund* 13(4):1–11.

Wilkinson, Charles F., and John M. Volkman. 1975. Judicial review of Indian treaty abrogation: "As long as the water flows and the grass grows upon the earth"–How long a time is that? 63 *California Law Review* 601.

Williams v. United States. 1946. 327 U.S. 711.

Williams, Robert A., Jr. 1990. *The American Indian in Western legal thought: The discourses of conquest*. Oxford Univ. Press, New York. 352 p.

Wills, Gary. 1991. "Native American" or "Pope"–let's use preferred names. In *Record-Eagle*, Traverse City, Mich., Sept. 30.

Wiminuche Band of Southern Ute Indians. 1913. Congressional ratification of 1911 agreement. P.L. 63-4, 38 Stat. 82.

Winters v. United States. 1908. 207 U.S. 564.

Worcester v. Georgia. 1832. 31 U.S. (6 Pet.) 515.

Worcester, Donald E., ed. 1975. *Forked tongues and broken treaties.* The Caxton Printers, Ltd., Caldwell, Idaho. 470 p.

Workman, Bill. 1991. Indians aren't rushing to make tribal lands nuclear waste dumps. *San Francisco Chronicle.* Reprinted in *Arizona Daily Star,* Dec. 8.

Worl, Rosita. 1988. Alaska Natives today. *In* Fitzhugh, William W., and Aron Crowell. 1988. *Crossroads of continents: Cultures of Siberia and Alaska.* Smithsonian Institution Press, Washington, D.C. p. 319–325.

Worton, Stanley N. 1974. *The first Americans.* Hayden Book Co., Inc., Rochelle Park, N.J. 181 p.

Wrone, David R., and Russell S. Nelson, Jr., eds. 1973. *Who's the savage: A documentary history of the mistreatment of the native North Americans.* Fawcett Publications, Inc., Greenwich, Conn. 576 p.

Yakima Nation Treaty. 1855. 12 Stat. 951.

INDEX

This index contains the names of Indian tribes, bands, etc., only if they are specifically referred to in the text. Appendixes 2 and 3 contain the names of all federally recognized Indian tribal entities.